C000175028

WHO KILLED POLLY PECK?

Who killed Polly Peck?

THE CORPORATE ASSASSINATION OF ASIL NADIR

ELIZABETH FORSYTH

SMITH GRYPHON
PUBLISHERS

First published in Great Britain in 1996 by
SMITH GRYPHON LIMITED
Swallow House, 11–21 Northdown Street
London N1 9BN

A CIP catalogue for this book
is available from the British Library

The right of Elizabeth Forsyth to be identified
as author of this work has been asserted by her in accordance
with the Copyright, Designs and Patent Act 1988

ISBN 1 85685 113 3

Typeset by Computerset, Harmondsworth
Printed and bound in Great Britain by Butler & Tanner Ltd, Frome

To my family and friends

CONTENTS

ACKNOWLEDGEMENTS AND SOURCES

I would like to thank the following people for their help. Sheila Aitken, Mehmet Ali Akpuar, Jonathan Bekhor, Aisling Daly, David and Jo-Rae Dahl, Hopie and Peter Dimond, David Fawcus, Abide Gonultas, Richard Holmes, Barbara Jackson-Smith, John, Peter Knight, Peter and Jean Krivinskas, David Lake, Bruce Matthews, Michael Mates MP, Liz Moore, Asil Nadir, Fehim and Bilge Nevjat, Ozgul, Jenny Pitman, Roger Ratcliffe, Anthony Scrivener and Mark Surridge. I would also like to thank the researcher and writer.

Barchard, David: *Asil Nadir and the Rise and Fall of Polly Peck* (Gollancz, 1992)

Hindle, Tim: *The Sultan of Berkeley Square: Asil Nadir and the Thatcher Years* (Macmillan, 1991)

Widlake, Brian: *Serious Fraud Office* (Little, Brown, 1995)

1. The Raid on South Audley Management

'GET OFF THE line. The SFO is here.' I could hardly believe what I was hearing when I phoned my office to pick up any messages. My company was in the middle of a full-scale raid. When the Serious Fraud Office occupied South Audley Management on the morning of 19 September 1990, I was snatching a few days' holiday. I had not taken a break since I had started work for Asil Nadir three years earlier, and I had promised a Swiss friend that I would spend a few days' holiday with him.

When I told Mr Nadir that I needed a few days off until a bankers' meeting in Switzerland scheduled for the following week, he was sympathetic – although he looked worried. It certainly was not the best time for me to be going away. For weeks there had been a non-stop series of stories in the national press about an Inland Revenue investigation into his affairs, and rumours that Swiss-administered offshore-company dealings in Polly Peck shares were being investigated variously by the Serious Fraud Office, the Stock Exchange and the Department of Trade. Much of the media speculation had centred on South Audley Management, the private company set up by Mr Nadir and run by me to organise his family's financial interests.

I had spent most of August in Switzerland trying to pacify our bankers who were understandably nervous at the impact of all this attention on the shares they had as security for loans. The Polly Peck share price had been well over 400p earlier that summer, but it had fallen steeply as stories about share dealings and investigations appeared in the press. Like most entrepreneurs, Asil Nadir had borrowed against the value of his shares.

As SAM chairman I knew that its affairs were in order, and I assumed, naively as it turned out, that the press hysteria would eventually peter out, and life would return to normal. I had even told my mother that she should buy some PPI shares, so convinced was I that the share price would recover as soon as all the fears created by the press reports were dispelled. The tax investigation was being handled by our advisers, and we had received no inquiries from the Serious Fraud Office, despite the press reports. We were under orders not to talk to the newspapers.

That morning I made my usual phone call to the office just after nine o'clock to check if there were any queries or urgent mail. I was stunned when my assistant Barbara Jackson-Smith told me the SFO was there. Barbara had arrived at 8.30 that morning and was immediately hustled into the boardroom on the ground-floor by two policemen who were manning the front door. No explanation was given either to her or to the other office staff who were already there, wondering what on earth was going on.

Hassan, the general office hand and chauffeur, had turned up to work at 7.30 am to be greeted by several policemen on the doorstep of the pretty Georgian terrace house in Berkeley Square that SAM occupied right across the square from the PPI headquarters. As other members of staff arrived they had been taken to the boardroom and told to stay there. It was a frightening experience – particularly for the younger ones.

A full-scale police raid was soon in progress. While two policemen kept an eye on the staff, several others could be heard thumping around upstairs as cupboards and files were ransacked. Plastic bags of documents were brought downstairs and taken away. When Barbara realised what was happening, she tried to go upstairs to our office but found policemen barring her way. The staff couldn't even use the toilet without an escort.

The SFO didn't want anyone inside the office to have outside contact. All phone calls were diverted to the boardroom. When our telephonist, Shelly, took my call she mouthed 'Elizabeth' to Barbara, who leapt to the phone and warned me of the situation before her two 'minders' realised what was happening. They were furious, as they were obviously waiting for me to come into the office.

Barbara was promptly marched upstairs to be interviewed by a couple from the SFO. There she was served with a Section 2 notice – which overrides the right to silence – and told she had no alternative but to answer their questions concerning my whereabouts. Barbara told them I was travelling, and that the only contact she had with me was when I telephoned regularly into the office to pick up any messages.

In fact I was in Scotland with my friend, a Swiss banker. We were staying at the Gleneagles Hotel and getting ready to fly to Switzerland that day. After my brief phone conversation with Barbara, I immediately called Peter Knight at Vizards, our company solicitors, and told him about the raid. I then phoned Mr Nadir to alert him. He was obviously stunned. I told him I had asked Peter Knight to contact him once he found out what was going on. For the time being I suggested he send one of his Turkish bodyguards over the square to SAM to see what was happening.

That afternoon SFO case controller Lorna Harris, who was at the raid along with her colleague Robert Wardle, told our lawyer that she wanted to interview both Mr Nadir and me. Meanwhile Peter Knight accompanied another SAM director to the SFO's offices in Elm Street, where she was interviewed. But by the end of the afternoon neither of them was any the wiser about what the Serious Fraud Office was after. From the start Peter Knight was suspicious about the way the raid was mounted. He believed that it had a lot to do with the tax investigation. He had been concerned about the press reports since they had focused on the Inland Revenue investigation into Asil Nadir's tax affairs, with which he had been dealing for over a year. He had already had angry exchanges with the tax office over alleged leaks to the press. Negotiations with the taxman were supposed to be private. The Inland Revenue had always been very clear on this point, as had the advisers with whom they dealt.

Up in Scotland I was in a state of shock. I didn't know what to do. Both Mr Nadir and my friend insisted I should carry on to Switzerland, where I was due to meet bankers. That was the top priority now more than ever. In retrospect I should have gone back to London immediately, because by going to Switzerland it looked as if I were running away. But my companion took the initiative and booked two flights from Glasgow airport – in the name of himself and his 'wife'. I was terrified. I knew I would not be allowed on the plane if the name on my passport were different from the name on the flight ticket, but surveillance was slacker than usual that day, and we got through.

But disaster struck the next morning. As soon as the London stock-market opened for business, the Polly Peck share price started to fall. Wild stories circulated in the City among investors and stock-brokers. One news service reported that Asil Nadir had been assassinated; another rumour suggested that he had committed suicide in Hong Kong. There were reports that he had been arrested – and that the company had lost a huge amount of money in Turkish bonds. At one point Mr Nadir's sister Bilge was telephoned by a City acquaintance who offered his condolences on her brother's death. Fortunately Bilge had just seen Asil a few minutes before, but that gives an indication of the way the rumours hit the world and the stock-market that morning. There was pandemonium as the Polly Peck share price plunged swiftly from its opening price of 243p.

The telephone lines to PPI's headquarters were jammed as brokers and institutional investors tried to find out what was happening. The morning edition of the *Evening Standard* carried the news of the raid on SAM the previous day, but callers to the SFO's headquarters in Elm Street were already being told about the raid while PPI shares were still see-sawing on the stock-market. It was chaos. The combination of wild rumours and reports of the SFO raid on Asil Nadir's private company were devastating for the PPI share price. With SAM having featured so much in the news over recent weeks, the raid seemed like final confirmation that the reports were true.

With the phone lines to PPI jammed, I had great difficulty reaching Mr Nadir from Switzerland. When I eventually got through, I told him I was particularly alarmed because I had just discovered that very morning that Citibank, one of the biggest American banks and one of his major personal lenders, where I had worked before joining Asil Nadir, had recently placed a 'put' option on some 7.9 million shares of his family holding pledged as security against the bank's loans. It was a way of securing the bank's money if the share price should fall. Through the 'put' they could offload the shares on to Phillips & Drew, the stockbroking counterparty. The loan had existed for some years. The 'put' had only been in place for two or three months. And until that morning I had not known anything about it.

I told Mr Nadir the 'put' was at 200p. If the price fell to this level, it could mean a sudden dumping of all those shares on the market when whoever had taken the put found itself required to buy them. He told me not to worry as the shares would be suspended long before then. In fact he had been trying in vain to get the shares suspended since breakfast time that morning. He had made several phone calls in an attempt to get trading in Polly Peck suspended. The rumours were creating a false market in the shares. A suspension was clearly in order, but inexplicably nothing had happened.

Aisling Daly, Mr Nadir's personal assistant, still shudders when she recalls that morning when he made constant phone calls for four hours to try and get the share price suspended. At some point during that time he received a message from one broker to say: 'The Stock Exchange says it isn't in the habit of suspending shares on volatility.' Asil Nadir's reply was: 'This isn't volatility – this is free fall.' When he called the Stock Exchange itself, he was told that the company brokers had to request a suspension – yet he had been asking them to do just that since early morning. It was a chaotic muddle.

At around one o'clock, one of the other PPI directors managed to contact someone at Shearson Lehman who agreed with him that a suspension would be in the best interests of the shareholders. But it took another 90 minutes to raise anyone at the Stock Exchange, during which time the shares fell a further 50p – a huge drop in percentage terms. Lehman's had difficulty finding anyone with some authority at the Stock Exchange, but someone was eventually pulled out of a lunch. By the time the shares were suspended at 2.15 that afternoon, however, the price was 108p. Some 40 million PPI shares had changed hands in the panic.

It was a black day for the stock-market as the leading market indicator, the FTSE-100 index, slumped to its lowest point in 18 months. Investors were already worried about an impending Gulf War. The previous month Iraq had invaded Kuwait, and there was speculation that Turkey, where some of the major PPI companies were based, might take military action. There were anxieties, too, about an American banking crisis. Many substantial British companies suffered sharp falls in their share prices that day. Yet no one has ever explained why it took so long to suspend the PPI shares, despite what was happening in the market and the repeated requests from Mr Nadir to do so. And questions must also be asked about communications between the Stock Exchange and the Serious Fraud Office. If there was to be a raid, surely the Stock Exchange should have been standing by to suspend. It should have been properly informed by the SFO, which, I discovered later, had conducted informal meetings earlier with the Stock Exchange and the Department of Trade to discuss Polly Peck.

The PPI share-price collapse was a disaster, described later by one commentator as a 'lynching'. Mr Nadir, who then owned around 27 per cent of PPI shares, lost £160 million of his wealth in just over four hours. It was the huge block of Citibank shares that finished off the Polly Peck share price when they went through the market that morning. Several other banks who held Nadir family PPI shares also sold and added to the chaos. But it was the Citibank option that really hit the share price. Never had a major UK public company seen its shares fall so far so fast. Shareholders saw their investment devastated. Polly Peck had just announced some good half-year profit figures. There was no suggestion that there was anything wrong with its businesses, which included the well-known Del Monte fruit group and the Japanese electronics company Sansui. Yet the shares, which had been over 400p earlier that summer, were now, according to next day's *Financial Times*, showing a 'death bed rating'. The company's founder and chief shareholder, on his way for an interview with the Serious Fraud Office, was effectively ruined.

As subsequent events were to demonstrate the SFO had committed a major error by raiding SAM and triggering the devastating fall in the share price of Polly Peck. The SFO did not seem to know what it was looking for, despite all the press reports. And it had paid scant regard to the impact of its actions on thousands of Polly Peck shareholders. The speculation that had centred on South Audley Management over the previous few weeks had made it inevitable that an SFO raid would prove seriously detrimental to the Polly Peck share price, the confidence of PPI's bankers and Mr Nadir's own personal financial position, not to mention his 22,000 shareholders. It was an appalling blunder. But quite how appalling only became clear years later.

In the weeks that followed Peter Knight asked the SFO repeatedly for a copy of the warrant for the raid on SAM. He knew that this document and the accompanying affidavit would have to show the reasons for the SFO's action. The magistrate who granted the warrant had to be informed first of the SFO's concerns – raiding a company was not something to be undertaken lightly. Peter Knight suspected that the SFO had done little digging of its own and had relied on information emanating from the tax investigation he had been handling on behalf of Mr Nadir. He was never to receive a copy of the warrant from the SFO. It was only when I was preparing my own case five years later that the SFO finally gave in to my lawyers and produced the elusive documents – as I was chairman of the company they could hardly refuse. When I eventually saw the warrant it was quite clear to me that the SFO raided SAM on the wrong assumptions, the implications of which I will deal with in Chapter 3.

At that time the Serious Fraud Office was a relatively young organisation, set up in the late 1980s to provide a more effective way of fighting City fraud. Its lawyers and accountants work together with the police. This combination of specialist skills was reckoned to be the answer to the problems of prosecuting the clever financiers who were adept at covering their tracks.

The SFO was given draconian powers. Its accountants and lawyers can interrogate suspects and witnesses under the Section 2 provision that overrides the right to silence. The SFO's Section 2 directives are unique and controversial. In all other kinds of criminal investigations suspects have the right to remain silent. But anyone served with a Section 2 has to answer any questions put to them and to supply and explain documents. To refuse is a criminal offence, as is to give false information.

Originally Section 2 was designed as the ultimate measure to coerce unwilling witnesses to talk – in fraud cases documents and statements are all important. Until the establishment of the SFO, only Department of Trade inspectors officially appointed to investigate a company had the authority to demand answers from witnesses who did not have the right to silence. Giving that mandate to the SFO was considered an important part of the new fraud-busting regime. The police do not conduct Section 2 interviews, and information given under Section 2 is not admissible in court as evidence unless a defendant contradicts his or her previous statements, or gives false information.

As the Serious Fraud Office established itself, Section 2s were employed routinely by its officials in what many lawyers then and now claim is an abuse of its powers. Critics claim Section 2 enables the SFO to go on 'fishing expeditions' – questioning individuals who have been targeted for one reason or another in a random fashion in the hope of finding something – and creates an overly enthusiastic attitude on the part of the SFO.

The SFO is also unique because it both investigates and prosecutes. Critics claim this is one reason for its poor success record in major fraud trials. Evidence in other criminal cases has to be sent to the Crown Prosecution Service, a separate body, which decides independently whether there is enough evidence for a prosecution. The SFO is not accountable in the same way. Hence, in part, its current reputation for chronic misjudgement.

But back in 1990 there was an enormous will for the new organisation to succeed, particularly on the part of the British government, which had been criticised for its previous failure to either preempt or successfully prosecute fraud. The government had embarked on its huge privatisation programme, and it was important to assure everyone that the share market was well regulated. As the stockmarket boomed in the frantic take-over activity of the 1980s and the yuppy emerged as the symbol of the decade, there was also the feeling that City types were once again getting away with breaking the rules. In the United States investigators were getting to grips with the junk-bond promoters and uncovering huge insider-dealing networks. One thread of the US investigation led the UK authorities to uncover the share-support operation that lay behind the successful Guinness take-over of the Distillers drinks company, when some prominent business personalities were paid fees to prop up the Guinness share price while the bid went through.

The first Guinness trial was a major success for the UK authorities. Leading City figures were put in the dock and found guilty of participating in an illegal share-support scheme. It was a great triumph, too, for a then little-known woman QC, Barbara Mills, who was the leading criminal lawyer for the first Guinness prosecution. That ended in a victory for the authorities on the 27 August 1990, when the defendants were sentenced. Barbara Mills, fresh from her Guinness triumph, took over as head of the SFO just before the raid on SAM. It was a high-profile appointment on a salary far below what she had been earning as a successful Queen's Counsel. But, as she made clear in a series of interviews, Mills was determined to make her mark as a 'hands-on' SFO director. Many believe she wanted to make the SFO as feared and forceful as the Securities and Exchange Commission in the United States.

The SFO was conscious of the role of publicity in highlighting the work of the organisation. Showing that you were prepared to be tough on City crime was a real deterrent to potential wrongdoers. If it wanted to become a high-profile operation, it would certainly not have been displeased that the pressure on Asil Nadir in Elm Street was not confined to the interview room that first afternoon on the day of the SFO raid on SAM. The pavement outside the SFO had been deserted when he arrived. Half way through the interview, someone came in to say that press and television reporters were outside – one news agency had apparently been 'tipped off' that Mr Nadir was attending for an interview. By the time he came out, there were dozens of press and cameras to greet him. Even his other PPI directors did not know he had gone to the SFO until they heard and saw it on the evening news.

The raid on SAM must have been one of the new director's first initiatives in office – Barbara Mills had arrived at the SFO by early September. But she would later point out that the PPI investigation had been started not by her but by her predecessor, John Wood. The sworn statement accompanying the warrant also makes this clear, in a curious fashion. Lorna Harris had stated:

> I am a member of the Serious Fraud Office. I have been autho-rised by the Director of the Serious Fraud Office to exercise on her behalf all the powers conferred by Section 2 of the Criminal Justice Act 1987. On the 28th August 1990 I was authorised by her to investigate the affairs of Polly Peck International.

Strangely the word 'predecessor' is handwritten under the last sentence, which is supposed then to read 'her predecessor'.

But the SFO were by no means the only ones with cause for

alarm over the way Polly Peck shares had crashed in the wake of the raid on SAM. On 21 September, the day after the devastating PPI share-price collapse, Peter Knight of Vizards was surprised by a request from Inland Revenue officials to come and see him. The men both worked in Special Office 2 of the Inland Revenue, set up to target wealthy, high profile individuals. We had been negotiating with them over Mr Nadir's tax affairs since early the previous year, and they wished to discuss with us the alleged leaks about this to the media over the previous few weeks.

Press reports had been totally misleading, muddling up the perfectly proper Nadir family-trust holdings with share dealings by Swiss companies, the names of which I had never heard before. These had nothing to do with South Audley Management, although the media, which had got wind of the tax probe, implied that they were. These leaks continually fuelled an increasingly damaging press campaign that weakened City confidence in Asil Nadir and the company he created.

Over the previous few months there had been angry exchanges between the Inland Revenue and our advisers over the way they had conducted their investigations. Mr Nadir's tax advisers, Coopers & Lybrand, had suggested we retain the solicitors, Vizards, because they were so alarmed by the Revenue's actions, which were very different from anything they had ever encountered.

Coopers' tax department were very experienced in the ways of the Inland Revenue, having acted for individuals in dozens of investigations over the years. They were used to the process of cooperating with the Revenue on behalf of their clients. But from the beginning they were wary of what appeared to be an exceptionally aggressive investigation and insisted that Mr Nadir be legally represented.

For a start the inquiry had been mounted without any attempt to approach Mr Nadir or Coopers about whatever queries or claims the Inland Revenue might have had in mind. We only became aware of the investigation in August 1989 when one of SAM's bankers told me about a letter he had received from the Inland Revenue. The inquiry, I discovered, had been going on since that spring, and I immediately informed Coopers & Lybrand, who had been Mr Nadir's personal tax advisers for years.

The taxmen were issuing Section 20 notices to our bankers and several firms of stockbrokers, demanding documents and information about SAM. They were perfectly within their rights to approach third parties, but what alarmed Coopers was how many Section 20 notices appeared to have been issued on a 'scattergun' basis. The Revenue even sent one to Rutland County Council, where no financial transactions were involved. Rutland was simply the local authority dealing with Mr Nadir's application to turn Burley-on-the-Hill, a dilapidated historical pile near his country home of Baggrave Hall, into a hotel and conference centre.

At one point in the negotiations the Inland Revenue had proposed to go round to SAM uninvited and demand to see Mr Nadir in person. On another occasion, in the spring of 1990, a senior Revenue official told our advisers that they were dissatisfied with the amount of information given to them. He then said there would be an extensive investigation into Polly Peck and Mr Nadir unless information was provided to the Inland Revenue by a certain time.

Coopers took this to mean that the Inland Revenue was cooperating with other agencies, notably the Serious Fraud Office and the Department of Trade. At a meeting the previous autumn with Stoy Hayward, PPI's auditors, our advisers had discussed the possibility that the Inland Revenue investigation was linked to a Department of Trade inquiry into share dealings. When one of our advisers was shown pages and pages of share transactions by the Inland Revenue, he became convinced that the information could only have come from the Stock Exchange.

At one time during the tax investigations Coopers & Lybrand became so incensed that the firm wrote to Sir Anthony Battishall, the Chairman of the Board of the Inland Revenue, threatening to suspend absolutely all cooperation with it. This was unprecedented – Coopers had a major tax practice.

Following the first article in the *Sunday Times* at the beginning of August about an Inland Revenue investigation into Mr Nadir and Swiss-company links with SAM, the taxmen were challenged by our advisers. Our advisers had even been told at one point that the journalist who wrote the piece claimed to have a tape-recorded conversation with an official of the Inland Revenue. As each weekend brought forth more damaging press reports about the Inland Revenue investigation, relations between our advisers and the Revenue reached boiling point.

So the day after the PPI share-price collapse the Inland Revenue were anxious to make it clear that they had not supplied information to any regulatory body (such as the SFO) or leaked stories to the press. An astonished Peter Knight ushered the officials into Vizards' boardroom. They told him that they had investigated the leak allegations by checking phone calls, and they assured him that no information had been given to the press by the Revenue. They indicated that there were others who had duplicate copies of some of the documents acquired by the Inland Revenue under Section 20(3) notices, which had been the basis of lengthy and detailed articles in the *Sunday Times* over the previous few weeks. They had already told our adviser at Coopers & Lybrand that if he looked through his files he would find evidence of this.

They also pointed out that a national newspaper had identified a stockbroker as having released information to the regulatory authorities. To make the point they showed Peter Knight a letter they had received from another newspaper, the *Sunday Times*, dated the day before the raid on SAM, confirming that the Inland Revenue had not been the source of their information. In fact another of our tax advisers had already been shown two letters from the *Sunday Times* – one signed by the paper's editor, another by the journalist who had written the original article about the tax investigation. The letter shown to Peter Knight said that the newspaper had received no information about Mr Nadir's tax affairs from the Revenue itself. The taxmen had clearly gone to a lot of trouble to clarify the situation.

One of the tax officials then went on to deny that the Inland Revenue had passed any information to the SFO. And he offered proof that far from colluding with the SFO the Inland Revenue had refused to have anything to do with its investigations into Polly Peck. Peter Knight was astonished when they handed him a note that detailed a telephone conversation a month earlier between Michael Chance, Deputy Director of the SFO, and Dennis Parrott, a very senior Inland Revenue official in charge of Special Office 2.

The note detailed the following: Michael Chance had phoned Dennis Parrott on 21 August and said that a meeting had been arranged the following Thursday between the SFO and the Department of Trade, with a member of the Metropolitan Police also in attendance. The consultation was precipitated by recent disclosures in newspaper articles. According to the note: 'Chance had invited the Inland Revenue to attend at that meeting for the purposes of chairing and exchanging information which would assist the SFO in their enquiries.'

But Parrott declined the offer. He said the Inland Revenue's own 'investigations were proceeding satisfactorily towards a monetary settlement. As far as the Inland Revenue were concerned they had not identified and were satisfied that no offences had been committed of a revenue nature that would give rise to any prosecution. They were therefore satisfied that there was little point in their attending such a meeting,' he told Michael Chance. The Revenue memorandum went on to reveal that Parrott had then 'told Michael Chance that he regarded the SFO as being on a fishing expedition led on by the newspaper articles and that they had nothing to go on and were unlikely to find anything.' Apparently Chance had agreed.

This new information was devastating. It showed that the SFO had been warned off raiding SAM by the Inland Revenue but had still gone ahead regardless. It seemed to indicate that Michael Chance, one of the SFO's most senior men until he left its employ a few weeks later, had doubts about his own organisation's investigation. Why then had he phoned Parrott to suggest a meeting in the first place? And why had the Inland Revenue been asked actually to chair the meeting? It seemed to show that the recent newspaper articles were wrong. While they had been huffing and puffing about the Inland Revenue investigation into Asil Nadir and getting excited about mysterious Swiss companies, it appeared that the Revenue itself had decided nothing was amiss.

In their meeting with Peter Knight, the Revenue went on to describe the events of the past two days as a 'monumental disaster' caused by the SFO, whose actions they criticised in the most damning terms. They said that they could see no purpose whatsoever in the search warrant having been executed at the premises of South Audley Management, knowing what a disastrous effect it would have and realising, as they did, that nothing of any consequence or evidential value would be obtained by such behaviour. They seemed to be suggesting that the SFO had acted precipitately.

In their effort to clear their own names the Inland Revenue had confirmed all Peter Knight's suspicions that the SFO was indeed on a 'fishing expedition' when it had raided SAM. And his view was that there had been collusion between the various City regulators and the Inland Revenue. Embarrassingly enough the taxmen's damaging revelations would soon become known to the SFO itself. Peter Knight's note on this bizarre meeting was among privileged documents seized by the SFO when they raided Polly Peck a month later. By that time deputy-director Michael Chance, whose invitation to the Inland Revenue raised so many questions about the conduct of their investigations, had left the SFO.

In time I would discover that the men from the Inland Revenue had, in fact, played a key role in the Polly Peck saga. Indeed, one senior investigator, in later television and newspaper interviews, would claim to have been a prime mover in the events that led to the SFO investigation of PPI and Asil Nadir.

All of this throws light on a very murky period in the Inland Revenue's history, when the organisation, or parts of it, did cooperate with other authorities as a matter of policy. The taxmen had been working closely for months in the Stock Exchange, scrutinising sales and purchases of Polly Peck shares by offshore companies for evidence of share dealing and a share-support operation, which they had believed was organised by South Audley Management. It was one of a number of wide-ranging covert City investigations started in the wake of the Guinness scandal. And the original impetus, it appears, came from 10 Downing Street.

Sometime in 1987 a meeting had been arranged between a senior Inland Revenue official and a senior Stock Exchange investigator. It was an informal lunch to discuss cooperation between the two organisations and how they could best pool their resources to combat City crime. These talks had followed a sensational article in the *Financial Times* alleging that there was a huge insider share-dealing ring in the City of London, making millions of pounds illegally, which the Stock Exchange could not bring to book. This story had caught the eye of the then Prime Minister Margaret Thatcher who wanted to know if it were true. Word came back from the Stock Exchange that it was.

Although insider dealing was illegal, the Stock Exchange, which had the job of keeping the markets in order, could not track down the specific individuals behind the flotillas of offshore companies whose share dealings looked suspicious. The existence of these kind of operations had come sharply into focus during the Westland saga in 1986, when a fierce political and City battle was fought over who should rescue the failing helicopter company. A handful of anonymous shareholders, hiding behind offshore nominee names, dramatically swung the crucial shareholders vote in favour of the American deal at the very last minute.

The Stock Exchange had also been mightily embarrassed by a television documentary that showed City dealers boasting how easy it was to break the rules, while the Exchange was claiming to police the markets successfully. Bob Wilkinson, who headed the Stock Exchange's surveillance department, was furious about the slant of the programme, in which he appeared in a particularly unfortunate light.

The Stock Exchange believed that offshore companies, registered in exotic places such as the Cayman Islands, Bermuda and, of course, Switzerland, were 'fronts' for UK insiders and speculators who wanted to conceal their identities. It could identify suspicious share trades efficiently enough, but it had no powers to extract information about the ultimate owners of the share-dealing companies. Their identities were hidden behind a web of offshore corporations. The stockbrokers who bought and sold the shares for these companies did not necessarily know anything about who actually owned them.

There were three aspects to this. First, the question of illegal share dealing and insider trading. Second, the point that these unknown individuals evaded paying tax on their profits. Third, the Stock Exchange's desire to find out whether these offshore companies were actually operating on behalf of partners in stock-broking firms as well as their clients. If Stock Exchange members themselves were financially exposed through their own dealings, it would affect the solvency of their business. One of the Stock Exchange's tasks was to check that member firms obeyed the regulations in the interests of investor protection.

The Stock Exchange could not get behind the offshore companies – neither could the Department of Trade and Industry, which followed up the Stock Exchange's referrals. But the Inland Revenue was armed with much more effective powers. The purpose of this discreet high level lunch, therefore, was to see how the regulatory authorities could combine their efforts. Although there was a strict procedure for one regulatory authority to pass information it had gleaned in the course of a bona-fide investigation to another, using one regulator to 'fish' on behalf of another was an altogether different matter.

The policy had to be kept on an informal basis, and the niceties had to be observed. But the system was wide open to abuse, and individuals could be targeted. A tax inquiry was a powerful weapon, and if anyone had anything to hide, the taxman would find it – just the threat of investigation was often enough to ensure an individual's compliance. This cooperation between the Inland Revenue and the Stock Exchange may have been set up with the best of intentions, but it had the makings of a disaster. The collapse of Polly Peck was that disaster.

Sometime later a senior Inland Revenue investigator turned up at the Stock Exchange and issued a number of Section 20(3) notices requiring information on share trades, companies and member brokers from the Stock Exchange's newly installed computerised data base. He had already contacted various stockbrokers and banks, but he soon realised he could be more effective by going to the Stock Exchange direct.

The Exchange decided to cooperate. Gratifyingly enough the Revenue appeared to be after the very people who had caused the Stock Exchange such frustration, and the Exchange was only too delighted to help. The view, according to one Stock Exchange official was: 'If we couldn't get these chaps in the jug for insider dealing it made us feel better knowing they would be done for a lot of tax on their share dealings.' But, bearing in mind the cooperation discussed over lunch, the relationship with the Stock Exchange was possibly not so straightforward.

For in reality the Stock Exchange was deeply envious of the way the US Securities and Exchange Commission had managed to crack arbitrageur Ivan Boesky's insider-dealing activities and prosecute the likes of junk-bond king Michael Milken. The UK Guinness share-support operation, mounted in secret to ensure that its unwelcome takeover offer for drinks company Distillers in 1986 was successful, had only been revealed because of the SEC's investigations. British regulators had not managed to uncover it.

It was widely believed that similar share-support operations had been mounted in other major UK takeovers, which made our regulators look pretty limp on the detection front. Even after the creation of the SFO, which was given unprecedented powers to investigate and prosecute large-scale fraud, detection remained the weak link in the fight against City crime. The SFO relied for its cases on referrals from other agencies, such as the Stock Exchange and the Department of Trade, both of which had limited powers of investigation and great difficulty in getting enough information to back up their suspicions.

The Inland Revenue not only had greater routine powers of its own, but also its Special Office 2 operation brought it face to face with individuals – individuals with complicated financial arrangements who could perhaps be persuaded by the prospect of a massive tax demand to talk informally with IR investigators in a way they never would with either the Stock Exchange or the Department of Trade and certainly not with the SFO.

The Inland Revenue, on the other hand, rarely prosecuted its targets – comedian Ken Dodd, who was acquitted, and jockey Lester Piggott were very high-profile exceptions. Prosecution usually meant the destruction of someone's business – from the Inland Revenue point of view this was tantamount to killing the goose that laid the golden eggs. But it was clear that they came across a lot of interesting information during the course of their investigations – information that might be vital to other investigators. A little-noticed change in the 1989 Finance Act eased the Inland Revenue's rules on confidentiality, and Section 182 now enabled information not relevant to tax to be passed on in some circumstances.

The Inland Revenue's Special Office operation had been formed in 1976. Its investigators were not orthodox tax inspectors. Their brief was to target certain areas, such as horse racing, or casinos. They were wheeler-dealers – very much left to their own devices in comparison with the rest of the Inland Revenue. Many in the Revenue were dismayed at the ethos that developed in Special Office, where investigators often lacked the detailed technical knowledge of their colleagues in Enquiry Branch, whose inspectors were not allowed to do deals with their targets. Special Office 2, on the other hand, was set up on different lines, and its investigators were given much more latitude.

Michael Allcock, then in his early 40s, was a crack investigator at Special Office 2, celebrated for his success in collecting more tax from the most unlikely places than any of his contemporaries. Before joining Special Office 2 he had made a name for himself as a local tax inspector in Colchester, where he conducted what was known as the 'business economy exercise' in restaurants – examining the constituents of a meal and estimating what the profit was on its sale – and reassessed their tax position on this basis. But that was small fry, quite literally in some cases, and he was ambitious. At Special Office 2 he and his team were reckoned to pull in as much as £100 million a year in extra taxes.

Allcock homed in on the City, attracted by stories about massive profits routinely made on share deals by stockbroker folk and their clients. He was prepared to be tough and unorthodox. If a stockbroker wouldn't give him the names of clients doing deals, he would suggest that maybe it was the brokers themselves who were making the profits that were liable to tax. And in many cases he might have been right.

He seemed to like the City life – the lunches, the trips to meet his millionaire targets – and he dressed the part in smart suits and good shoes that marked him out from the normal run of tax inspector. And he was hated. His crusading, investigatory style made life very uncomfortable for his wealthy, high profile targets. Our advisers regarded him as something of a bully, and there were few tears shed among the accountants and lawyers who had dealt with him when he was suspended from duty in autumn 1992. At the beginning of 1994 he was charged with defrauding the Inland Revenue. So was a wealthy businessman, whose tax affairs he had been probing. Michael Allcock is expected to come to trial in autumn 1996.

One of Allcock's first City investigations started at the stockbroking firm of A. J. Bekhor, run by Jonathan Bekhor, who had originally taken the lead in providing a cut-price dealing service to investors back in the days when Stock Exchange commissions had been rigidly fixed. Jonathan Bekhor, Allcock discovered through the Stock Exchange, bought and sold shares for a large number of offshore companies – some of which appeared to deal in PPI shares. He has claimed that this was the starting-point for the Inland Revenue investigation of Mr Nadir, whom he seems to have believed was using all these companies as a 'front' for some kind of share-dealing or share-support operation. Michael Allcock later claimed in interviews that he provided the vital information to the Stock

Exchange and the Serious Fraud Office that opened the way for the Polly Peck investigation.

Peter Knight of Vizards was always convinced that documents presented to Mr Nadir at his first interview had been given to the SFO by the Inland Revenue, because they were identical to the ones that had featured in the tax investigation. Although the SFO had acquired copies of them by issuing a Section 2 notice to the London branch of the Finnish bank, Kansallis-Osake-Pankki (KOP), the day before the SAM raid, the short amount of time between that and Mr Nadir's interview convinced him that someone had identified particular documents from the volume available at KOP.

Subsequently, in 1991, MP Michael Mates, then a back-bencher, before his appointment in April 1992 as Minister for Northern Ireland, came to know about the case and took up the issue with two successive Attorney-Generals – Sir Patrick Mayhew and Sir Nicholas Lyell – as well as the Director of the Serious Fraud Office George Staple. All denied that documents had not been passed directly from the Inland Revenue at that stage or that the investigation into Mr Nadir had started initially on the basis of information from the Revenue. Sir Nicholas Lyell pointed out that the referring authority was the Stock Exchange, which had given the SFO a report outlining its suspicions of insider dealing.

This was odd because insider-dealing investigations are usually conducted initially by the Department of Trade and Industry, and it takes some months before a decision is made about whether or not to prosecute. But it was late 1992 before the authorities revealed that the PPI investigation came about because of a referral from the Stock Exchange.

The Stock Exchange had indeed called an informal meeting to discuss Polly Peck some weeks before the meeting discussed in the Inland Revenue note shown to Peter Knight. John Wood, then director of the Serious Fraud Office, had been there as well as officials from the Department of Trade and the Stock Exchange. Everyone apparently had their own concerns about Polly Peck. None the less the Stock Exchange official who called this meeting said he was astonished to discover, some four years later, that the SFO had raided SAM as a result of information received from the Stock Exchange.

Then, in an interview to provide background for a *Panorama* documentary that was never shown, Michael Allcock gave his own explanation of how the investigation started:

> The regulatory bodies had been looking at Polly Peck for years, but could find nothing substantial. But there were lots of rumours about insider trading, share ramping. It was a volatile share, ripe for that sort of thing. Lots of people were sceptical about the profits. The DTI and the old Surveillance division in the Stock Exchange were all suspicious, but it was considered too difficult. If it wasn't for the relationship I had with the Stock Exchange in that last few years, which was all totally unofficial incidentally, Polly Peck would never have been broken.

In the same interview Allcock stated that it was he who asked the Stock Exchange to bring in the Serious Fraud Office in 'early to mid-1990' specifically to investigate suspicions that Mr Nadir was engaged in a major share-ramping operation. The three organisations – the Stock Exchange, the Inland Revenue and the SFO – he claimed had had an informal meeting. In the *World in Action* programme and in an interview with the *Financial Times*, Allcock had stated that he passed on information about Asil Nadir and Polly Peck to the Stock Exchange. Most sensible people accept that this kind of informal discussion does go on and probably approve if it helps bring wrong-doers to justice.

In the case of Polly Peck, however, Allcock's belief that Mr Nadir was behind the share-dealing activities of a string of the Swiss-administered companies was unfounded. Within a few months of the raid on SAM that was effectively admitted when the Inland Revenue agreed a settlement with Mr Nadir's advisers. None of the 'Geneva airport' companies alleged by Allcock and later the SFO to be fronts for Mr Nadir was shown to be his. The IR agreement for a comparatively modest sum of £5 million undermined the whole justification for the raid on SAM that collapsed Polly Peck.

It was small wonder no one wanted to accept the truth: that the raid on SAM was effectively mounted on the back of an Inland Revenue probe, and that it happened as the result of a policy of cooperation between the Inland Revenue's Special Office 2 and the Stock Exchange. The fact is that no charges of insider dealing or share support were ever brought against anybody.

The SFO had been led to believe by the Stock Exchange that Asil Nadir was behind the Swiss companies' purchases of shares that had been highlighted in the press articles and that they would find the evidence of this when they raided SAM. They were wrong. But the media blitz, combined with the misconceived raid on his private company, had led directly to the collapse of Polly Peck.

The SFO's action had backfired disastrously: a FTSE-100 company had been brought to its knees. What happened was more than a mistake. It was a catastrophe that threatened the very existence of the Serious Fraud Office, whose activities were already coming under scrutiny.

It threatened also the reputation of the Inland Revenue, whose investigators appeared to have led the City regulators to believe that they would find the evidence they wanted when they raided SAM. The Inland Revenue had amassed huge powers over the years. It wasn't loved, but it was respected. Many of its more orthodox inspectors disliked the way Special Office operated. They regarded it as 'an accident waiting to happen'. Now it had.

The raid on SAM resulted in one of the most bizarre and disturbing prosecutions ever. Everything about the case has proved controversial. Nothing was right, and the eventual charges against Asil Nadir had no link with South Audley Management. Privileged documents were seized and wrongly circulated by the SFO. The SFO lawyer in charge of the investigation was assigned elsewhere in the Civil Service. A Government Minister, Michael Mates, lost his job when it was revealed that he had complained to the Attorney-General about this and other aspects of the SFO's handling of the case. And the Attorney-General, the highest law officer in the country, eventually had to apologise for unwittingly misleading Parliament over Mr Nadir's prosecution.

To cap all this, Asil Nadir's trial on charges of theft and false accounting was overshadowed by shocking allegations that he had conspired to bribe the judge – allegations for which the SFO eventually apologised and admitted there was no evidence. Surely none of this is a coincidence. How could so many things go wrong with one man's prosecution?

By the time Asil Nadir left the UK in May 1993 he had despaired of ever getting the chance to prove his innocence. Polly Peck shareholders and creditors, too, have not had their day in court – and are unlikely to – as a result of the SFO's extraordinary management of his case. They have been persuaded that PPI collapsed because Asil Nadir was a crook who had stolen their money. The truth is otherwise, and no company could have survived such an onslaught. But the SFO's future depended on justifying the raid that brought down the company.

2. The Rise and Rise of Polly Peck

I FIRST MET Asil Nadir in 1985 through a former banking colleague Ted Petropoulos who was working for him as a financial adviser. I was then a manager at the West End branch of Citibank in London. Ted felt that Asil needed the services of a major bank with expertise in managing trusts for foreign residents of the UK. Many British do not appreciate it, but for foreigners Britain is one of the most rewarding of all tax havens. Of course I had heard of Asil Nadir and Polly Peck, by then well on the way to becoming one of the decade's stock-market success stories, but I didn't know much about the company. I remember my mother buying me a Polly Peck dress at Affleck & Browns in Manchester as a child – it was a very well made garment that never seemed to show any signs of wear – and I assumed that PPI's main business was still textiles. At that time Polly Peck was based in the garment district of Commercial Road in the East End of London, a rather seedy area on the edge of the City.

As I was to discover, PPI was now a major international producer and trader in fruit. It also owned Vestel, a large Turkish electronics company, which manufactured many well-known consumer electrical products under licence. Outside the PPI headquarters there were flags representing the Queen's Award for Industry, a source of enormous pride to the Nadir family. I entered a sumptuous office –

a vast room with cream carpets overlaid by Turkish rugs and containing a tasteful mixture of antique and modern furniture. Asil Nadir was courteous, charming and immaculately dressed in a dark suit, silk tie and impeccable white shirt. Over many cups of Turkish coffee Ted and I discussed his situation with him and the pros and cons of the British tax system in relation to his financial affairs. Although he held a British passport Asil Nadir was a foreign resident, which could hold a potential tax advantage for him.

The success of Polly Peck, founded several years earlier following the construction of a packaging factory in Asil Nadir's homeland of Turkish Northern Cyprus, had made him and his family very wealthy. With an international company to run he needed help to manage the family's financial affairs properly. When several weeks later we met again, I took two experts along to outline what I had in mind. One of them was my boss at Citibank, Bernard Stalder, a Swiss national who was number two at Citibank's private-banking operation. The other was Carl Stibolt, a US lawyer who ran Confidas, Citibank's Swiss Trust Management Company, based in Zurich. We were given the go-ahead to prepare proposals for managing the Nadirs' financial affairs, and we celebrated winning an important new client with lunch at the Chesterfield Hotel. There we dined on Dover sole, and henceforth DOVER became the in-house code-name for any dealings with the Nadirs – something that several years on one newspaper decided was distinctly fishy in its hunt for significant data.

A few months later Citibank invited Asil Nadir to lunch at its offices on the corner of Berkeley Square – Bernard Carl and I were also there. During lunch he kept looking out into Berkeley Square, where a large For Lease sign could be seen on one of its elegant Georgian buildings. For some time Ted had been trying to persuade Mr Nadir that PPI should have more prestigious offices to enhance its market image. A few days later Ted told me that Polly Peck had leased the building. Unlike the open-plan Citibank offices, 42 Berkeley Square had a traditional interior, which Mr Nadir filled with beautiful antiques.

The death of Asil Nadir's father, Irfan, in April 1986 accelerated the need for the family to organise their financial affairs. Irfan Nadir had brought his family to England in the 1960s to escape the troubles in Cyprus. In the years following independence from Britain, attacks on the Turkish minority were commonplace – the beginnings of what we now call ethnic cleansing. Irfan was an entrepreneur, who built a thriving textile business in London's East End. He and his equally entrepreneurial son, who together ran Wearwell, the family textile company that floated on the stock market in the early 1970s, did not always see eye to eye, although the family was exceptionally close. Asil Nadir once told me that at one stage he had told his father that England was too small for both of them. When Irfan had returned to Northern Cyprus with his wife, Safiye, to supervise the businesses there, he left Asil to run those in the UK.

Despite the clash between two strong personalities, Asil Nadir had great love and respect for his father, who was much admired in his native Cyprus and is still remembered there today, where annual memorial services are held in the mosques on the anniversary of his death. Irfan Nadir owned a lot of property in Northern Cyprus and London. To complicate matters, some of the Nadir family were UK residents, while others lived in Northern Cyprus. Asil Nadir realised that he faced considerable tax liabilities if these matters were not organised – like many entrepreneurs his personal affairs took a poor second place to corporate business. Several times he suggested that he needed someone to look after his affairs full time. In May 1987 I agreed to leave Citibank and join him.

Almost as soon as I started my new job he insisted I should visit his native country. 'If you don't get to love my people, you will not be able to work for me,' he said.

I flew to Cyprus on the private jet with Mr Nadir, his son Serhan and other members of the family. It was the last holiday I would have until September 1990, the time of the dramatic SFO raid on my office.

There was a wonderful welcome for us at Ercan Airport, where I was presented with a huge bunch of flowers. Many dignitaries turned out to greet us, and I realised how well regarded Asil Nadir was in his homeland. I also got my first inkling of some of the problems Northern Cyprus faced, recognised as it was by no other country than Turkey. At passport control an official offered to stamp a piece of paper slipped inside in case I ever wanted to go to the South. This seemed very odd, and I remember telling him that if the Greek

Cypriots objected to a Turkish Cypriot stamp in my passport then I didn't want to go there.

Northern Cyprus is a country of flowers, and the scent of jasmine is always in the air – a garland of jasmine is the traditional welcome for visitors. Along the north coast the Kyrenian mountain range sweeping down to the sea with its three Crusader castles is spectacular, taking on a different aspect as the seasons change. Delightful though the island is, it became clear that Northern Cyprus had many problems because of its lack of recognition as a country. There were no direct flights there except from Turkey; international newspapers were almost impossible to get, and there wasn't even a good Turkish daily newspaper, let alone anything in English – despite the existence of a significant expatriate community. I decided that if there was any opportunity, I would make sure there were decent newspapers available in both languages.

I remember a wonderful evening spent with Asil Nadir at a restaurant inside the grounds of the famous Bellapais Abbey. It sits halfway up the mountain, from where we were able to gaze at the sea several miles below. The night air was warm, the stars were out, and my new employer was in an expansive mood. We talked for five hours about his plans, about his vision of Cyprus becoming an offshore tax haven for Turkey and the eventual emergence of Russia and China into the democratic world. It was fascinating to listen to him. A friend who had accompanied me on the trip declared afterwards: 'I am a hard-nosed journalist and not easily influenced by people but that was one of the most memorable evenings I have ever spent.'

When in Cyprus Mr Nadir spent the mornings at his office in Nicosia and his afternoons on a boat called *Serhan* after his younger son. I arranged to meet him one day on the beach at the Zephyros Hotel for lunch. I arrived as his boat dropped anchor, and he started swimming towards the shore. I waded in to join him, and we had a business discussion as the waves washed around us about the prospects of launching newspapers in Cyprus. 'Elizabeth,' he said, 'if you can produce a newspaper on this island you will have worked a miracle. I've been trying for years but getting people together without continual arguments is something else.'

Asil Nadir owned newspapers in Turkey, and in July 1989 *Kibris*, a Turkish-language daily paper, started up in Northern Cyprus, followed by an English weekly. I was involved in its research and planning for the Cypriot market, and I felt immensely proud when the first issue rolled off the presses. Bruce Matthews, once a key figure in newspapers such as the *Sunday Times* when he was managing director at News International, came on board as a consultant.

There had been a last-minute panic when one of the printing machines broke down on the day before the launch, and the spare part had to be flown in from Holland in Asil Nadir's private plane. Bruce, an Australian who had been in the hot seat at News International during the Wapping dispute, remarked that there had been difficulties distributing the *Sunday Times* because of transport problems. Here in Cyprus we had the transport, but no newspaper. We started printing the first issue of *Kibris* with a handmade part rustled up from an old radio by one of the Turkish engineers.

Asil Nadir did not have his own house on the island at this time. When visiting Northern Cyprus he stayed with his mother or other relatives. One day I heard there was a house on the market at Lapta, in which he had once expressed an interest. I went to have a look. From the outside it was unremarkable, but inside it was beautiful – built around a square courtyard full of plants and shrubs. With its elegant stone arches it had a peaceful, monastic atmosphere. The large sitting-room, once a camel stall, was spectacular, with its Gonyeli stone floor and two large fireplaces. The house once belonged to Lawrence Durrell's architect friend Austen Harrison, and it is mentioned in his famous book *Bitter Lemons*. Asil Nadir could not resist it. Filled now with solid oak English furniture it is a perfect blend of Levant and English country-house style, a welcome refuge for him when he returned to Cyprus in May 1993.

Back in England after my first trip to Cyprus we needed to establish an office and get on with finding the right advisers. Polly Peck was no longer a family business, and with its high stock-market profile the company now had a structure of professional directors and managers appropriate to a company of its size, although some of the Nadir family resented what they regarded as a take-over by outsiders.

Asil Nadir was aware of the important part his parents and his younger sister, Bilge Nevzat, had played in the early growth of the company. He wanted to give his family all the help he could to set up new businesses in order to diversify the family's interests. Bilge and her husband, Fehim Nevzat, had prospered in the travel and textiles business, and they wanted to find a suitable stock-market vehicle. Eventually they bought a 'shell company' that became Noble Raredon – Bilge, a beautiful woman five years to the day younger than her brother, became one of the few women in the UK to run her own publicly quoted company.

In the autumn of 1987 South Audley Management was established with me as chairman and named after the street in Mayfair where we had our first offices. SAM would take over the running of Mr Nadir's private financial affairs with advice from outside professionals who had nothing to do with the corporate side of his activities.

Rawlinson & Hunter, the accountants, were retained to study the tax situation. The UK can be a tax haven for individuals whose domicile of origin is considered to be outside Britain. As Asil Nadir was born in Northern Cyprus, he only paid UK taxes on his UK earnings, with his foreign income exempt. But there were a number of problems. If he were to die his worldwide assets would be liable to UK tax; if his mother were to die Mr Nadir and his two sisters who lived in the UK would be taxed on their inheritance; and there were always rumours that the Government was considering altering the tax advantages for overseas residents. Many people are opposed to these arrangements – they believed their continuance had something to do with the large sums of money given to the Conservative Party by certain wealthy individuals who benefited from and supported their policies. It was important to set up offshore trusts to hold the family's assets both here and abroad in order to protect them legally from any potential liabilities. My job was to see that this was done. South Audley Management was a service company that managed the family's UK properties.

One of my first tasks was really bizarre. Mr Nadir wanted help to obtain a divorce from his wife Aysegul. 'Can you imagine anyone being so stupid as to marry the same woman twice?' he used to ask me. Asil Nadir's relationship with the attractive woman he twice wed and twice divorced fascinated the gossip columns in both the UK and Turkey. They had married first when they were both very young, and she had borne him two sons. Although they had been separated for a number of years they were still very fond of each other. I wondered how I could possibly help in such a personal matter, but I had been divorced twice myself so I had some practical experience. I phoned a lawyer friend and said, 'I have a bit of a problem. I have to get a divorce, but this time it's not for me.'

Mr Nadir did not want a nasty divorce, although he was hurt by the stories of Aysegul's numerous affairs that had been appearing in the Turkish press. He simply wished to formalise the end of his marriage – but on grounds of incompatibility, not adultery. The problem was that Aysegul did not want a divorce, and as a Turkish subject she could return to Istanbul and sit there for seven years before a divorce could be achieved. I knew that the parting could not be as amicable as he wanted – and so did the legal team I took to lunch with Mr Nadir at his home in Istanbul.

The Yali, Asil Nadir's home in Istanbul, is a 300-year-old Ottoman summer palace right on the Asian bank of the Bosphorus. Set in a tranquil garden, it is hard to believe that it is so near the heart of Istanbul, a famously noisy city. The water laps its walls, and the interior was painted by Venetian artists of the day. The Nadir family had restored it beautifully.

Our lunch was almost over when I finally broached the difficult subject we had come here to discuss. I explained to Asil that if he wanted to divorce Aysegul the grounds would have to be adultery. By this time Aysegul was having an affair with Oliver Hoare, a London antique dealer now better known as a friend of the Princess of Wales. Asil was visibly upset by the thought of hurting Aysegul, and there were tears in his eyes as he reluctantly accepted our advice that the grounds for divorce had to be adultery.

Back in London the divorce lawyers hired a private detective to shadow Aysegul. We found out that she and her friend Oliver were going to Istanbul, where Aysegul was holding a party at the Yali. The investigators travelled on the same plane and took photographs. What they didn't anticipate was the vigilance of the Turkish police who kept a close eye on the Nadir home, and there was nearly an international incident when a British private detective was found lurking in the shadows of the Yali in the early hours of the morning. Fortunately one of Asil's employees at Vestel was the former head of the Turkish police, and he was able to sort things out.

Despite the fact that she knew I had been instrumental in helping Mr Nadir obtain his second divorce without another financial settlement, Aysegul was always very charming to me. Once called 'the most beautiful woman in Turkey', she was not classically beautiful, rather tall and sensual with the ability to make a stunning impact when she entered a room. She was never short of male admirers who found her great fun.

Despite the divorce Asil and Aysegul remained good friends. She came forward in December 1990 to put up part of his £3.5 million bail and vigorously defended her former husband. I saw a lot of her after the collapse of PPI because she acted as a liaison between Mr Nadir and me at a time when he was prevented by his bail conditions from speaking to any of his former staff.

In the summer of 1991 Aysegul decided to go back to Turkey, and I helped her to organise her move. She sorted through her massive piles of paperwork, gaily tearing up handwritten letters from the great and the good, including one from Princess Margaret, who had once stayed at the Yali. I suggested she should really keep some of these letters in case she ever wanted to write her own, very colourful, life story. Her entire apartment was crammed with cardboard boxes topped by her white Persian cat, all set to go to Istanbul by plane.

Aysegul never travelled without masses of luggage, but this was ridiculous, and British Airways would not take everything. So I offered to run some 20 boxes to Gatwick to go by Noble Air, the Nadir family airline that was still operating, and see them on the plane. The operation went smoothly until one box was set aside for further inspection after going through the X-ray machine. The box was opened and out came an extraordinary outfit from Anouska Hempel, one of Aysegul's favourite fashion designers. It was a Wild West outfit complete with real, spent cartridge shells sewn into the bodice and waistband.

Having spent the previous few months hounded by the press and the Serious Fraud Office, I could just see the headlines, NADIR AIDE SMUGGLES ARMS TO TURKEY, as two very tall policemen bore down upon me. I was told that I was contravening the Firearms Act, since the shells could be refilled. Well, this would be a new and bizarre addition to the list of my alleged misdemeanours, I thought. But they saw the humour of the situation and told me they would not be pressing charges this time.

My work for Mr Nadir was not always this extraordinary. At the beginning it mostly involved a hard slog through piles of documents with the family accountant, trying to sort out his neglected personal affairs and initiate some projects.

In October 1987 there was a global stock-market collapse. Black Monday, as it became known, did not affect PPI significantly, but many in the City had a rough ride. One young man, Jason Davies, a stockbroker friend of Asil Nadir's eldest son, Birol, from the days when they had both worked in a stockbroking firm called Giles & Overbury, found himself owing a colossal debt of £200,000 when one of his clients could not honour a transaction following the market collapse. On top of all that his wife was three months pregnant.

One day Birol came to me and told me what had happened to his friend. He wanted me to meet him because Jason was a versatile sort of person who might be helpful in the office. My staff at that time only consisted of a Turkish Cypriot accountant and a secretary, and SAM had lots of projects with which to cope. I told Birol to introduce Jason Davies to his father with the suggestion that we employ him as a consultant. Asil agreed to hire Jason as a part-time consultant to SAM and allowed Jason's company, Birchward Ltd, to rent an office from SAM in South Audley Street. Jason would continue his stock-broking activities with a firm called A. J. Bekhor, to whom he owed the debt, as well as dealing with other brokers. He was what was known as a 'half-commission man', which meant that he was not employed by a stockbroking firm, but he split the commission on his clients' share transactions with the firm through which he placed orders. He had a large number of Turkish clients, whom he had met through Birol, and investing for them would bring him in additional income to help him pay off his debts.

Initially Jason Davies assisted me at SAM with project development for the Cypriot newspaper and the purchase of Baggrave Hall as Asil Nadir's country home in Britain. He also bought considerable quantities of Polly Peck shares for Safiye Nadir's companies. The family wanted to increase its holding in Polly Peck, and Mr Nadir made no secret of his wish to take the company into private ownership again. One of my first tasks at SAM was to organise the bank loans for these share purchases by Safiye Nadir through a private trust company administered from Switzerland and set up by our advisers. It was all perfectly legitimate, and the shares were part of the declared Nadir family holding. But these share purchases, and the role of Jason Davies, were later to become the focus of the investigatory and media blitz that resulted eventually in the collapse of Polly Peck.

In retrospect, asking Jason to purchase Safiye Nadir's shares was probably not a good idea. We should have approached Asil Nadir's usual stockbrokers – Shearson Lehman, Kitcat & Aitken and BZW had all bought for him and the family in the past. But Jason was Birol's friend, and he was desperate to pay off his debt at A. J. Bekhor. Buying all the shares for Safiye Nadir on a commission-sharing basis made him a lot of money for little effort. And he made himself extremely useful at SAM when we were dealing with the Cypriot newspaper project and the purchase of a country home and farm for Asil Nadir. Most of the time Jason was just a consultant – he was a director for only six months, and that was only because our accountants said that we needed some more bodies on the board.

Mr Nadir's father, Irfan, had been the owner of a country estate in Sussex. He had been generous to his Cypriot friends, allowing them to overshoot his lands, and whenever Asil Nadir went to visit there was never a bird in sight, which upset him. Another of my concerns at SAM became to acquire a country estate for Asil Nadir himself, with the underlying instructions that it must be managed properly. When he bought his own estate, Baggrave Hall in Leicestershire, new coverts were established for the pheasants, but everyone was under strict instructions that no birds were ever to be shot.

I went to see Baggrave in the spring of 1988, having aroused Asil Nadir's interest through the glossy brochure presenting the sale. It was set in wonderful countryside near Market Harborough with good road links to London, but both the house and the farm had seen better days, and I could see that restoring it all would be a mammoth task. But when Mr Nadir went to see it he could see its potential and decided to go ahead, despite its dilapidated state.

When we stayed at Baggrave initially, Asil Nadir lived in one of the cottages we had renovated. We concentrated on the farm first and established a breeding programme for Aberdeen Angus cattle. Being Scottish I thought that Scottish beef was the best in the world and could not understand the popularity of imported foreign beef in the UK. I then discovered that the carcass of the native Aberdeen Angus was considered too small for the catering industry, so we brought over larger Canadian Aberdeen Angus, descendants of the cattle that went to Canada with Scottish emigrants at the time of the Highland

Clearances, to breed with them to produce a bigger animal on a commercial basis.

Asil Nadir used to wander round in the early morning looking at his cattle. He hated the idea of them being sent for slaughter. I think he was somewhat relieved when I explained to him that the cattle he had been visiting weren't going to be slaughtered as they were our prizewinning pedigrees. However, I couldn't hide the fact that another hundred or so animals in the next barn were being bred for beef, albeit in possibly more luxurious conditions than the less fortunate of their species. After all, the farm was intended to pay its way, and it would have done.

Irfan Nadir had also owned race horses, racing them in the UK under his own colours. The family had enjoyed race-going in Northern Cyprus under British rule, and Mr Nadir liked the idea of re-establishing horse racing there. I knew Jenny Pitman, the famous trainer, and the two of us met one night to discuss it. During dinner I suggested that Mr Nadir might be interested in having a racehorse and resurrecting his father's old colours. He didn't object, and I felt it would encourage him out of the office.

Jenny found a horse for us called Golden Freeze, which Mr Nadir bought. It won several races, but my hopes of getting its owner out of the office and on to the racecourse to watch it run came to naught. He just installed a television set in his office and watched the racing from there. The only race he went to see was the Cheltenham Gold Cup. Golden Freeze had been expected to win – all the Nadir family had turned out – but the horse was pulled up, and Asil Nadir rushed back to work threatening to sell it as he was so disgusted.

By the time I started work for Mr Nadir, he and his controversial Polly Peck company had become a City legend. In February 1980, although then still running Wearwell, the family textile firm, Asil Nadir had decided to expand his business by buying a small 'shell' outfit called Polly Peck. The company was a well-known women's wear manufacturer, but its basic business was losing money and going nowhere. Under City rules, Mr Nadir had to make a formal bid at 9p a share. The word quickly went round that he was nursing ambitious plans to expand the company, and the shares began to roar ahead. By July 1980, before he had done anything, they hit a breath-taking 85p, simply on the strength of rumours of what he might do. Then he announced that Polly Peck would buy control, at cost, of

Unipac, a cardboard box-making plant he had set up in the Northern Cypriot port of Famagusta.

Polly Peck raised £1.5 million by selling new shares and bought the Cyprus factory. Although Northern Cyprus was a major grower of citrus fruit – mostly oranges and lemons – Mr Nadir had realised that there was always a shortage of low-priced packaging. He knew the citrus business well, as his family had acquired acres of citrus groves in the west of the island, and he understood the opportunities for exploiting the rich, fertile land.

Encouraged by the Turkish Cypriot government, and with the support of his father, then one of the most prominent businessmen in the area, he felt he could make money and help his homeland prosper by providing proper packaging and bringing a more commercial approach to the export of citrus. Put together in a large building by the waterfront, the new Polly Peck plant had been established after a detailed business plan by London accountants Coopers & Lybrand, and the revived Polly Peck was confident enough to predict profits of £2 million in the first year of operation under Nadir ownership. The plant had teething troubles, and the factory was completed too late to supply boxes for the first year's citrus crop. But it soon had a virtual monopoly of the packing business, and, with favourable tax treatment from the Turkish Cypriot authorities, it began making handsome profits – so handsome that some in the City doubted they were real.

The packaging plant was merely the start. Asil Nadir had a profound belief in the capacity of business to change lives for the better. He claimed that underdeveloped countries did not need aid – they needed capital and expertise to establish export industries that could compete with the rest of the world. He saw Turkey and Northern Cyprus as a prime example of a region ripe for development. Soon Asil Nadir was busy developing other plans for marrying the resources of Northern Cyprus and Turkey with capital raised in London.

Although he had his critics and was subjected from the early days to constant sniping from Greek sympathisers in London, Mr Nadir quickly built a sizeable fan club of investors delighted to share his vision – and to enjoy a soaring share price. That made Polly Peck the hottest stock in the City. It was an investor's dream come true, rocketing from 9p to £36 inside a few years. Anyone who put £1000 in Polly Peck as Mr Nadir moved in would have had shares worth £1 million by the end of the decade. It was a stock-market sensation.

The cardboard-box plant was the springboard for a series of more ambitious investments. In addition to the citrus business Polly Peck went into electronics, building the Vestel television and consumer-electronics manufacturing plant near Izmir in Turkey. The first significant local company, it challenged the import of expensive television sets into Turkey. Polly Peck also bought Russell Hobbs, the British domestic utensils company, and the Taiwan-based Capetronics group. Mr Nadir liked the high-tech business, and PPI later purchased a controlling stake in Sansui, a Japanese audio group that had invested a great deal in research and development. It was the first time that an outsider had been able to buy a significant stake in Japanese industry.

Nadir had also decided that PPI should have a stake in the growing tourist industry, and not just in Turkey, where he was planning a sumptuous new hotel in Antalya, on the Mediterranean coast. He believed that tourism could transform the economy of Northern Cyprus, which had suffered enormously following the partition of 1974.

His greatest coup, however, was the acquisition of Del Monte, the North American fresh fruit business, in 1989. That gave his substantial fruit operations an internationally known brand name, and he himself became known as 'the man from Del Monte'. Del Monte was the largest pineapple producer in the world, and the third largest supplier of bananas, which made it a perfect fit with his existing citrus-fruit business. The acquisition of Del Monte for £550m was the high point for Polly Peck. It provided the company with international status and made it far less dependent on Turkey and Cyprus. But, after the early flurry, he always thought that their achievements, and the share price, were undervalued.

The City of London never quite knew what to make of Mr Nadir. Despite the company's dramatic profits growth and the evidence of Mr Nadir's energy and imagination in building up an international company, there were plenty of sceptics. Critics pointed out that PPI was very secretive about the breakdown of its profits, and there were worries about the high level of inflation in Turkey and the continual decline of the Turkish currency. Asil Nadir himself also seemed rather mysterious and enigmatic – he rarely gave interviews to the press, which, of course, encouraged their interest, and he made very few close friends in the City, although there were many happy to tag along, enjoying the fortune his initiatives had made for them.

I suppose some people regarded him as an upstart – and a foreign upstart at that. People liked to think of him as *nouveau riche*, but the family had been prosperous for many years. In fact his was second-generation wealth, and he was confident in his own taste. He was also at his ease with women and admired those with brains and character. He has an almost naive sweetness that women find very attractive. He was wonderful to work for because he let you, and expected you, to get on with things.

He was, however, never much good at taking advice or disclosing his plans, and his board of directors found him charming and courteous but very determined when it came to having his own way – particularly as his own way appeared to work so well in terms of business and profits. They marvelled at his range of contacts – people were so intrigued by him that doors opened everywhere.

His management style was eccentric by the standards of most public company chairmen and owed much to the Ottoman policy of divide and rule – one senior London director who was temporarily out of favour once found he could not get to see the chairman for three months. There were several boardroom bust-ups, and one criticism I will make of him is that he found it hard to take criticism, even constructive criticism. But however frustrating his fellow directors found him they could not help liking him – he was and still is a very kind man.

He quickly grew disillusioned with the City of London, where stockbrokers and their analysts seemed to look no further than the next set of profit figures. Often their forecasts were highly specu-lative, which caused problems for the shares, particularly in the early 1980s. At that time Polly Peck was rated very highly on the stock-market, with its price:earnings ratio, the barometer of stock-market anticipation, in the stratosphere – and higher even than the price:earnings ratios of other 'growth' stocks such as the Body Shop. The downside to all this was that the shares were intensely sensitive to rumour and gossip in the markets. While it was immensely flattering for the company to be given such a high rating, it created huge expectations among its City followers.

Asil Nadir is always tremendously optimistic – a trait that has got him into trouble. He wants to keep everybody happy and sometimes promises things that, with the best will in the world, he can not deliver. But, without that optimism he would not have survived what happened to him later, although it created problems for him.

On more than one occasion he felt that the City had wrong-footed him by jumping to conclusions. Particularly in 1986 when a stockbrokers' profit forecast for PPI was revised downwards, triggering off panic selling by some investors and causing the Stock Exchange to inquire about what looked like a remarkably well timed bout of institutional share selling.

It was incidents like this that made him cynical about the City and gave the share price a reputation for volatility that did not find favour with the Stock Exchange. The Polly Peck shares were also very popular with Turkish investors. The Istanbul stock-market was in its infancy, and Polly Peck was becoming one of the most dynamic commercial operations in Turkey. Because of the almost constant devaluation of the lire, many rich Turks liked to invest in hard currency, and PPI shares represented the best opportunity for investing in the growth of their own economy. They were great fans of the shares. This, too, attracted the attention of stock-market cynics who thought that all these investors were some kind of a front for Asil Nadir. There was a good measure of racism and snobbery in all this, and it helped to contribute to his downfall.

On top of that Polly Peck shares proved very vulnerable to a politically motivated attack. If Mr Nadir were now invited to identify one single event that marked the turning-point in his fortunes, he would probably say it was his meeting in mid-December 1989 with Nelson Ledsky, the US State Department official whose task it was at that time to find a solution to what the Americans thought of as 'the Cyprus problem'.

By then I had made numerous trips to Northern Cyprus, and I had begun to realise just how much hostility there was between the Greek South and the Turkish North and how sensitive an issue the small island was internationally. Britain, its former colonial ruler, still has military bases in Greek Cyprus, but the Americans have always been far more concerned about the reunification of the island. There is a large and vociferous Greek lobby in the USA, which has ensured that the matter is always on the political agenda, and successive American Presidents have promised to find solutions – only recently the US State Department said that Cyprus was its biggest concern after Bosnia. In the UK, where many remember the troubles of the late 1950s and early 1960s, it has always seemed far less of an issue, although each side of the island has support committees among British Members of Parliament. An additional problem for the USA is the fact that it has important military bases in Turkey. So this, plus the domestic Greek lobby, means that it is under pressure from both sides. Hence the US Government's constantly stated objective to broker some kind of an agreement.

Nelson Ledsky's approach to Asil Nadir came through the US embassy in London, and after consulting the Turkish and Northern Cypriot governments Mr Nadir agreed to see him. It was not surprising that Ledsky wanted to talk to him – his Turkish newspapers backed the then Prime Minister Turgut Ozal and his Motherland Party, while in Northern Cyprus he was one of the main supporters of the Turkish Republic of Northern Cyprus (TRNC) President Rauf Denktas, who was a personal friend. Ledsky was clearly dissatisfied with Denktas's uncompromising attitude towards suggestions of reunification. During their one-and-a-half hour meeting he suggested that Mr Nadir should meet George Vassiliou, the Greek Cypriot President. His idea seemed to be that if Mr Nadir, then the most powerful economic force in Northern Cyprus, could be persuaded of the wisdom of a settlement, then it might happen. Essentially Ledsky was seeing if Mr Nadir would be prepared to ditch Denktas. That, at least, was the way Mr Nadir interpreted the meeting.

Needless to say Asil Nadir would not be party to such a deal, and he already had strong views on what was in the best interests of Turkey and Northern Cyprus. Many people in Turkey saw and still see their future in the European Community, and there is enormous resentment that the country is not a member – while Greece is – despite its key role in Western defence. But Mr Nadir told Ledsky that he envisaged instead a powerful economic union of Turkish-speaking states, stretching from Europe to the borders of China once the USSR had fallen apart. He hated the idea that Turkey had to humble itself to be 'accepted' by the EC countries; that its human rights record, which was admittedly not brilliant, was given such prominence, and its real achievements were overlooked.

Asil Nadir was well aware of the threat of Muslim fundamentalism long before most of us in the West had ever heard of it. A friend remembers sitting with him on the little iron balcony of the Yali in Istanbul one evening in the mid-1980s. The sun was going down over the city, and huge ships bearing the hammer and sickle of the USSR were making their way through the Bosphorus from the Black Sea. They were so close to the USSR, his friend remarked – wasn't that worrying? No, said Mr Nadir. It was religious fanaticism that was the real threat to the state and economy of Turkey. It was this kind of thinking that he outlined to an astonished Ledsky.

Mr Nadir was not, in fact, opposed to the idea of a settlement over Cyprus. But he believed it should only take place when the Turkish Republic of Northern Cyprus could stand on its own feet economically. The Greek South was immensely prosperous. It had built up a thriving tourist industry with the help of international aid money and soft loans after the 1974 division of the island. Polly Peck, the major employer in the North, was transforming the economy, but there was some way to go before the Turkish Cypriots could negotiate as equals.

At the time of the Ledsky meeting Asil Nadir told his fellow PPI directors that he thought a Cyprus settlement was about eighteen months away. What the board of PPI was focusing on was the huge rise in value this would mean for PPI's businesses in the North of the island. Settlement on the right terms would mean political recognition – and with political recognition would come vastly increased financial possibilities for the company.

Mr Nadir believes that his meeting with Ledsky brought the political importance of PPI sharply into focus. From then on he believes he was a target, not just for the Greek Cypriots, who kept up a barrage of anti-Nadir propaganda, but also for the US Government, who regarded him and his support for President Denktas as an obstacle to their much longed-for settlement. It was after the Ledsky meeting that he received a warning from Government sources in Ankara, Turkey's political capital, that there was going to be an attack on him and his company. In March 1990 he told his board that he believed that there would be a massive onslaught against Polly Peck.

British journalists have always dismissed Nadir's claims that there was a politically motivated plot against his company as a paranoid fantasy. But the Greek Cypriots had already tried, and nearly succeeded, in bringing down Polly Peck several years before. Mr Nadir never forgot that. It brought him and his company to the brink of destruction. At the beginning of 1983 the PPI share price had crashed dramatically after doubts were cast on the favourable tax exemptions enjoyed by Unipac, Polly Peck's Northern Cyprus packaging company. By this time the operation was a substantial success, with pre-tax profits at around £25 million and institutional investors beginning to take a keen interest.

By 1983 Polly Peck had become one of the best-performing shares ever on the stock-market. More importantly the company not only brought employment to the war-torn economy of Northern Cyprus but also gave it access to hard-currency earnings and capital. The Greek Cypriots were alarmed. Already PPI had revived the citrus industry, marketing the fruit abroad, and was beginning to diversify into other areas. At one point in the panic the shares halved from £36 to £15 before being suspended. The stock-market was rocked by Greek Cypriot claims, which started with an article in the *Financial Times*, that the Polly Peck assets in Northern Cyprus included lands 'stolen' from them in the partition of 1974. These were the citrus groves at Guzelyurt, one of the most fertile areas on the island and now firmly in the Turkish half. The Greek Cypriots claimed that Polly Peck was not disclosing important information to shareholders, in breach of the Companies Act. These facts were that profits from its Northern Cyprus business would vanish into thin air when the 'Cyprus problem' was resolved. Any settlement would mean that the citrus groves would be returned to the Greek Cypriots, and that the company's monopoly of cardboard-box production would end.

The Greek Cypriots approached selected members of the press, although the authors of the damaging allegations were initially not anxious for their part in the affair to be disclosed. Polly Peck was lucky to survive the onslaught. Its shares plummeted, and although they eventually recovered, confidence in the company was badly dented, never to return completely. After that Greek Cypriot attack, the price was always more sensitive, more vulnerable than most to unsettling rumour and gossip. It never regained the high rating it had enjoyed in its earlier years. There were threats of legal action, and the

Cyprus High Commission went to the Foreign Office in London and asked the British Government to investigate Polly Peck, claiming that the business had broken UK company law. Many investors lost money in the crash.

Ironically it was a childhood friend of Mr Nadir's who spearheaded the 1983 campaign against him. George Iacovou, by now Permanent Secretary in the Foreign Ministry of the Greek Cypriot Government, had lived in the same Famagusta street as the Nadir family back in the late 1940s. The families were so friendly that they often spent New Year's Eve together singing carols, accompanied by Asil on his violin. Iacovou, then seven years old, was the only other child present at Mr Nadir's Islamic circumcision ceremony – the only anaesthetic being a piece of Turkish Delight.

Asil Nadir recalls that they were the best of friends until EOKA, the Greek anti-British terrorist movement started in the mid-1950s. 'When the Greeks started accusing the Turks of helping the British, the Iacovous changed their attitude,' he told me. 'It was as though we had never been friends.' However, when Iacovou's sister was arrested for throwing stones at British troops, Mr Nadir's mother, Safiye, pleaded with the local Turkish chief of police for her release.

In 1960 Cyprus became independent. In the years that followed many Turkish Cypriot families like the Nadirs left the island. They were an ethnic minority and felt threatened by their Greek Cypriot neighbours, who considered them 'traitors' because they had supported the British, whom the Turks regarded as their protectors. Those in the UK who now back the claims of the Greek south against the unrecognised TRNC have conveniently forgotten that the Turkish community were, rightly or wrongly, loyal to the British during the troubles of the 1950s. That, as much as the ancient enmity of Greek and Turk, resulted in the oppression of the Turkish community in the 1960s after independence. Mr Nadir can sound quite bitter when he talks about this.

The final crunch came in the summer of 1974 when President Makarios was removed in a coup, and a former EOKA terrorist, Nikos Sampson, became head of state. Years ago the Nadirs had known Sampson, and Mr Nadir and his sisters had played with him in the streets of Famagusta. Now he was known as a notorious gunman, and a passionate advocate of Enosis, the movement for union with Greece, where the military junta was then installed. The

Turkish Cypriots were terrified. They huddled into enclaves, and tens of thousands took shelter inside the old walled town of Famagusta as they were encircled by the Greek Cypriots. Turkey invaded the north of the island to protect them, and Cyprus was partitioned. Turkish Cypriots from the south went north, Greek Cypriots in the north went south. There was bloodshed and bitterness on both sides.

Turkey's invasion was condemned by the international community, which has refused to recognise Northern Cyprus. In the years after the war the economy dwindled, and the citrus fruit rotted on the trees. Few people were prepared to invest serious money in business there, since the country was not recognised by anyone except Turkey, and there was always the threat that any goods you wanted to export might be embargoed. But in the late 1970s increasing numbers of Turkish Cypriots, such as Mr Nadir's parents, decided to go back home and see what could be done. The partition looked pretty permanent, and they felt more secure – particularly as Turkey continued to maintain a large military presence on the island.

The Nadirs return was initially linked to the Wearwell rag-trade company in London. It was arranged that Wearwell would ship cloth by the container-load to Northern Cyprus. There it would be sewn, to be returned to London. Both sides benefited: Wearwell had dresses produced cheaply, and the Northern Cypriots enjoyed a labour boom. Later, working from an office in Nicosia festooned with flags celebrating the Queen's Award for Industry, Irfan and Safiye Nadir were involved in the establishment of the packaging plant in Famagusta, on which Polly Peck's business was founded.

In 1984 when Northern Cyprus established itself as the Turkish Republic of Northern Cyprus, staking its claim to be a separate independent state, there were worries that PPI would be hit by embargoes on its exports. Every time United Nations or US-sponsored settlement talks were mooted, there were concerns in the City of London that 'peace would break out' in Cyprus, and reunification might spell the end of Polly Peck's power and profits there.

The Greek Cypriots made no visible, official attack on Polly Peck following the mischief they managed to stir up in 1983. But, they did set up a government committee to monitor Mr Nadir's activities, and he became convinced that Greek Cypriots were behind press attacks in *Private Eye* and some British national newspapers. What really caused them to swing into action again, however, was Polly Peck's acquisition of Del Monte in 1989. In an interview in 1993 with a member of the BBC's *Panorama* team (for a programme that was never shown), George Iacovou discussed freely the anxieties of the Greek Cypriot Government about Mr Nadir's growing status and influence.

> After the acquisition of Del Monte he could not be stopped. We knew he would get a knighthood through his charitable contributions . . . We knew he was going to No. 10 Downing Street. He suddenly had enormous political leverage and had started to influence the British Government on its policy towards Cyprus, especially Northern Cyprus – the occupied lands. There was no such Greek Cypriot wielding such influence. This concerned us. We had another meeting and assessed the situation in late 1989.

Iacovou went on to explain that his Nadir Committee had provided reports and documentation to the Department of Trade, the Institute of Chartered Accountants, the Stock Exchange and the Serious Fraud Office on a continual basis, as well as encouraging their contacts in the British media to keep up a offensive against the company. Quite what all these worthy bodies thought, or did, about these reports is not known, although Iacovou boasted in this interview that the SFO and the Polly Peck administrators had used the results of the investigations.

Both Iacovou and George Vassiliou, who became Greek Cypriot President in 1988, reckoned that their machinations had managed to upset Polly Peck's planned flotation in early 1990 of the Del Monte fruit business in the USA. Vassiliou told the *Panorama* interview: 'We were able to tell the Securities and Exchange Commission that Nadir was talking of phantom profits on his Cyprus operations. And that Del Monte, since he was putting into it all the fresh-fruit operations including those of Northern Cyprus, would be challenged in the US courts. You see, we had some success in the US courtrooms a year or so earlier in establishing our claim to some mosaics that had come from Northern Cyprus. So we managed to do in America what we couldn't do in the UK and European courts. On Del Monte we found that it was not necessary to be successful. We didn't really need to get the rightful owners of stolen properties in the North, Greeks going to the courts in the United States. It was sufficient just to cause trouble behind the scenes, to ensure that the flotation of Del Monte was not successful. To frustrate it.'

I don't know to what extent the Greek Cypriots managed to frustrate the flotation of Del Monte, which was certainly expected to take place some time in 1990. But, speculative rumours that there was some problem with the expected US flotation did put pressure on PPI's share price in London that summer. The Greek Cypriots were not the only ones concerned by the PPI acquisition of Del Monte. One banker who had been involved with Polly Peck told me that Israeli investigators had been looking at the company, too – Israel has an important fruit export industry.

Meanwhile Asil Nadir and PPI were increasingly being identified as a major obstacle to the Cyprus solution so much sought after by the USA. In an article he wrote for the *New Statesman*, former MP Christopher Price, a member of the Friends of Cyprus, the British parliamentary group that supports the Greek Cypriot Government, quoted the text of what he claimed was a confidential paper submitted by the American Ambassador in Ankara to the Turkish Government. It stated the US position.

> Turkey and the USA should enter into closer relations. Our wish is to offer you support. But there is a Greek lobby in the USA. You know their influence. If they get angry they withdraw their vote support from the US Congress. First we have to silence them. This will be achieved by a solution to the Cyprus problem. As far as Denktas remaining in his arm chair, this is impossible. Denktas and the National Unity Party should be ousted from the administration. But, if this is to materialise, Nadir, who is their most important supporter, should be neutralised.

Asil Nadir has often been described as some kind of paranoid fantasist. But, having lived in Cyprus for a couple of years and witnessed the Greek Cypriot obsession with his activities, I can understand why he believes that 'the other side' had a hand in his collapse.

Christopher Price's article was published after the start of Asil Nadir's prosecution. He claims that the turning-point of Nadir's political fortunes was August 1990, when Iraq invaded Kuwait.

George Vassiliou, as the new Greek Cypriot President, he suggests, had made some headway in persuading the international community that it was the Turkish community that was delaying progress towards a settlement. Then came the Gulf crisis.

Western reaction to the Kuwait invasion made defence of the Turkish position on Cyprus more difficult still. A switch in policy by the US and the UK became more noticeable. While they stayed solid with Ozal in Turkey, as a necessary Gulf ally, they were disposed to ditch both Denktas and Nadir. Suddenly Polly Peck became, officially, a dicey share.

When Nelson Ledsky came to London in 1989, he also met a number of supporters of the Greek Cypriot side. They told him that Polly Peck's 'illegal' activities on the north of the island were standing in the way of a reasonable agreement with the Greek Cypriots. I believe, too, that this idea had support amongst some influential Turks who regarded the commitment to Northern Cyprus as an expensive nuisance and resented Asil Nadir, a Cypriot, as an outsider who had achieved far too much power and prosperity on the mainland.

Mr Nadir had critics, too, among the country's grander industrial families who resented the way he had opened up Turkey to European commercial interests. Turkey maintains, to this day, a substantial army in the TRNC to guard the Turkish community. But it has been less willing to provide the investment funds needed to help its economy, seemingly content to let it scrape along as a much poorer relation to the mainland. A significant number of Turks, then and now, would like to see a solution to the Cyprus problem on almost any terms, if it would give Turkey access to the EC. But, Mr Nadir was firm in his belief that there should be no settlement until the TRNC was economically independent, when he envisaged Cypriot entry into the EC as a federated state.

Looking forward to the opening of PPI's new international-class hotels in Antalya, on the Mediterranean coast of Turkey, and the Jasmine Court, on the outskirts of Kyrenia in Northern Cyprus, Asil Nadir was formulating plans for a swift expansion of the tourist industry in Northern Cyprus. Substantial sums of PPI money had gone into these projects, as well as the restoration of the battle-scarred Palm Beach Hotel in Famagusta and another hotel just up the coast from Kyrenia, called the Crystal Cove. This again was calculated to rattle the Greek Cypriots, who work very hard to keep alive, within their own community and the outside world, a sense of injustice about what happened in 1974. The fact was that every new project sponsored by investment through PPI was regarded by them as another nail in the coffin of a Greek Cyprus.

The PPI board were against any further developments in tourism, but Asil Nadir intended to continue to develop the industry in Northern Cyprus. The Nadir family could see the potential there, and Mr Nadir's sister had developed a new holiday village near Kyrenia as well as a small airline company. The North is beautiful, and far more unspoilt than the Greek South. Lack of investment had held back the development of its tourist industry, and it still does. The Greek Cypriots became alarmed by reports that Asil Nadir might be looking at the possibility of redeveloping the ghost town of Varosha, which was, and remains, a major bone of contention between the two Cypriot communities.

Varosha, a high-rise holiday resort built right next to old Famagusta in the 1960s on the beautiful Bay of Salamis, was abandoned by its mainly Greek owners when the Turkish army landed in 1974 and took control of the North. Nowadays, it is an eerie sight for holidaymakers, who can get a close-up view of it from Mr Nadir's luxurious Palm Beach Hotel, which sits right on the edge of the divide and was also part of this bombed site when I first saw it in 1987. It is a modern, empty town, rotting behind barbed wire manned by soldiers, where civilians may not enter. The remnants of curtains still flap from hotel windows, and there are stories of tables bearing the remains of breakfast. The high-rise blocks look perfect, but closer examination shows that one or two have great gashes in the side, with staircases blown open to the elements.

The Greek Cypriots have always made it clear that they want Varosha back as part of any settlement. Early in 1990 they heard rumours that Mr Nadir had started informal discussions with the UK hotel group that held a major stake in one of Varosha's largest hotels before the 1974 invasion. But, by the beginning of 1990 Mr Nadir must have felt pretty invulnerable. He was high on the list of the richest men in the UK – he once told the press he was worth over £1 billion. He was courted by politicians and made substantial donations to the Conservative Party.

• • • •

A February 1990 internal credit report by Citibank, one of the banks that had lent money to his mother's trust company to buy PPI shares, gave the Polly Peck company a clean bill of health, pointing out that the stock-market was pleased that it had strengthened its senior management and acquired two major brand names – Del Monte and Sansui.

Interestingly enough the bank revealed that it had asked two agencies to investigate Mr Nadir's personal life. There were always unconfirmed rumours that he was somehow involved with guns or drugs, which Mr Nadir believed was one way his enemies had tried to smear him. Obviously these stories had reached his bankers, but the investigation concluded: 'Both report nothing negative can be evidenced . . . Much of market rumours stem from competition and the "fear of the unknown" in the early 1980s when much of the corporate activities were based in Turkey.'

The report did mention an Inland Revenue inquiry and concluded, 'There is no evidence for this being a front for a wider investigation.' Among other risks assessed by Citibank was the danger of an inquiry into insider trading. 'Our shares have not been traded. After each acquisition the SE conducted investigations as normal into share dealings conducted during the close season. No negative results.' It appears that the lending bank, which was holding PPI shares as collateral for its loan, was entirely happy that the shares bought for Safiye Nadir were on a legitimate basis. They had good reason to know: the shares had to be sent to them when they were bought, and they knew every purchase was straightforward. There was nothing particularly sinister about Citibank's investigations. It was standard practice for US banks. But, strangely, in the summer of 1990, just before the raid on SAM and the share-price collapse, rumours of a damning bank investigation of Asil Nadir and PPI were circulating on the London Stock Exchange.

Meanhile I had been busy organising a Swiss residency for Mr Nadir. Since our very first meeting his advisers were convinced that he should move to Switzerland. We knew that his long-term residence in England might eventually bring his worldwide assets into the UK tax net, and he had been living in England for over 20 years, normally the benchmark after which the Revenue would dispute whether overseas residence status was valid, and his status might therefore be queried. Later the press thought there was something sinister about this – that it demonstrated he was planning to move the Polly Peck company to Switzerland, too. But it was a pre-emptive move to protect his own and the family assets. It did not affect Polly Peck.

I was in touch with accountants Rawlinson & Hunter's Swiss office and spent a day exploring the various French-speaking cantons, where I thought that Mr Nadir, with his Levantine background, might feel more at home, rather than in one of the more austere German states. I liked the canton of Vaud, bordering Geneva, and discovered that one way of cutting short what would have been a five- to seven-year wait for Swiss residency was to buy a Swiss company, which held a residence permit. PPI had an electronics manufacturing subsidiary, Vestel, in Turkey and the Nadir family had a substantial shareholding in Harland Simon, the British electronics company. Buying a small company in the same business with a residence permit would make sense, and Alp Technology was for sale. We bought it. Asil Nadir also needed a nominal home in Switzerland to establish his residency, and we found a converted farmhouse in Givrins that could double as an office.

We needed someone to administer our Swiss interests and build up operations there. If SAM were directly to manage and control a foreign company, its business could then be brought into the UK tax net, which would ruin the whole point of what had been set up. Jason Davies, Birol Nadir's young stockbroker friend, seemed the ideal candidate, as he had previously been involved with the development of our UK and Turkish operations. He was willing to live in Switzerland with his family and help buy the computer company and form Nadir Investments SA, the legally required holding company for Alp Technology and Mr Nadir's residency. Jason went to Switzerland in autumn 1989 when the stockbroking firm A. J. Bekhor ceased trading. He carried on buying shares for Safiye Nadir when required and still had the Turkish clients he had met through Birol, whose investment companies were administered by Rhone Finance, the Geneva-based group that looked after a string of offshore companies.

The final requirement for Asil Nadir's residency permit was a chest X-ray. Always a heavy smoker, he was very nervous that it would show something wrong with his health. But it was all clear, and finally he got his permit.

We were sitting in the garden at Givrins on Friday, 10 August 1990, enjoying the sunshine after a very pleasant lunch with one of our advisers. It was a beautiful setting, and we could see Lake Geneva in the distance with the Swiss Alps beyond. Asil Nadir had been in London, worried about the impact that the invasion of Kuwait might have on PPI, but that afternoon he was happy and relaxed. He was a workaholic and did not often take time off, but in the late afternoon he went off to view a house, which he admired, overlooking Lake Geneva. I remember thinking how peaceful it all was. It just couldn't last. It didn't.

3. Countdown to Disaster

ASIL NADIR HAD just left for Lake Geneva when I received a fax message from my assistant Barbara Jackson-Smith, at the South Audley Management office in London. A Michael Gillard of the *Observer* had phoned SAM asking to speak to me. He wanted a comment on South Audley Management's dealings in PPI shares. The fax read: 'Could he speak to you in connection with dealings in Polly Peck shares by a number of Swiss companies with which he believes SAM has a connection?' Gillard had left his number for me to call him back that evening or the following morning, so I put it to one side for the moment. About an hour later I received a call from William Grosvenor, Asil Nadir's PR man in London. He had just been phoned by Dominic Prince of the *Sunday Times* asking the same kind of questions. It was teatime on Friday, 10 August.

I rang Mr Nadir on his car phone, told him what had happened and suggested he should come back to the office. In the meantime I phoned our lawyer Peter Knight. When Asil Nadir arrived I told him what had happened. He was absolutely furious. In fact I had never seen him so angry, and the mere mention of Gillard's name was enough: 'Do you know who this man is, Elizabeth?' I hadn't got a clue. Asil Nadir went on to explain that Gillard had become a sworn enemy. The *Observer* had published photographs of an empty field, which Gillard had claimed was the site of the Niksar waterbottling company set up by PPI. There had been years of legal wrangling with Gillard over this and other anti-Polly Peck articles.

After Asil Nadir calmed down he spoke to Vizards. They were

prepared to try to stop the newspapers printing. He talked to Peter Knight, but then he decided, 'Let them print. I was warned a few months ago by Turkey that there would be an attack on the company. This is it.' The press could print whatever story they liked.

The previous weekend there had been snippets in the news about a tax inquiry and share dealings. A few months before that there had been an article in one of the Scottish Sunday newspapers about an Inland Revenue investigation into Asil Nadir. Peter Knight, who had been handling tax matters for SAM, was furious. He believed someone in the Inland Revenue was leaking information to the press. I had not taken much notice of any of this, but what Mr Nadir did next completely astonished me. Suddenly, he announced he was going to move to take Polly Peck private. He would make an offer for the shares – right now – so could I phone and assemble our advisers for a meeting in Geneva tomorrow morning?

I had known that he wanted to take PPI private for some time – there was no secret about that – and he had nearly done so the previous summer, dissuaded only by his fellow directors. I was aware that he had looked hard at the proposition in general and had talked to bankers. He frequently said that they were ready to give him whatever money he needed. We had both discussed this issue with our bankers. Rawlinson & Hunter, the accountants, had advised that the parent company should be incorporated in Bermuda, and the acquisition of Mr Nadir's Swiss citizenship had been an important step.

Nothing had been done, however, to construct the bid in any great detail. There were no UK merchant-banking advisers on board, although Asil Nadir had gone to a lunch at Hambro Magan the previous week. They had invited him several times and were keen to meet him on the basis that if he was doing something in the future they might like to be considered. But that was as far as it went.

But the threat of what might appear in the press was not the only explanation, not even the main reason, for his hurried decision. The newspaper stories were going ahead anyway. The share price was around 400p, not quite its peak but well above the level for his loans. Earlier that day he had spoken to the office of the Turkish President Ozal. It was possible then that Turkey herself might invade Iraq – she was the strongest US military ally in that part of the world. In August 1990 the Gulf crisis was making everyone nervous, and Turkey shared a border with Iraq. Whatever happened could have a devastating impact on PPI's businesses there and the confidence of its bankers. The Turkish lire was already weak, and it would get weaker. I believe that this, combined with what appeared to be a media attack in Britain, moved him to act as he did.

I knew we were not really ready for an announcement that weekend, although we could have been in a very short space of time, and I told him so.

'The timing is right,' he replied. 'If we are not ready now we never will be,' and he rushed headlong into the biggest mistake of his life. It was a disastrous error of judgement that shook his own and his company's credibility to its foundations. If there was one thing, looking back, that he might have done differently this was it. I telephoned our advisers, then told him that I hoped his mother was burning the olive leaves, a Turkish Cypriot ritual to bring good luck. 'I am going to tell her to burn a whole forest of them,' he told me.

Next morning Asil Nadir met our advisers from Rawlinson & Hunter at the Richmonde Hotel in Geneva. They had flown out to meet us and Jurgen Schnabel, formerly of the First National Bank of Chicago, who was now in business on his own and had been working to organise the finance for the bid. Some Citibank people were there, too, and I knew that the backing was in place for a £5 a share bid. I am not sure that at that stage there were enough assets committed to cover the PPI debt, which would have to be rejigged if the company were to become private. But Jurgen had certainly got a consortium of banks and investors behind the deal, when Mr Nadir flew back to London with Phillip Prettejohn of Rawlinson & Hunter later that day.

PPI directors were roused from their weekend break and summoned to a board meeting on the Sunday. It was all very rushed, and when George Magan of Hambro Magan was contacted by Asil Nadir and told of the plan, he was horrified, pointing out that it was just not feasible to charge off and launch a bid overnight. But Mr Nadir had prepared his letter to the board, which stated that he was writing at this early stage, before either the formal structure or the methods of its financing had been determined, to tell them that there was a possibility of an offer being made for PPI by Mr Nadir and his family interests. He was doing so at this stage to avoid creating a false market in the shares. The offer, if made, would be at a price that reflected the value of the company and would exceed the level at which the company's shares would otherwise trade in the foreseeable future. He added that he would provide a more detailed proposal as soon as he could.

This was a very provisional letter – a proposal for a proposal. There was no possibility of a firm offer with a price attached emerging for the best part of a month, until the company's half-yearly results were published. It stated quite clearly that the financing had not been completely organised, so when Asil Nadir told the astonished PPI board of his plans, he did not expect them to reveal the offer at that stage. But they insisted on putting out a statement on that Monday after taking advice from their lawyers. After the decision was taken to make it public Mr Nadir asked one of his directors why it had been necessary. The answer was that the board wanted to be absolutely in the clear as regards any suggestions that there was a false market in the shares.

The share price had been 393p on the Friday, and the statement from the PPI board sent the price up to 452p briefly, but it closed at 417p on the Monday. The stock-market did not seem terribly convinced that any offer would succeed. Much mention was made of the fact that the estimated £1.5 billion deal was a larger buy-out than anything the City had so far seen. Although Richard Branson had floated Virgin on the stock-market and then taken it private again the fashion for such things had definitely turned. The financial climate was thought to be against such deals. Interest rates were high, and the junk-bond market, which had financed so many of them, had collapsed in the USA the previous year. In fact, there were no US banks in Schnabel's consortium – a lot of the funding was Arab and Middle East money. There was the distinct feeling that Mr Nadir had reacted impetuously to the unfavourable weekend press reports, and as the Lex column of the *Financial Times* put it: 'He would not be the first chairman to get into a tizzy about trigger-happy market makers, or the cocky British media.'

Meanwhile Asil Nadir was discovering that he might have difficulty getting all the shares he needed. David Fawcus, the PPI deputy chairman, was phoned by a fund manager at Friends Provident, one of the largest of PPI's institutional investors and long-term fans of PPI shares. A couple of their fund managers knew Asil Nadir personally. They had just under 5 per cent of the shares, and they told Fawcus – and several others in the City – that they were not happy about the bid and were unlikely to accept an offer; they would like to stay as minority shareholders.

Asil Nadir needed acceptances of 90 per cent of the shares he did not own. Furthermore he planned to sell some of the companies in order to reduce the finance he needed as part of his offer – that was crucial to his plans. When he discussed the situation with Fawcus later that week, however, he decided to withdraw his proposal. Everyone, including me, told him that he should go through the motions: if the bid failed, it would still leave his credibility intact; if he withdrew, it would be a catastrophe. Nevertheless, he said that he was not prepared to go through weeks of rigmarole, delaying the company's progress, if he was not going to get what he wanted. Against everyone's advice he withdrew the proposal to bid.

Just five days after his proposal had been made public he made another statement:

> Since the time of my letter to the board I have received approaches from both significant institutional and individual shareholders who have indicated that they would not wish to see Polly Peck become a private company ... Therefore I have decided to discontinue my approach made last Sunday and do not intend to proceed with the possible offer.

The impact on the share price was instantaneous: it plunged to 324p. The City was bewildered. So were his board. After years of on-going suspicion, Polly Peck was being taken seriously in the wake of the Del Monte deal, but its new-found credibility was now severely dented.

Quick off the mark, the Stock Exchange mounted an official inquiry. During the next week there was a steady parade of bankers and brokers before the Exchange's Quotations Committee to explain the events of the past few days. Mr Nadir went along to be inter-viewed, as did David Fawcus. They were told that they would be sent the report from the Stock Exchange before it was published. When it was sent to PPI headquarters on the Friday afternoon, it contained very serious criticisms of Asil Nadir: he had not prepared for the bid properly; he had ignored advice; he had held that fatal weekend board meeting at extraordinarily short notice. It also criticised the board itself for not making it clear that the bid proposal was still at a preliminary stage.

There were several errors in the Stock Exchange's coruscating report, but the board had been told that there would be a chance to correct any mistakes. In the afternoon David Fawcus phoned the Stock Exchange with some amendments. In the event the damaging statement went out with only one alteration.

There was a nasty sting in the tail at the end of the report: 'The Stock Exchange has conveyed these findings and the supporting papers on which they have been based to the relevant authorities.' The Stock Exchange offered a nod and a wink to the media, and everyone assumed these to be the Department of Trade and the Serious Fraud Office, both of which were reported in the press as looking into share deals in Polly Peck, separately from the SE inquiry.

Two senior lawyers acting for Asil Nadir concluded that he had broken no rules or regulations, but for some in the Stock Exchange, the aborted bid had just been the last straw. They didn't particularly like Mr Nadir or his company as there had been too many upsets with PPI's share price in the past. The companies in the FTSE-100 index are assumed to represent stability and best practice, to be the cream of the British stock-market. It appeared to them that Mr Nadir had thumbed his nose at everyone. The shares had gone up and down like a rollercoaster for a week, and FTSE-100 companies are expected to manage their affairs better.

There were those in the Stock Exchange who had watched what they regarded as strange dealings in PPI shares for years. They believed that Asil Nadir had just announced the bid to raise his share price. To many others, even those fond of him and the company, it served to demonstrate why his desire to bid to take the company private might have been the right move. He was temperamentally better suited to running a private enterprise. And although PPI had a £2 billion market value, the shares had none the less been shown to be extraordinarily volatile.

Mr Nadir would eventually have lived down his censure from the Stock Exchange, but the real damage was being done by a series of articles in the Sunday press. Both the *Sunday Times* and the *Observer* had produced stories that the Inland Revenue Special Office 2 had been investigating his tax affairs. My company, South Audley Management, was supposed to have links to a number of Swiss companies that had bought and sold PPI shares over the last few years. The name of the companies mentioned in the press reports were Tristan, Forum, Gateway and Riverbridge. Jason Davies, the newspapers pointed out, had placed orders with London brokers on behalf of these companies to buy and sell PPI shares, and the authorities were reported to be investigating.

I certainly knew about the two operations named Tristan and Forum, which were companies formed for Safiye Nadir, Asil's mother, who lived in Northern Cyprus. They were indeed administered from Switzerland. By the summer of 1990 Forum had replaced Tristan as the main trust company holding some of Safiye's PPI shares.

Since joining Asil Nadir, one of my tasks had been to arrange the finance for Safiye Nadir to purchase PPI shares because the family wanted to increase its holding. Over the past two and a half years Tristan and later Forum had bought some 7.9 million PPI shares on her behalf, through margin loans I had arranged with KOP and Citibank, my old employer. With a margin loan, a bank will typically take shares as security for a half or more of a loan, so that the borrowing is conservatively covered. If the share price falls it may ask for part of the loan to be repaid or for extra security on it. This was the arrangement I had made for Safiye Nadir's trust companies, but extraordinarily the newspapers kept talking about 'dealings' in PPI shares by the Swiss companies. I knew the shares purchased for Mrs Nadir were pledged as security to the bank; they were bought, not sold or 'dealt in', as the newspapers kept claiming, and were part of the overall Nadir published shareholding in PPI.

The other companies cited in the press reports were Riverbridge and Gateway, apparently registered at a PO box number at Geneva Airport. They had nothing to do with SAM or Asil Nadir, although they were certainly among Jason Davies's clientele. He had continued to act for his other clients, whose companies were administered by Rhone Finance in Geneva. Jason had also bought the PPI shares for Safiye Nadir's two companies, Tristan and Forum, and this was the link that the press and the authorities thought was so significant.

Jason knew Rhone Finance from his time at the stockbroking firm of Giles & Overbury, one of whose former partners, Roger Leopard, was now a director at Rhone. Clearly the press believed that the Swiss letter-box companies, and maybe Rhone Finance itself, were some kind of a front for Asil Nadir. Jason had, after all, rented an office from SAM and bought shares for Safiye Nadir's companies. What everyone overlooked in the speculative excitement, however, was that Tristan and Forum were administered by Confidas in Zurich, the trust arm of Citibank that lent money to buy the shares. And, furthermore, that Mrs Nadir's shares were never traded but firmly held by the bank as security. Whatever Jason was doing for his other clients, his buying for SAM was completely straightforward. But, here we were, the unhappy focus of unrelenting press speculation.

In the wake of the calamitous bid episode newspapers reported that the authorities were looking at insider deals or a long-term share support operation in PPI shares. The reporters tracked Jason Davies down in Switzerland, but Jason and I were both told by Asil Nadir and his advisers to say nothing. I was very frustrated that the newspapers were clearly imagining some giant share-support operation where there was none, and there was a perfectly simple answer to the questions about South Audley Management that vexed the newspapers. In retrospect I should have just put an end to all the nonsense and tried to explain it to the more sensible members of the press. But I had other things on my mind.

By now the PPI share price had slipped below 300p, and the banks were getting agitated. I stayed on in Switzerland trying to pacify them. One particular Swiss creditor rang me every morning at 7.30 am at my hotel in Geneva, threatening to sell at the opening of the Stock Exchange in London. At the end of August, one of the major banks that had lent money to Restro started to sell PPI shares. Restro Investments (Jersey Ltd) was the Nadir private investment company that held their PPI shareholding. The price slipped to around 260p by the first week in September. By this time Mr Nadir was in the market buying PPI shares himself. Bankers were calling for him to put up extra cash against the loans they had granted him with PPI shares as security. He reasoned that if he used cash to pay these margin calls from the banks for extra money it would not help the share price. Much better to get the shares through the market. But how long would the media assault go on? And what did the allegations of Swiss company share dealings all mean?

• • • •

This was the question everyone – bankers, stockbrokers, PPI company directors, members of the press, not to mention Asil Nadir's own family – was asking themselves as they flew from Luton to Turkey on the second weekend of September 1990. They had been invited to celebrate the opening of the new Polly Peck hotel, the Sheraton Voyager, in Antalya on the south coast, a beautiful marble and glass structure in the shape of a wave.

The hospitality that weekend was lavish. Mr Nadir arrived late on the Friday night, striding through the dining hall as one of Turkey's top pop stars paused in her act. On the Saturday a police convoy escorted the guests along the coast to a barbecue lunch, where they swam in a lovely cove around the ruins of an ancient classical town and harbour. There was a nervous edge to the *bonhomie*, however, and one PPI director was heard to say in a loud voice, 'There is only one Asil Nadir. Thank God.' It was not meant unkindly, but just summed up the frustration felt by many close to the company over the events of the past month.

In the evening there was an open-air dinner in the beautifully landscaped gardens of the hotel, following a stupendous fireworks display. American pop star Randy Crawford topped the bill, which featured a band from Latin America performing the latest dance craze, the lambada. It was a fabulous night, the climax of the opening celebrations. President Denktas was there, with other politically well-connected figures, and most of the Nadir family were present, too, including Safiye. All the Nadir women looked spectacularly beautiful, and Asil Nadir was resplendent in a white dinner jacket. There is still a photograph of them all, taken that evening, displayed in the main sitting-room of Asil Nadir's house in Lapta.

There were echoes of a scene from *The Great Gatsby*, with a similar sense of foreboding. One of Asil's friends remembers it as the worst weekend of his life. Just before he had left London for Turkey, this friend had lunched with a stockbroker he had known for years, an old acquaintance. The broker knew he was friendly with Asil, and he had something on his mind. On the afternoon of Friday, 10 August, Jason Davies had rung from Switzerland to buy 1 million Polly Peck shares for a company called Newbridge – another company administered by Rhone Finance in Geneva.

The broker had been about to leave – he was just putting his jacket on – when Jason phoned at around 4 o'clock. The broker had known Jason and dealt for him before, but there had been a break in their business together, and the link had only recently been renewed. The deal was large, but not unprecedented. Jason had purchased PPI shares for Safiye Nadir over the previous three years, sometimes through this broker, and Newbridge was not linked to Mrs Nadir, so the broker thought nothing was amiss, dealt and went home without a care.

His calm was shattered early on Monday morning, when the PPI board put out the statement that Mr Nadir was proposing to make an offer for the company. The broker was taken aback, fearful of what the Stock Exchange would make of his transaction on Friday when it was spotted on the dealing records. The PPI market-maker, only too happy to supply the stock on the Friday, was absolutely furious now and complained to the broker and the Stock Exchange. On the Tuesday, the day after the bid was announced, Jason rang the broker again and gave an order to sell the Newbridge PPI shares. This was done, at a profit of £198,500. Three days later Asil Nadir announced that he was withdrawing his proposal, and the share price fell dramatically. It looked, the broker thought, like the most blatant piece of insider trading he had ever seen – and he had been around the City a long, long time.

The broker was quite convinced that Mr Nadir was somehow involved. He had met Jason Davies through Asil Nadir's son Birol – at one point I had lunched with all three of them. This broking house had bought some of Safiye Nadir's shares, for which I had arranged the settlement with money drawn on bank loans, and the shares were registered in the bank's nominee name. What I did not know was that Jason had transacted a lot of business for his other clients through this firm. The broker had the impression that Jason dealt for Asil Nadir – although he had never been actually told that and had never received instructions to buy shares for him. He obviously knew that South Audley was something to do with Tristan, for which Jason had bought shares. The broker just assumed that all Jason's accounts were something to do with Mr Nadir.

Over lunch, Asil Nadir's friend had said he did not believe that Nadir was involved, but he agreed with the broker that it looked very suspicious. The newspapers had been full of reports about mysterious Swiss companies dealing in PPI shares. Now Asil Nadir's friend had been told first hand about a deal that appeared highly suspicious and that the Stock Exchange was investigating. He was upset and worried, and he had been trying to see Asil on his own since the previous day when he had flown to Antalya from Luton.

Halfway through that Saturday evening Asil Nadir arrived suddenly at his table, complete with bodyguards. He sat down, and while the other diners went off to dance, the two men talked intensely for about ten minutes, hunched together over the table. The friend explained what he had heard about the deal that the Stock Exchange was investigating. He told Asil that if he did not find out and expose whoever was really behind it, suspicions could not be laid to rest. Unresolved, the mystery could spell the end for him and for Polly Peck. He also believed that the press articles would continue until it was known who owned the Swiss-administered companies. He had the broker's permission to give Asil Nadir his name and telephone number, which he passed on. The purchase and sale of the PPI shares had to be confronted and investigated, even if the answers were painful when Mr Nadir unearthed them. The friend was practically in tears.

Asil Nadir was clearly under pressure, too. He had already been faxed the early editions of the Sunday newspapers that contained more articles attacking his company. He told his friend that he had nothing to do with the share sale and purchases, so he had nothing to worry about. His friend was nevertheless distraught – he simply could not make Mr Nadir understand that this was beside the point. The problem was not so much the reality – but what the City thought it to be. Polly Peck shares were sliding under the weight of media speculation focusing on SAM and the Swiss companies. Now there were clear signs of what looked like a case of insider trading. In the current climate of suspicion it would be enough to bring down Asil Nadir.

The fact was that Newbridge was another Rhone Finance managed company, not Mr Nadir's, and the deals were innocent of any insider information. Mr Nadir did not decide to go ahead with his intention to bid for PPI until well after the London stock-market closed on Friday, 10 August. When Jason Davies placed the Newbridge buy order, he could not, therefore, have known of Mr Nadir's proposal. I know this because I was there, and I also have the faxed message that gave us the first warning about the newspaper articles, the time of transmission of which is four o'clock in the afternoon, several hours before Mr Nadir decided to propose a bid. I do not know why Jason Davies sold the Newbridge stake a few days later, before Mr Nadir dropped his idea to bid. Maybe he was nervous about having bought a big block of PPI shares just before the bid. Maybe he could just see a quick profit for his client. But, it was this deal that led directly to the raid on SAM and the subsequent collapse of PPI.

With the discovery of the Newbridge deal the Stock Exchange thought it had established a link between Newbridge, Mr Nadir and SAM. In the normal course of events these transactions would have been investigated by the Department of Trade, which would establish if there were any grounds for prosecution. This kind of inquiry takes some time. Instead, however, the results of the Stock Exchange's investigation, and other information it had collected on dealing in PPI shares, was passed to the Serious Fraud Office.

Unknown to me, one of the stockbrokers through whom Jason had bought shares for Tristan and Forum had been discussing his concerns over purchases of PPI shares with the Stock Exchange some months before. He had told the Stock Exchange's head of surveillance, Bob Wilkinson, about a conversation he had had with me that he had considered deeply suspicious. What worried him was this. At one point I had trouble in getting the payment for Tristan's and Forum's share purchases made on time. Although I had established loans at Citibank and the London branch of the Finnish bank Kansallis Osake Pankki (KOP), there were problems drawing down the money before I established a line of credit. But I was often away abroad and not able to sort things out. As CGS had complained about late payment – several times as I recall – I gave them the direct telephone number of Aisling Daly, Asil Nadir's personal assistant at Polly Peck because Mr Nadir, like myself, had authority to act for his mother over Tristan and Forum. When the stockbroker phoned up Aisling one day, he realised that he had got through to a Polly Peck number and Mr Nadir's personal assistant, and he jumped to the conclusion that there was something fishy about the share purchases.

This stockbroker had been trying to find out who was behind Forum. I had lunched with the CGS people and he knew Jason purchased the shares for them and that he was connected to SAM and me. He also knew that Forum was administered by Confidas Finance et Placement in Zurich, the trust management arm of Citibank from where the money to purchase the shares came. He had written to Confidas in 1988, asking for details of the company's directors, shareholders and beneficiaries, but Confidas had no obligation to disclose that Safiye Nadir was the beneficiary. He was told that Forum was a personal investment company, owned by an individual resident and domiciled outside the UK, which was correct.

All this he told the Stock Exchange, and later the SFO, who apparently regarded him as a prime witness in their case against Asil Nadir. Several newspaper reports, in fact, highlighted the stockbroker's role in the PPI investigation, as did the Inland Revenue, when they went round to see Peter Knight at Vizards the day after the PPI share-price collapse.

I had no idea at the time that Jason Davies dealt for his Rhone Finance company clients in a way that stockbrokers and the Stock Exchange found suspicious. He would 'cash and new' shares, which meant he didn't pay for them following the end of the Stock Exchange account but would roll them over, at extra cost, to the next account. It appears that this way he, or his clients, could hold Polly Peck shares for weeks without paying for them. It also emerged that he would transfer PPI shares from one Rhone Finance client to another. I only discovered this much later, when I was preparing for my own trial.

As press speculation mounted a former Polly Peck executive went along to see the SFO. Tim Wood had worked for PPI twice in the previous few years, and in between times he had worked for SAM. Mr Nadir had liked Wood, which was why he had employed him at SAM when he left PPI the first time. He was subsequently re-employed as the company's head of investor relations, but he had not got on with PPI's senior directors, whom he believed had blocked his progress to a directorship.

Wood told SFO that Jason Davies was buying PPI shares for Asil Nadir through the Swiss-administered companies. He also said that I knew about it. This informal meeting between Tim Wood and the SFO took place on 18 September, the day before the raid on SAM. But by then the die was cast: on the previous day, the 17th, one of the SFO lawyers, Lorna Harris, had obtained a Section 2 warrant to raid South Audley Management.

The decision to raid was a serious misjudgement. Quite how serious only became clear some five years later when the SFO was finally forced to supply a copy of the warrant, and the affidavit supporting it, to my solicitors. When I eventually saw the documents in November 1995, I realised they were riddled with mistakes and inaccuracies, which confirmed all my suspicions that the raid, with its devastating impact on the PPI share price, had been a disastrous error on the part of the SFO.

The affidavit sworn by Lorna Harris states that the SFO investigation was concerned with dealings in PPI shares by two companies, Blade Explorations and Newbridge Investments, which had bought shares prior to the announcement of Asil Nadir's intention to bid for PPI and had sold them before the bid proposal had been withdrawn. Clearly Mr Nadir was suspected of orchestrating an insider deal. His friend, who had talked to him about the Newbridge share deals at the Antalya hotel opening, had been right.

It emerged later that Blade Explorations had sold PPI shares on the day Mr Nadir's proposal to bid was announced. Blade was another of Jason Davies's Rhone Finance clients, and a holder of some 4 million PPI shares, of which it had sold 425,000 that Monday. If this had been, as the authorities contended, an insider deal why hadn't Blade sold more, or all, of its stake?

I later discovered that neither of the brokers who negotiated the Newbridge and Blade transactions was ever interviewed by the SFO before the SAM raid. The authorities had simply not done their homework with regard to that or any of the other crucial aspects of the warrant.

The SFO affidavit also states that:

> It is suspected that Asil Nadir controls or owns the companies involved which thereby profited from the price rise. Blade Explorations and Newbridge Investments both have an address at PO Box 324 Geneva Airport. Both are managed by a company called Rhone Finance. Rhone Finance also controls the following companies, all registered in the Cayman Islands, Riverbridge Investments, Gateway Investments, Tristan, Forum, Fax Investments and Equities Investments.

In fact Tristan and Forum were not controlled by and quite separate from Rhone Finance and had nothing to do with addresses at Geneva Airport. The suggestion was that all these companies had a common owner – Asil Nadir. This was, of course, what the newspapers had been strenuously implying for the previous few weeks.

The affidavit then went on to outline the role of Jason Davies, who had given the orders to buy and sell the Newbridge and Blade shares:

> Jason Davies is a close associate of Asil Nadir, having been the stockbroker who handled his account at Giles & Overbury. When Davies left that firm he retained control of the Nadir portfolio.

This was nonsense, of course, and as far as I am aware Jason Davies never met Mr Nadir until he worked for SAM as a consultant in 1987. He did not have control of 'the Nadir portfolio', not then, nor at any other time. It was well known in the City that Asil Nadir bought shares through three much larger stockbroking firms, two of them brokers to the PPI company.

It is clear from the warrant that the SFO thought that my company, SAM, was at the centre of some kind of illicit share-dealing operation in PPI shares. And that when they raided they would find all kinds of documents that would link SAM, myself and Asil Nadir to Newbridge and Blade, the two companies whose share transactions they were investigating, and the other Rhone Finance companies.

The affidavit states:

> The specified documents are a crucial link between the ownership or control of the companies concerned and the dealings in PPI shares.

The SFO could have come along any time and served me with a Section 2 notice and asked me anything they liked. But they chose to raid. The fact was that when they raided SAM, the SFO found none of the evidence they had so eagerly anticipated. Not then. Nor when they later grilled SAM's bemused staff in the hopes of finding something that would back up that wretched warrant. What they found instead was that they had toppled a FTSE-100 company without any justification.

They had collapsed Polly Peck and had ruined its investors but with nothing to show for it. It begged all kinds of awkward questions about the source, not to mention the accuracy, of the information upon which they had acted.

On the afternoon of the PPI share-price collapse Asil Nadir had the first of what was to be numerous meetings with the Serious Fraud Office at their Elm Street headquarters. Already it was clear that they were in a muddle. His inquisitors had piles of documents in front of them, and Mr Nadir was told that one large bundle came from one of his bankers, Kansallis Osake Pankki (KOP). The documents were in fact identical to the papers the Inland Revenue had acquired during the protracted negotiations over his tax affairs, and the SFO questioning went over much of the ground already covered by the two taxmen, Cook and Allcock, over the previous eighteen months. Asil Nadir was asked about the ownership of a number of Swiss-administered companies, including Gateway, Fax, Riverbridge, Newbridge, Blade, Tristan and Forum, that had bought and sold PPI shares. The SFO told him that all these were registered at a PO box number at Geneva Airport.

This was, of course, the crucial mistake they had made in the warrant. Mr Nadir told them that Tristan was a family operation, and that he thought Fax was owned by some Cypriots. He had only seen the names of the other firms in the newspaper reports of the previous few weeks.

The SFO also questioned him about bank loans given for PPI share purchases by Tristan, something the two taxmen had also inquired about and about which the SFO now seemed to think there was something sinister too. The SFO inquired about SAM and even queried the number of trips I had made to Switzerland, where I had raised the margin loans for Safiye Nadir's share purchases. What on earth was suspicious about that? In the final stages of the interview the SFO raised the question of share purchases the previous summer before PPI's major acquisition of the Del Monte fruit company, as well as the events, including share purchases, surrounding the recent bid-proposal débâcle.

By the end of the three-hour grilling neither Mr Nadir nor his advisers were any the wiser about what the SFO wanted to know or what it was he was suspected of doing. They were never shown the warrant and accompanying affidavit that demonstrated that the SFO were looking at evidence of insider dealing and some kind of share support operation conducted by SAM. So who or what had misled the SFO into believing that South Audley Management was the centre of an illicit share-dealing operation in PPI shares? That when they raided SAM they would find evidence linking the suspect Rhone Finance company share deals in PPI to SAM and Mr Nadir?

Mr Nadir's legal advisers believed, I think wrongly, that Inland Revenue documents had been given directly to the SFO. In fact the SFO had served a Section 2 notice for documents on KOP the day before the raid on SAM and had acquired some photocopies. But it was clear from the note of the telephone call that had been shown Peter Knight that the Inland Revenue was believed by the SFO to have important information – important enough to have asked the Inland Revenue actually to chair the SFO meeting.

But it was the Stock Exchange that had actually given that information to the SFO. The SFO had confirmed in a letter to my solicitor that

> the information sworn on 17 September 1990 supporting the warrant to search the premises of South Audley Management was based on information received from the Stock Exchange and enquiries made of them. The documentation is contained in the reports from the Stock Exchange and, to a lesser extent, in the notes of conferences held at the Serious Fraud Office.

So the question is: from where did the Stock Exchange get its information? Information that proved to be wrong and misleading. The Stock Exchange has few investigatory powers of its own, so insider-dealing cases are referred by it to the Department of Trade for investigation and usually take months. Unusually, however, in the case of PPI the Stock Exchange had itself done the background work for the raid on SAM. Why?

In the wake of the successful result of the first Guinness case, the Government was anxious to show that a new City fraud-busting regime had been established. That the Stock Exchange was not the feeble body that its critics claimed. Polly Peck was the first major 'test' for a new approach that would bring City wrongdoers to justice much more speedily. The Stock Exchange had, in fact, been cooperating for months with the Inland Revenue, who believed they had found evidence of a PPI share-support operation – evidence that was eagerly seized upon by the Stock Exchange. The trail that led to the collapse of PPI had started some eighteen months before in the spring of 1989 when the Inland Revenue launched an investigation into Asil Nadir's tax affairs.

4. The Taxman Cometh

THE FIRST THING I knew about the Inland Revenue investigation was a telephone call in the summer of 1989 from SAM's bank manager at the National Westminster branch in South Audley Street. He said he had received a letter from Richard Cook at Special Office 2 of the Inland Revenue about a number of companies that might have appeared in SAM's banking records. He was surprised that I knew nothing of the investigation, as he had been aware of it since March. The companies concerned were Tristan and Fax. I asked him for a copy of the letter, and I phoned Richard Cook at Special Office 2 and asked if we could meet. According to his handwritten note, which turned up in a pile of papers from the SFO when I was preparing my own case, I was rather aggressive and complained that Britain was becoming a police state.

Cook came to my office that afternoon and spent about half an hour there. He wanted information on a company called Fax Investments. I had no idea what that was. He said that he understood that SAM had been passed a payment for Fax through our bank account. I said that as far as I knew there was no payment to a company called Fax. I was shown a cheque to the stockbrokers A. J. Bekhor for £352,294.88 signed by me and dated February 1988. I then knew what Mr Cook was talking about, because this was one of the few occasions when a SAM cheque had just my signature – two people usually used to sign – but I had no idea that the cheque I had signed had anything to do with Fax. How could I?

I had been phoned by SAM's Turkish accountant, Arseven

Gumush, who was in the Isle of Man on business at the time. He told me that a Turkish gentleman who had done some consultancy work for Unipac, Polly Peck's Cypriot subsidiary, wanted to be paid in sterling rather than Turkish lire. He wanted SAM to give him a cheque in return for a credit from Unipac. I was happy to do this so long as SAM got its payment first. Arseven had to phone our bankers to tell them to honour the cheque. The company name Fax wasn't mentioned. I told Cook that I would try to find out more.

I eventually discovered who the owner of Fax was: a client of Jason's and Birol's from their days at Giles & Overbury. In fact one of the first tasks I had done when I started reorganising Mr Nadir's lending arrangements was to find a bank to refinance a small loan to Fax Investments that had been guaranteed by Asil Nadir as part of one of the major loans against PPI shares held by the family in Restro. I had forgotten all about it. I assumed the loan was for Birol, or one of his acquaintances, and found Fax and whoever owned it another bank. It had been a side issue for me at the time, as my main purpose had been to reorganise Mr Nadir's loans.

Until the end of 1989 Jason was acting on behalf of Fax and other clients buying shares through A. J. Bekhor, and I was absolutely right to tell Cook that Fax had nothing to do with SAM or the interests we managed for Mr Nadir. At that stage I didn't see anything particularly sinister in the Inland Revenue's approach.

At the beginning of September 1989 I received a poisonous letter from Cook. It was headed: FAX INVESTMENTS LTD TRISTAN LTD AND RELATED ACCOUNTS AND COMPANIES CONNECTED OR ASSOCIATED WITH THE NADIRS. This was the first time I realised that for some reason the IR wanted desperately to show that this Fax company was part of Asil Nadir's interests administered by SAM.

Initially Cook disbelieved me when I told him earlier I knew nothing about Fax – despite the fact that neither the cheque nor the faxed letter sent by Arseven to our bank to facilitate the cheque mentioned the name of the company. Then he claimed, 'You've had various discussions and meetings, both with other banks and with firms of stockbrokers about Fax Investments.' He continued in an accusatory fashion, claiming I had denied that Jason Davies was an employee of South Audley Management (he was at that time a part-time consultant) and had stated that Jason was now an employee of Citibank, which was complete nonsense, as Jason never had anything to do with Citibank. I myself, of course, had worked for Citibank before joining Mr Nadir.

It was an extraordinary letter, and more threatening still was Cook's final point: 'You told me that Asil Nadir was definitely not connected with these accounts. As I said then I have direct evidence showing a link with Asil Nadir, and this remains my position.' He demanded a written report from me about Tristan and Fax, detailing their investments, financing and ownership. By this time our advisers had been alerted. When they saw the letter they realised that Special Office 2 really had their teeth into the investigation.

What I didn't realise at the time was just how wide-ranging the Inland Revenue inquiry was. Our advisers were in no doubt that the investigation had resulted from an IR review at the stockbrokers A. J. Bekhor, through which PPI shares were bought for Safiye Nadir's trust companies, Tristan and Forum. But by that autumn Special Office 2 had been to several other banks and stockbrokers as well as PPI's auditors, Stoy Hayward, and I was really baffled about what the Inland Revenue was looking for.

When Dennis Robertson, a senior partner of Stoy Hayward, met Richard Cook in September 1989, Cook told him that he was concerned with UK residents dealing in shares through offshore companies – but not only that. He also explained that he was investigating various share transactions connected with Asil Nadir and Polly Peck, which had connotations of insider-dealing. Cook had told him that he had served a Section 20 notice on A. J. Bekhor, which had revealed the names of a number of letterbox companies based at Geneva Airport. These businesses, including Fax Investments, had traded in PPI shares.

There was no mention of Mr Nadir, but it was clear that Special Office 2 thought that Mr Nadir was behind Fax and the other companies on the list, which included Riverbridge, Gateway and the other operations that eventually turned up in the warrant for the raid on SAM. All in fact were administered by the Geneva-based company Rhone Finance. Our advisers were now getting to grips with the fact that the taxmen were convinced that the whole lot were a front for Asil Nadir.

There were two aspects to this. Firstly, if it could be shown that these offshore businesses did indeed belong to Asil Nadir and that a UK company, South Audley Management, was administering them in some way, then everything could be brought into the UK tax net. That was my main concern at the time. Secondly, from Cook's comments to Dennis Robertson, it seems that the Inland Revenue was looking for evidence of some kind of illegal share dealings. This, of course, I only discovered much later. Right then I was just heartily sick of Mr Cook and his accusations. Tristan had bought a great number of shares, all by way of margin loans from two banks, Kansallis-Osake-Pankki and Citibank. So far as I was concerned Tristan had been established as Safiye Nadir's company, with the PPI shares later transferred to another trust company, Forum, which replaced Tristan when our advisers realised there might be some technical problems with Tristan's incorporation.

It was important to establish Safiye Nadir's independence from her son to protect Asil's tax position. Safiye lived in Cyprus, but Mr Nadir and I had the authority to act for her, and I used to fly regularly to Cyprus to discuss her trust with her. There was no reason why her situation should be of interest to the UK tax authorities at all. She was a bona-fide overseas investor who was not liable for UK tax.

The Inland Revenue mounted a blitzkrieg in the City, scattering Section 20 notices everywhere in their efforts to find evidence for their investigation into Asil Nadir. Among the stockbrokers they contacted was a small firm called Douglas Le Mare and, at the end of October, their investigator, Richard Cook, sent me an accusing letter insisting that 'copies of contracts and statements were sent to you by Douglas Le Mare Ltd in respect of Fax Investments.'

This was simply not right. I knew that Jason had bought some shares for Tristan from these stockbrokers, but I later discovered why Cook thought he had found something significant. A DLM-client card index dated 2 October 1987 and headed FAX INVESTMENTS showed me and SAM as the recipients of copy contract notes. Confusingly the same card shows that the registration of shares should be made to Tristan, which was shown, correctly, as care of Confidas Finance et Placement SA Zurich – the Swiss trustee arm of Citibank, where I had arranged the loan. It is clear to me that the brokers were initially confused by the fact that Jason bought shares for Tristan, for which settlement was organised by SAM, as well as for Fax, and they had thought both companies had one and the same owner.

The administration in stockbrokers' back offices is not brilliant, but a DLM card-index entry, date 15 October 1987 – just two weeks after the first botched one – shows the client quite clearly as Tristan, care of Confidas, with instructions to send copy contract notes to me at SAM. This was correct, but the Inland Revenue, for some reason, were just convinced that Fax was something to do with SAM and Asil Nadir. It became obvious where the confusion lay with much of the Inland Revenue inquiry: Jason Davies bought shares for Tristan, and later Forum, through the same stockbrokers that he used to buy shares for the other clients he had acquired.

Douglas Le Mare was not the only stockbroker with a confused back office. Shares purchased by Jason on behalf of Safiye Nadir were incorrectly registered in the name of Fax by A. J. Bekhor several times. For instance A. J. Bekhor bought 60,000 Polly Peck shares in the middle of February 1988 that were registered wrongly to Fax. As well as the Citibank loan there was a smaller facility at KOP for Safiye Nadir's purchase of shares. A payment of £118,138.20 went out to A. J. Bekhor from KOP on the same date as the 60,000 PPI share purchase. There is a letter from me at SAM to KOP specifically requesting this very same payment be sent to A. J. Bekhor's 'against delivery of Stock Notes in the Name of Tristan Ltd'. There is also a letter from KOP confirming that the loan had been drawn down to cover that amount. It is quite clear that the money from KOP was destined to help the purchase of PPI shares for Tristan, Safiye's company, and not for Fax.

It is well documented that Tristan did have an account at Bekhor, and that the shares were not dealt in furiously as the newspaper articles implied but pledged from the beginning to the banks and only rarely sold. The main margin loan I had arranged for Safiye Nadir's PPI share purchases was with Citibank in Zurich – Confidas, as its trust arm, held the shares purchased by Tristan. The correspondence shows clearly that A. J. Bekhor bought shares for Tristan with this money. A letter dated October 1987 from Confidas to Jason Davies at A. J. Bekhor reads:

> Please transfer 2.1 million Polly Peck Int 10 pence ordinary shares, which are owned by Tristan, to Citibank NA, London, for account of Citicorp Investment Bank (Switzerland) Zurich, for account of Tristan Ltd.

This confirms a request from SAM to Confidas, stating that the shares are at A. J. Bekhor. There is a letter from A. J. Bekhor itself to Citibank referring to the registration of PPI shares in the name of Tristan. If Bekhor's didn't have an account for Tristan, why was it that both Citibank and KOP were attempting to register shares bought by the stockbroker in that name?

What is clear is that these shares bought for Tristan were sometimes registered incorrectly. There were several occasions when shares bought for Tristan through Bekhor ended up logged in the name of Fax instead. The immediate effect was to set the lending bank, who needed them as collateral, off on a paperchase for the missing stock. At a meeting I went to in mid-September 1988 at the Confidas office in Zurich, the problems are clear from the minutes. There were discrepancies between Rawlinson & Hunter's, Tristan's accountants, estimate of the number of PPI shares held by Tristan and those shown by the main lender Citibank, or rather Confidas, which managed Tristan and monitored the shares.

One of the missing blocs of shares that the bank was trying to track down appears to be the 60,000 purchased by Bekhor in the name of Fax the previous February. It is clear from the minutes that Rawlinson & Hunter had been counting and re-recounting Tristan's shares and that they knew some had gone astray.

In July 1989 there was a message from Confidas in Switzerland to Rawlinson & Hunter in London regarding the authorisation of payment for two purchases of PPI shares by A. J. Bekhor for Tristan. The message read:

> Please find attached copies of Tristan's authorisation letters re payments of (1) £1,056,300.60 (2) £551,506.25 to A. J. Bekhor for purchases of Polly Peck shares in November 1987. Please note that no mention of Fax Investments Ltd has been made in these letters.

Clearly, from the last sentence, Confidas was getting a little irritated by the registration problems regarding Tristan shares. At one point, I remember, I told Jason to sort out the mess at A. J. Bekhor.

There is a further letter, one signed by Mr Nadir (who like me was a signatory for Safiye), to Confidas giving instructions for the purchase of shares by A. J. Bekhor.

> Please would you arrange for the Securities Department of

> Citibank NA 41 Berkeley Square London W1 to issue a draft today for an amount of £1,056,300.60 to A. J. Bekhor & Co. In return please accept 350,000 Polly Peck International Ordinary 10p shares. The shares to be registered in the name of NCB Limited, your nominee company, until we have met with Citibank Geneva on Thursday.

NCB, Citibank's nominee company, would hold shares, that, like the Tristan shares, were security for a loan. Yet the corresponding contract note from A. J. Bekhor, showing the £1,056,300.60 purchase of PPI shares dated 16 November – the purchase referred to the Confidas note – shows Fax Investments as the client. This is fairly typical of the sort of mix-up that happened several times as I recall.

Since Jason Davies appeared to be buying PPI shares for several different clients as well as Tristan, one can see how the problem arose. Safiye Nadir bought a huge number of shares with the Citibank loan – some 7.9 million in total were managed by Confidas in Zurich by the end. It is perfectly clear from the documentation that there was a Tristan account at A. J. Bekhor, despite what the taxmen thought. A letter from Confidas dated 12 October 1987, sent to Jason Davies at A. J. Bekhor, says:

> Please transfer 2.1 million Polly Peck Int 10p Ordinary Shares, which are owned by Tristan Ltd, to Citibank NA London for account of Citicorp Investment Bank (Switzerland) Zurich for account of Tristan Ltd.

The share-purchase schedules for Tristan, compiled by Confidas from the end of October 1987 till November 1988, show that the purchases through three stockbrokers, Douglas Le Mare, CGS (later Whitefriars) and of course A. J. Bekhor, took Tristan's holding from around 1.3 million PPI shares to over 6 million. There were dozens of separate purchases and only two or three sales. That is a fact. The impression given by the newspaper reports was that there was something fishy about these 'dealings', but there were no 'dealings' by Tristan in PPI shares. The shares were bought and held. It was a perfectly straightforward effort to increase Safiye Nadir's holdings of PPI shares, partially financed by loans from totally respectable banks.

• • • •

By the spring of 1990 SAM's advisers were being asked by Special Office 2 about other Rhone Finance operations as well as Fax. The taxmen were clearly looking for evidence that Gateway Investments, Newbridge Investments and Blade Explorations, as well as Fax, were fronts for Asil Nadir. They obviously believed that all these companies had the same owner. This was why the issue of the Tristan account was so crucial. If it could be shown from the brokers' records that Fax and Tristan were really the same account, then Asil Nadir could be shown to be the common owner, which in turn linked him to the other Rhone Finance companies.

The Serious Fraud Office were plodding along the same route that the Inland Revenue had taken before. In my first interview with the SFO in January 1991, I was questioned at length about the purchase of PPI shares by Fax. The SFO claimed in that interview that Tristan did not have an account at A. J. Bekhor. There was only an account for Fax. I knew of course that they were wrong. I also knew that this particular piece of misinformation must have originated from the Inland Revenue investigation at A. J. Bekhor, when they had earlier majored on this point.

By the time the SFO started its investigation in August 1990, A. J. Bekhor, and its computer files, had been closed down for nine months. Hence the incorrect statement in the warrant and the affidavit for the raid on SAM that Tristan and Forum were administered by Rhone Finance instead of by Confidas.

Of course the SFO did not have the Confidas documentation when it decided to raid SAM. It was 1992 before they got most of it from Switzerland, and it contradicted everything they had assumed about SAM. Far from proving that South Audley Management was the hub of some illicit share-dealing ring, the Confidas documentation shows that we merely arranged the finance and settlement of share purchases for Safiye Nadir's trust. Jason Davies may have been dealing for his other clients – and dealing in PPI shares – but it was nothing to do with SAM or Mr Nadir.

It was quite ridiculous for the authorities to jump to the conclusion that there was some kind of share-support operation going on in PPI. There were 400 million PPI shares – 300 million if you excluded the Nadir family holdings. Jason Davies used to buy or sell in lots of between 200,000 and 1 million shares, it appears, which is a volume nowhere near the huge amount required for the kind of share-support operation that Asil Nadir was supposed to be orchestrating.

But, there was another reason why the Inland Revenue had stuck so long to their inquiry. Their investigator Richard Cook had queried a £2 million draft that had been paid to A. J. Bekhor by Unipac, the PPI subsidiary. In fact they discovered several payments from Unipac's Jersey bank account to individuals and stockbrokers. It was clear to our advisers by then that the investigation was very wide-ranging.

In fact Unipac frequently acted as an exchange route for Cypriots who either wanted paying in hard currency for work done or goods supplied for PPI or just wished to invest their money abroad. The TRNC was not recognised internationally, and it was a slow and very expensive procedure for Cypriots to get hard currency. Unipac was almost certainly the largest centre of hard currency in the TRNC, so there was effectively a secondary banking operation within Unipac, which held more than 90 bank accounts outside Cyprus, to facilitate the transfer of funds for third parties who would pay Turkish lire in Cyprus and get sterling from Unipac.

There was absolutely nothing wrong with this, but the PPI accountants were worried, quite rightly as it turned out, that it was yet one more thing for the Inland Revenue to chew over, particularly as several of the transactions went to purchase PPI shares on behalf of Cypriot investors. Dennis Robertson of Stoy Hayward informally warned Asil Nadir in October 1989 that it just might arouse suspicions that these were not genuine investors but fronts for himself. It was illegal, of course, for a public company to buy its own shares.

I think Asil Nadir took no notice of the warning. Unipac made sizeable profits from its local foreign-exchange business. What the Revenue thought, and later the SFO, however, was that money was going from PPI to pay for all the Tristan shares. They did not have access to the Confidas documentation that showed how a very large margin loan had been established by me in Switzerland to fund the share purchases by Safiye Nadir. When the SFO eventually received these documents from Switzerland in 1992, they must have been appalled to discover that Tristan's and Forum's share purchases were validated by the Citibank loan and perfectly above board. But, it would be years before I discovered just how extensively the Inland

Revenue had pursued their investigations into Asil Nadir – how zealous it had been in its attempt to prove that he was behind the offshore companies that traded in Polly Peck shares.

In November 1995 I flew to New York with my lawyer, Peter Krivinskas, to meet Jonathan Bekhor, the former owner of the stockbroking firm that had been the initial focus of the Inland Revenue investigation. Wild stories had circulated for years in the press about the collapse of his stockbroking firm and his subsequent decision to move to the USA in the wake of the tax investigation.

Jonathan Bekhor was believed to have given the Inland Revenue information about whoever was behind many of the offshore companies for which A. J. Bekhor had dealt. All I knew was that our advisers had thought that the tax investigation into Asil Nadir had started from a review at A. J. Bekhor. Several newspaper articles suggested that it had been at his firm that the Inland Revenue had come across offshore companies dealing in Polly Peck shares, whose owners were thought to be Mr Nadir and a prominent politician, among others, and that Bekhor had fled to the USA because he feared some kind of retribution. While in the States he had, indeed, been attacked twice.

I had met Jonathan Bekhor a couple of times when Jason Davies was working for his firm and had bought large quantities of shares for Tristan back in the late 1980s, and I had joined him for lunch at his office on one occasion. In the early days of SAM there had been those delays in drawing down the loan in time to meet payments for share purchases, and Bekhor had asked me to do something about it because it was causing problems for his firm.

The SFO had interviewed several former members of his staff in their efforts to prove that SAM was linked to some sophisticated share-support operation. One former Bekhor employee had claimed that I phoned up from Switzerland on a regular basis to place orders for shares, and that Mr Nadir was a frequent visitor to A. J. Bekhor. I knew both these things were completely untrue. It was a bizarre allegation.

I had to find out what had happened to Jonathan Bekhor, but it was all shrouded in mystery, and since leaving the UK he had never publicly given his own version of events. Many Fleet Street journalists had gone to San Diego, California, where he now lives, to pursue the scandalous story of the politician and his alleged offshore companies but had seemingly drawn a blank.

Bekhor is hardly a City smoothie. He is a large teddy bear of a man, whose firm once employed dozens of half-commission men, servicing thousands of clients, and accounted for between 7 and 10 per cent of all the bargains done on the London Stock Exchange. He was clearly nervous when we finally met, and he gave me the impression that he did not fully understand what had happened to him or why it had occurred. He was still traumatised – and no wonder. He had a dreadful story to tell.

In December 1987 the Inland Revenue had started investigating dozens of offshore companies for which A. J. Bekhor bought shares. The Revenue, which had clearly got its initial information from the Stock Exchange, wanted to know who the owners were. Jonathan Bekhor went to see his solicitor about this, who told him that the Inland Revenue was adopting the wrong procedure: individual requests had to be sent out to each company. Within seven days the Inland Revenue had done just that, but Bekhor said that he did not know the identities of the owners of all these companies. Bekhor had very little knowledge about or interest in who owned the companies, feeling that the principals, whoever they might be, were responsible for their own tax affairs after all.

It soon became clear that Asil Nadir was one of the main targets of the Revenue's probe. The Inland Revenue seemed to be looking for evidence that Mr Nadir was behind the offshore companies that purchased the PPI shares through A. J. Bekhor. But when I met him in November 1995 Jonathan Bekhor confirmed to me that he had never met or spoken to Mr Nadir in his life, that Asil Nadir had never visited the offices of A. J. Bekhor, and he had only met his son, Birol, in the company of Jason Davies, who was busy working off his debt by dealing for his Turkish clients.

The tax authorities were not alone in thinking that Jonathan Bekhor held crucial knowledge about dealings in PPI shares. Bekhor claims that Bob Wilkinson, head of surveillance at the Stock Exchange, warned him about dealing with Asil Nadir, telling him that it would come to no good. He had been friendly with Wilkinson in the past. But from 1987 onwards things had changed. Bekhor believes that the Stock Exchange helped the Inland Revenue in identifying who was dealing for offshore companies. A. J. Bekhor did, in any case, buy and sell shares for large numbers of offshore companies, several of which dealt in PPI shares.

The Inland Revenue investigation of Jonathan Bekhor and several of his clients went on throughout 1989, when Bekhor decided to sell what remained of his business to another stockbroking firm and go to the United States. By now Bekhor was alarmed and worried that the sale of his business would be blocked in some way. He was also concerned that the authorities might now find some reason to arrest him.

One of the more extraordinary results of the tax investigation of A. J. Bekhor was the handwritten compilation of a list of offshore companies together with a list of supposed beneficiaries. The name Asil Nadir, among others, was included in that list. However, Bekhor says that he had never dealt for Mr Nadir, nor as far as he knew was he a beneficiary of the offshore operations for which he bought and sold shares. He was worried that his clients would think he had told the Inland Revenue about them.

Inland Revenue officials visited Bekhor in the United States. Their first trip was in November 1990, after Bekhor had gone bankrupt in the UK, owing the Inland Revenue unpaid tax. Bekhor was under the impression that the Revenue wanted him to supply information in any future case against Asil Nadir. Shortly after, Bekhor was attacked by a man in a parking lot in Los Angeles, and his briefcase containing a copy of his handwritten note was stolen. Later he was accosted at Los Angeles airport, where he had a gun stuck in his ribs. He told me he had feared for his life – his wife had even been sent a wreath with condolences for her husband's death. He had already given his version of events to the British police.

Jonathan Bekhor had told me that he would be prepared to be a defence witness at my trial, provided my lawyers could ensure his 'safe passage' to the UK. I had first approached Bekhor because I had been alarmed that one of his former employees had told the SFO that Asil Nadir had been a client of A. J. Bekhor and had visited his office, and that I had phoned from Switzerland to place orders for shares. Although none of this had any relevance to the charges against me, the SFO was still trying to prove that the Rhone Finance companies were a front for Asil Nadir. This had, after all, been the basis for the raid on SAM and the collapse of Polly Peck.

When we got back to the UK, my solicitor wrote to the SFO to check if there were any reason why Jonathan Bekhor should not come back to the UK. The SFO replied that they had no intention of arresting him and that as far as they knew the Metropolitan Police had no wish to detain him either. But, there was a sting in the tail: 'I should also tell you that Mr Bekhor contacted the police following your visit and as a result it is intended to interview him.'

I already knew that Bekhor had contacted the police. He had told me that he would do so to see what information they could give me that might affect my own case. He had previously given them a long statement. Then a few weeks later Jonathan Bekhor was phoned out of the blue by a Sunday-newspaper journalist, who had originally revealed the details of the tax investigation into Asil Nadir in the summer of 1990, and asked what he had told the police. Just days before the start of my trial, the SFO travelled to the USA to interview him.

Once I had seen Jonathan Bekhor, a few other aspects of the Polly Peck saga that had puzzled me fell into place. It confirmed all my suspicions that the tax investigation had led to the raid on SAM and that Mr Nadir and Polly Peck had become caught up in a general City clean-up campaign of offshore companies. The result had been the collapse of PPI, following the raid on SAM, but no one wanted to admit that a mistake had been made. But, by then, the damage had been done.

5. The Arrest

WHILE ALL THE drama of the raid on SAM and the collapse of PPI was taking place in London, I was in Switzerland with a problem. The press was weaving a web of speculation around me. The first weekend after the raid, the *Sunday Times* reported confidently that the SFO had interviewed me. I was described as 'a director of the company, whose alleged role in the share-buying operations is at the centre of the investigation'. The article claimed that SAM was the 'real' headquarters of the Swiss letter-box companies dealing in PPI shares. I needed legal representation. I desperately wanted to come back and tell my side of the story.

During my initial few days in Switzerland, I actually met a couple of Jason Davies's Turkish clients, whom I believe did invest in shares through the Swiss-managed companies. Upset by what had happened in London, they had flown out to see Jason in Switzerland. The farmhouse at Givrins was encircled by the press, so we all ended up in a rented house up the road. It is a pity, in retrospect, that the press didn't meet the gentlemen whose investments in PPI had caused such speculation. Neither of them was Asil Nadir, and it was about their own money that they were worried.

I had every intention of returning to England as soon as possible. As Peter Knight of Vizards was SAM's lawyer, it seemed sensible for me to have separate legal advisers. Peter suggested Ludovic de Walden of Lane & Partners, and Ludo flew out to Switzerland to meet me. I told him I wanted to cooperate with the SFO, but I had no idea it would take the best part of three months to arrange an interview. Ludo wrote to Lorna Harris, the SFO case controller, a week after the raid on SAM, underlining my willingness to cooperate. The interview was fixed for the beginning of October. Ludo asked the SFO to give us an idea of the kind of offences in which I was suspected of being involved. He also asked for a list of documents taken from SAM's offices – some of the things removed were my own personal property, such as my diary.

I was becoming very concerned that the SFO seemed to regard me as a prime target. There was a large drawing in the *Sunday Times* that showed Jason Davies and me in a meeting with Mr Nadir at his Berkeley Square office. The caption read: 'Where he went wrong.' And I was further alarmed when, after fixing the October date, out of the blue the SFO had jumped on one of the staff in Ludo's London office and served her with a Section 2 notice. They had mistaken her for me. I began to wonder what they were playing at. Meanwhile the SFO refused to disclose the nature of its investigation and failed to supply the list of documents. I never did get my diary back. Ludo cancelled the first meeting.

A couple of weeks later Lorna Harris wrote to say they were proceeding as fast as they could to provide access to the documents. Could Ludo postpone making arrangements until the documents were ready for inspection? I was seething. It had been a month since the raid on SAM, and the UK press was implying that I was not cooperating with the SFO and intimating that I had something to hide. I was staying in a chalet in Gstaad. I had to laugh when a cartoon appeared in one newspaper diary column showing a typical Swiss chalet with smoke coming out of the chimney in the shape of my name with the caption: 'Come on out, we know you're in there.'

In London Polly Peck was now fighting for its financial life. The events of August and September had thoroughly unnerved PPI's bankers, and a cash crisis engulfed the company. PPI had always had high borrowings – its overseas subsidiaries had been expanding rapidly and it had raised money to finance the acquisition of Del Monte. But the real problem was that a lot of its loans were short term. Since the spring, long before its recent troubles, the company had been reducing its borrowings. It had sold and leased back the refrigerated ships acquired as part of Del Monte and realised about £80 million by floating part of Turkish electronics company, Vestel, in the Istanbul stock-market. These and other deals reduced debts by about £250 million.

There was no problem with the size of the borrowing – it was the structure of them that the board wanted to change. As PPI had grown, it had tended to borrow relatively small amounts on a short-term basis from a large number of banks. That had been advantageous as far as cost and flexibility was concerned, but it meant that the company did not establish a close relationship with any one bank. At the time of its collapse, the nearest PPI had to a 'lead' bank was Standard Chartered, whose borrowings were £50 million out of a total of £1 billion and whose merchant-banking arm had been corporate advisers to the company.

The refinancing plan was to convert around £700 million of these short-term loans into long-term committed borrowing. By the time Asil Nadir made his disastrous bid for the company in early August, some £180 million of the borrowings had been reorganised, another £200 million had been agreed and was ready for signature, while the rest was awaiting approval from the various banks. In another six weeks the process would have been complete, and the banks would not have been able to call in the loans in the way they did. Following the bid fiasco, the media blitz and the SFO raid on the company, the refinancing exercise ground to a halt. And the pressure on the company revealed the very weakness in PPI's borrowing structure that the refinancing exercise had set out to pre-empt. Instead of being content to roll over the loans every few months, as they had done happily for years, some of PPI's fifty bankers began instead to demand their money back as borrowings came up for renewal.

The share-price collapse and the dark cloud of suspicion that now hung over Asil Nadir as the result of the SFO investigation was destroying confidence in the company he had created. While the major overseas subsidiaries in the group were operating profitably, there was a growing crisis in London because of all the speculation. Something had to be done to restore faith, without which no company can survive. Within a week of the share-price collapse, it was becoming clear that PPI needed to get at least £100 million of short-term funding – maybe more. But, who was going to lend the company new or more money, when there was so much speculation about it and the position of its founder, Mr Nadir? After the raid on SAM and the collapse of the shares, the newspapers were full of stories about what the SFO was looking at. POLLY PECK SHARE SCANDAL GREATER THAN GUINNESS was the headline in the *Sunday Times* the weekend after the raid.

• • • •

A few days later PPI took the unusual step of asking the Department of Trade and Industry to investigate what had happened. The PPI board had already issued a short statement deploring the attacks on the company, but it now requested DTI Minister John Redwood to appoint independent inspectors under Section 442 of the Companies Act, as a way of clearing the air and allaying the suspicions of creditors and shareholders. There had been no explanation offered to them, beyond sensational stories that speculated about the SFO investigation into Asil Nadir's personal affairs.

The DTI was also asked to review the behaviour of the regulatory authorities – not a surprising request, considering the contents of Peter Knight's note, the implications of which had been much pondered meantime at PPI's Berkeley Square. The note detailed the unexpected visit of the two taxmen from Inland Revenue Special Office 2 the day after the share-price collapse and their unflattering assessment of the SFO's behaviour.

The sudden demise of Polly Peck raised all kinds of questions. Why had it taken the Stock Exchange so long to suspend the shares? Had the SFO approached the Stock Exchange before it raided SAM? And if not, why not? At the very least it looked as if the various regulatory authorities had a few questions to answer. A FTSE-100 company had collapsed following an SFO raid. That had never happened before. This, and the media reports that preceded it, indicated a serious flaw in regulatory procedures. A Section 442 investigation could inquire into all that.

It is difficult to envisage, in retrospect, how a DTI inquiry would have helped PPI to stay afloat. It would have taken some months to complete, and the company's financial life blood was quickly draining away. Presumably the very fact of inviting in the DTI inspectors demonstrated how confident the board was in the company's basic health and operation. Because Asil Nadir was so closely associated with PPI, everyone seemed to have lost sight of the fact that it was SAM, a private company, that had been raided, not the publicly quoted plc.

A couple of days later the DTI turned down the request, but in doing so it managed to twist the knife a couple more times. Minister John Redwood said an investigation under Sections 431 or 432 would be more appropriate, but it would be impossible for it to be completed before the SFO had finished its investigation. 'Moreover, were any court action to arise in relation to the matters under investigation, publication of the Inspectors' report would be precluded,' he pointed out, raising the spectre that criminal charges might be on the horizon. The Secretary of State was 'at present satisfied that the SFO have the necessary powers to investigate all the allegations of which we are aware'. Unusually, Redwood's letter was made public.

The appeal to Redwood was a final attempt to resolve the damaging speculation now surrounding the company by asking the DTI to investigate the recent actions of the authorities and any dealings it may have had itself with the Inland Revenue, the Stock Exchange and the SFO in the weeks and days leading up to the raid on SAM. There had been at least two meetings – the one on 23 August, mentioned in Peter Knight's note, and another before that called by the Stock Exchange. But, most of the board of PPI was unaware at that time of the fact that there had been unofficial discussions between all these worthy bodies in recent months, although some may have seen Peter Knight's note.

John Redwood said that he would be willing to consider an application for a Section 431 investigation, but PPI should bear in mind that the cost could exceed £1 million. The company could not justify spending that kind of money, so instead it commissioned accountants Coopers & Lybrand to review the business and report to the board. This, it was hoped, would keep the banks in line for the moment. There was talk, too, about strengthening the board with the appointment of a non-executive chairman. Earlier discussions between some directors about persuading Asil Nadir to take a six-month 'holiday' while his personal position was clarified came to nothing.

Meanwhile, commentators were taking the ice pick to the published PPI accounts issued over the previous few years. According to one analysis, exchange-rate losses amounted to over £300 million, while profits had soared. There was no secret that the Turkish lire had been steadily depreciating since PPI's inception. Nor that the company's currency losses were taken through reserves rather than profits – this was standard UK accounting procedure and clearly shown in notes to the accounts. Coopers & Lybrand had been asked at one point to give advice on how to treat the currency problem.

PPI's published profits, on the other hand, had benefited from the steady inflation that beset Turkey and Cyprus – that partly accounted for the high margins. But how real were those profits? If Polly Peck's Turkish and Cypriot operations had been financed locally by paying the very high rate of interest demanded by domestic lenders, the profits would have not been nearly so high, but equally there would not have been exchange losses in the reserves. The fact was that Polly Peck had been financed by raising stock-market money in the UK and borrowing there and elsewhere in Europe. That, plus the UK accounting rules, produced a very different financial result.

That thought now started to alarm the banks, although it was something about which they had known all along and was the main reason why PPI shares had a low rating on the stock-market from the mid-1980s onwards. Later Mr Nadir was said to have performed some kind of accountancy conjuring trick by getting hard-currency funding for the Turkish and Cypriot businesses. The fact was that the accounts were prepared according to the rules. That UK accounting regulations worked to enhance stated profits and earnings in a stock-market-orientated economy was hardly Asil Nadir's fault. But, it highlighted the fact that, more than most companies, PPI depended on confidence – and confidence was now ebbing away under the strain of a media onslaught and an SFO investigation.

There were hopes that support funds for PPI might come from Turkey, which it was believed had good reasons to consider helping. PPI was a UK public company, but over half its business was still in Turkey and Northern Cyprus and played a crucial role in the Northern Cyprus economy. A failure in London could damage the TRNC and its chances of ever being economically independent. This was an important political consideration for the Turks, who had begun to look forward to the day when they no longer had to subsidise the TRNC.

At the end of September, Asil Nadir flew to New York to see his friend the Turkish President Turgut Ozal, who was there for a meeting with other heads of State, including the British Prime Minister Margaret Thatcher. President Ozal had already sent one letter to Mrs Thatcher concerning Polly Peck earlier in September, warning about a Greek Cypriot attack on the company. On 28 September, the day Mr Nadir flew to New York, Gunes Taner, Turkey's Minister for Economic Affairs, sent a letter via the Turkish

Embassy in London to Douglas Hurd, Secretary of State at the Foreign Office. It sounded encouraging.

We are examining what support Turkey can give to Polly Peck International Plc at this time and would be grateful if Her Majesty's Government could assist by making arrangements for Polly Peck International Plc's banks to hold the situation steady in the meantime.

Taner said that Asil Nadir had been invited to Ankara the following week for talks with the Turkish Government.

Gunes Taner had asked for a standstill. The following week several dozen of PPI's bankers would be holding a meeting with the company in London to discuss their predicament. What would help enormously would be some sign that Turkey was prepared to support the company. The Turks, on the other hand, wanted to be reassured that their money would not just be used to pay off nervous UK bankers.

By that evening the Foreign Office had taken advice from the Bank of England, which in turn had taken soundings from some of PPI's lenders. According to one of PPI's main bankers who was consulted that day, the Bank did not want to get officially involved in a PPI rescue. It is easy to see why. It had not been approached directly, and it would have calculated that the collapse of PPI posed no threat to the UK banking system, which was its major concern. No one lender was so exposed that a collapse would spell disaster – or come anywhere near it. The answer from the Bank was to demand that the Turkish Government should arrange for £100 million to be available 'in a form acceptable to the banks' by eleven o'clock on Monday morning. Quite how this large amount of money, a huge sum in hard currency for the Turkish banking system to scramble together at the best of times, was expected to be organised over a weekend when the banks were closed is not clear. This condition, which sounded more like an ultimatum, seems to have been decided on by the Bank of England itself rather than the actual main lenders.

This, plus other conditions stipulated by PPI's four largest lenders, such as the appointment of an outside non-executive chairman, was the uncompromising message delivered to Ankara and thence to President Ozal in New York, just before he met Mrs Thatcher. It was, by all accounts, an angry meeting. Ozal was apparently furious at the high-handed tone of the letter – the British authorities thought Gunes Taner's missive had been equally blunt, but it is hard to see why. Apparently, Ozal had asked Mrs Thatcher if any allegations against Asil Nadir or PPI had been proved, and he had requested her assistance. She replied that it wasn't a Government matter – the Serious Fraud Office was investigating.

That was probably the end of any chance that Turkey would put up a rescue package. Neither was there much prospect of PPI repatriating money from Northern Cyprus, where the local companies had substantial cash sums on deposit earning a high rate of interest. Eventually, it would be alleged that there was something sinister in the fact that so much PPI cash was kept in Cyprus. But, commercially, it seemed to make sense. Sterling would be deposited with Cypriot banks, which would lend in Turkish lire at an interest rate of over 100 per cent. Interest rates were high because of inflation and the steady depreciation of the Turkish currency. Even after allowing for exchange risks, the return to the company was very high – around 40 per cent.

But, by the end of September, Asil Nadir was telling his fellow PPI directors that the Cyprus money was effectively 'blocked'. Seeing what was happening in London, the Northern Cypriot authorities were refusing to release the money and risk damaging the PPI businesses on the island. There is also the theory that at least some of the money was lent, via the banking system, to the TRNC Government, which might have had difficulty paying it all back at short notice. Whatever, the removal of £100 million from the TRNC would have been a hugely damaging blow to its fledgling economy – the equivalent, it has been estimated, of taking £5 billion out of Britain. It is hardly surprising that the TRNC, remote, unrecognised and starved of capital until the advent of PPI, took the view that its need was greater than that of the PPI creditors back in London.

After weeks of tension and bankers' meetings, the directors of PPI decided to put the company into administration on 24 October. £30 million of extra financing would probably have been enough to have kept things going over the next few weeks, but with the Cypriot money blocked bankers were nervous. There were still no charges against Mr Nadir or anybody else, but the company had been brought to its knees by speculation, innuendo, and the actions of the SFO. Through his solicitor Peter Knight, Asil Nadir had been asking the SFO to give him an outline of whatever it was they were investigating, so that he could answer any allegations and get on with the task of saving his business.

Over in Switzerland I was having similar problems getting any sense out of the SFO. Having initially agreed to let my solicitor, Ludo, inspect the documents taken from SAM, Lorna Harris eventually wrote back at the beginning of November to say she now considered that they revealed a 'clear conflict' between myself and SAM, and she now did not think it appropriate for Ludo to view them. I found it difficult to accept this explanation considering I was Chairman of SAM. The real truth was that they had found nothing to back up the suppositions that had led to the raid.

Meanwhile Mr Nadir and his advisers were becoming ever more angry and frustrated about the damage caused by the SFO. An FTSE-100 company had collapsed as the result of the fears roused by their raid – but there were no charges. What a way to bust a company. Wasn't the organisation accountable for its actions – to shareholders, creditors, employees, let alone Mr Nadir? Peter Knight had asked the SFO several times for a copy of the warrant and affidavit obtained before the raid on SAM and had been refused.

In that autumn of 1990, Peter Knight was deeply disturbed about what was happening to his client and his client's business. He is still very clear about what was in his mind. He felt it was outrageous that the SFO could destroy a company without first establishing reasonable grounds for raiding it. 'There was an important principle at stake here,' he said. Several times he asked SFO director Barbara Mills for a rough outline of what she was investigating. If necessary the information could be seen just by the lawyers, not even by Asil Nadir himself. Barbara Mills refused but gave no reasons for her refusal. So in mid-October Mr Nadir's lawyers applied to the High Court to force the SFO to disclose an outline of its investigations. He was asking the court for a Judicial Review of the refusal of Barbara Mills to indicate what transactions were being formally investigated.

The SFO had never in its short life been judicially reviewed – nor, indeed, has it ever been yet. The Polly Peck collapse had exposed some crucial flaws in its operations, which, while intended to protect investors, had clearly done quite the reverse. It would be an important test case. The idea of a Judicial Review is that a judge can rule on the fairness and legality of action taken by the authorities, and the first attempt to establish a case for a review failed. But Asil Nadir appealed at the beginning of November, and it was decided that there was indeed a case, which would be heard in the New Year.

In the meantime the SFO had raided PPI's Berkeley Square head office in a blaze of publicity on 30 October. The press knew in advance about the raid – journalists have since assured me that they were tipped off well beforehand. Television cameras were stationed outside the building ten minutes before the police arrived, hoping maybe to catch a glimpse of Barbara Mills and her by now famous red-painted fingernails.

Asil Nadir himself was in the City that day for a meeting. When his personal assistant, Aisling Daly, arrived she found herself dispatched to the Yellow Room, where visitors were usually asked to wait. The SFO spent some four hours searching Mr Nadir's office alone. Ersin Tatar, one of the PPI accountants, was terribly upset about the raid. He was seen nervously tearing up bits of paper from his briefcase and was frogmarched off to Elm Street for a Section 2 interview forthwith. Ersin's papers were patiently reassembled by the SFO. His reconstituted electricity and home telephone bills are solemnly recorded in the case documents.

It was hard to see why the SFO felt impelled to raid. However, it did raise the profile of an investigation that was looking a bit flat-footed. Asil Nadir was about to appeal for his Judicial Review, requiring the SFO to answer questions about their investigation. Maybe this was one answer, but it scarcely served any practical purpose. A team of accountants from Peat Marwick had already been working on behalf of the SFO inside Polly Peck for the previous three weeks, jostling for space with teams from the joint PPI adminis-trators, Coopers & Lybrand and Touche Ross, recently appointed by the court. Coopers had been reviewing the company's operations on behalf of the banks for several weeks. A couple of days before the raid, Michael Jordan, one of the three administrators, had told the press that they had found no evidence of fraud at PPI.

The next day the *Financial Times* reported on the PPI raid and pointed out: 'If evidence, leading to a successful prosecution of those involved, is not discovered, there are bound to be some sharp questions about the role of the SFO in the Polly Peck affair.' That raid did, indeed, lead to some sharp questions. Privileged papers, including notes and letters exchanged between Asil Nadir and his legal advisers, were seized by the SFO. These kind of documents are agreed to be off limits to the police and other investigators, and they should have been returned immediately the mistake was realised. They weren't. Instead the SFO denied any impropriety when Mr Nadir's lawyers tried to claim them – an oversight that in the end cost them dear in terms of reputation. Meanwhile the police seemed to be interested in far more exciting things than documents. Aisling Daly was amazed to see them take a comb from Asil Nadir's desk and put it carefully in a plastic bag. It was returned a few days later. When she told me this I realised that it had most likely been taken so that the hairs on it could be tested for drugs.

For the moment I stayed in Switzerland, convinced that the raid on PPI compounded the SFO's earlier ruinous action against SAM. In addition, my lawyer, Ludo, who had written to Barbara Mills complaining about the way the SFO was handling the investigation, received a letter saying she did not propose to take direct personal responsibility for the conduct of the investigation. It was in another letter to Peter Knight that Barbara Mills said the investigation had been mounted by her predecessor, John Wood.

All this time the press were trying to find me. Fortunately, they didn't know what I looked like, although I had a narrow escape one day in the dining-room of a Swiss hotel, where I noticed several men in jeans and leather jackets speaking English and suspected they were reporters. They turned out to be the *Sunday Times* Insight team. I regarded the press as real bloodhounds then, but they were only doing their job. I would have loved to have talked to them, but I had been advised by my lawyer to say nothing to the media until the interview with the SFO had been arranged.

It was distressing to see details of my private life all over the newspapers. It upset my family in England, and I got to the point where I could hardly bear to read the press reports at all, so worried was I about what the next 'revelation' would be. I used to phone Mr Nadir on Sunday mornings to find out what the media had to say. Eventually, I decided the press would track me down in Switzerland, so I opted to go to Northern Cyprus. I had my young secretary with me, and we stopped off on the way in Istanbul. We had a narrow escape at the Sheraton Hotel, where one floor was packed full of the press, and we ended up taking the lift down with David Barchard of the *Financial Times*. Neither he nor his colleagues recognised me.

In Cyprus I stayed for several weeks in a lovely remote farmhouse overlooking the sea, hardly venturing out at all. Asil Nadir was travelling in Turkey and Northern Cyprus, and he came and had lunch. It was lovely to see him again. He was already thinking about how he would rebuild a business. Where would we base ourselves once things got better? I asked him. 'Where you have been treated the best,' he told me – meaning Northern Cyprus. By the end of November, I had had enough, and I told Ludo to arrange an appointment with the SFO and not wait for the list of documents. I felt that whatever the lawyers said my absence from the UK was damaging to Mr Nadir. Just before we left the farmhouse for the airport, I realised that I had finally been tracked down. A woman had phoned asking for me by name. Our bags were packed and ready to go. I wanted to move before whoever it was that had discovered my whereabouts landed on the doorstep. I went ahead in the farm truck, putting on a headscarf to disguise myself as one of the local women. 'You certainly won't be mistaken for a local wearing a Hermès headscarf,' my secretary pointed out.

I knew the woman's phone call had been put through from the Dome Hotel in Kyrenia, and I phoned a Cypriot friend and told him what had happened. He informed the police. It was eventually discovered that a British couple, who had entered the island registering as a taxi driver and a secretary, were in fact a British journalist and a member of the Metropolitan Police. Turkish intelligence is rather good. Talking to British journalists later, I discovered they had all been amazed by the number of people who had come to check the air conditioning in their rooms.

Before going back to London I went to Zurich to see my Swiss friend. The events of the last few months had been quite devastating for him as well as me. His father had died, his mother was dying, and he had not been well. We were very fond of each other, but once I was back in London I didn't know when I would see him again. The minute I arrived at Zurich airport I heard my name being called repeatedly on the tannoy. I was terrified. Might I be arrested there and then? When I got through customs to the information desk, I discovered there was a message from my friend. He was too ill to come to the airport to collect me. Could I take a taxi? Later that night he became seriously ill, and I ended up driving him to hospital, before going on the next day to London. Fortunately, he recovered from his illness. And promptly married someone else.

No sooner had I returned to Britain following our protracted negotiations with the Serious Fraud Office – my interview with them had been fixed for early January – than I was in for another shock. The morning after I arrived back a friend phoned. Had I seen the newspapers? There was a photograph of me in *Today* alongside one of a very senior police officer. Assistant Commissioner Wyn Jones was being investigated following allegations of links with Polly Peck and Asil Nadir.

I was astonished to read that Wyn Jones, whom I had met a few times at the SAM offices, was alleged to have taken favours from Asil Nadir. The *Today* article was a follow-up to a front-page story in the *Sun* the previous day, which alleged Wyn Jones had received expenses-paid holidays from Asil Nadir in return for vetting staff and potential employees of Polly Peck. I knew it was utter rubbish but none the less damaging to both Wyn Jones and Asil Nadir, who had been rarely out of the headlines in the previous weeks. I was appalled that Wyn Jones, who had never met Mr Nadir, had been dragged into the Polly Peck affair but I knew immediately why they had made the connection.

When the SFO raided South Audley Management they seized my business diaries, which did indeed contain references to Wyn Jones. They also probably found his name in the SAM telephone records that had been taken during the raid. But it was all perfectly innocent. I had encountered Wyn Jones several times at SAM's Berkeley Square offices. He was a good friend of Bruce Matthews, the consultant who had set up the Cyprus newspapers. They had met when Bruce was managing director at News International, publishers of *The Times, Sunday Times, Today* and the *Sun*. Following Rupert Murdoch's controversial decision to move all his newspapers to a new high-tech plant at Wapping in the mid-1980s, there had been demonstrations and picketing for many weeks by employees who resented the new regime. Wyn Jones had been in charge of the policing at Wapping, and he and Bruce, who lived near each other, had become good friends. Wyn Jones used to pop into SAM's offices now and again to see Bruce when he was off duty, and they would go for a drink at Morton's wine bar nearby.

I used to pass Wyn Jones on the stairs from time to time. On one occasion I asked him if he had an idea where we could find retired police-dog handlers and dogs to employ in Northern Cyprus. I knew that Asil Nadir was worried about drug smuggling, and only a short time before one of the PPI ships that carried citrus from Famagusta had been stopped in an Irish port and searched for arms. Of course nothing was found, but Mr Nadir believed that his enemies, furious at the way he had resurrected the citrus industry, had planted the arms allegations. He realised that it would be all too easy for them to plant actual arms and maybe drugs on the boats in order to discredit Polly Peck. He wanted to find a team of experienced 'sniffer' dogs to check the ships before they left Famagusta.

Wyn Jones said he could make some enquiries and come back to us, while I would try and arrange a meeting with Mr Nadir, whom I knew was concerned enough to want to handle this delicate matter personally. The meeting never took place. I suspect Wyn Jones never intended to meet Mr Nadir and that my difficulties in arranging a discussion was his polite way of ducking the issue without seeming unfriendly. There was never any suggestion of a business arrangement. It just seemed to me that he was the right kind of person to ask for advice.

I also knew that Bruce Matthews did at one point pass on to Wyn Jones a very strange reference we had received from one of our security men. It claimed that he had been a SAS operative in Belfast – not the kind of thing anyone should bandy around about himself – and we felt suspicious and thought the police should know about it. So we passed the information on to Wyn Jones and never heard any more about the matter.

Bruce Matthews met up with Wyn Jones at Claridge's in London the evening before the *Sun* published its story, after Wyn Jones had been phoned by the paper earlier that day and asked for his comments on his Polly Peck links. Matthews was appalled by what was happening and talked to *Sun* editor Kelvin McKenzie, whom, of course, he knew well from his time at News International. But, the story went out next morning under banner headlines: YARD CHIEF IS QUIZZED OVER POLLY PECK LINKS, and the damage was done. The day after the *Sun* story Sir John Dellow, the acting Commissioner, asked the Home Office to launch an inquiry into Wyn Jones. The implications of it for him and Mr Nadir were horrific. One had allegedly bribed the other – and the two men had never even met. *Sun* editor McKenzie later suggested to Bruce Matthews that the story was justified by the fact that there was an investigation.

But there had been questions asked about Wyn Jones before the raid on SAM. Earlier in September, while Asil Nadir was opening the new PPI hotel in Antalya, the *Daily Mail* ran a story about a police officer who was being investigated over the allegation that his wife had been employed as a consultant by Asil Nadir to arrange a team of bodyguards. There are strict rules about serving police officers, or members of their families, being involved in private-security businesses. The officer to whom the *Daily Mail* referred had once served under Wyn Jones, who had for some reason not approved of his work and transferred him to administrative duties elsewhere.

This man now tried to implicate his senior officer, whom he probably knew was on friendly terms with Bruce Matthews. I don't know whether it was the security agency run by his wife that supplied the bodyguard with the suspicious SAS reference, but whatever was going on had nothing whatsoever to do with Wyn Jones. Presumably the discovery of his name in the SAM offices gave some credibility to the allegations, which were robustly denied by both Wyn Jones and Bruce, but I suspect that Wyn Jones had already been targeted for investigation for altogether different reasons.

Wyn Jones, considered to be a rising star in the police force, had made powerful enemies at Scotland Yard. He was an unusual kind of policeman, with a university degree, and he was committed to reforms that were resented by some of his colleagues. He wanted to recruit more police from the ethnic minorities and supported equal opportunities for women. He was encouraged by Sir Peter Imbert, the Police Commissioner who had promoted him earlier in his career, but at the time the investigation started Sir Peter was on leave, recovering from a heart attack.

It was mid-December 1990 when news of the Wyn Jones investigation appeared in the press, and Wyn Jones was told to take his Christmas leave a few days early. When he and his family returned to their home after their Christmas vacation, they found their house had been broken into. Nothing had been stolen, but all their papers had been ransacked.

Meanwhile there had been another development when the Home Office called in an outside force, the West Yorkshire Police, to make a full inquiry into the affair. A couple of days after the newspaper articles appeared, Wyn Jones was suspended, and the West Yorkshire inquiry was announced. The next thing I knew was that my lawyer was told that the West Yorkshire Police wanted to interview me about my 'dealings' with the Assistant Commissioner. By this time I had given up worrying about being dragged through the headlines yet again. I was just appalled that my casual encounter with Wyn Jones had resulted in such personal disaster for him. Bruce Matthews knew him to be a fine policeman and an upright individual. He was furious. If something like this could happen to him, it could happen to anyone.

I was interviewed by two West Yorkshire police officers in January. I had very little to tell them – just that I had met Wyn Jones a few times. They seemed sympathetic towards the hapless Assistant Commissioner, but they kept asking me whether I had ever given Wyn Jones a lift in my car. I didn't think I had, but I couldn't be certain. If it was cold or raining, Hassan, our chauffeur, would often offer to run visitors to the nearest station in my car.

Ironically, it was the two West Yorkshire police investigators who ended up having a trip in my car. After the interview we left my lawyer's Bloomsbury Square offices in the middle of a torrential downpour. The two policemen were only too happy to accept my offer of a lift to their hotel, which happened to be on my route home.

The next thing I heard was that the report on Wyn Jones had been sent to the Director of Public Prosecutions for him to decide whether there was any case for pressing charges. A month later, in May 1991, the DPP announced: 'There is insufficient evidence to justify criminal proceedings against Assistant Commissioner Wyn Jones in relation to any of the matters investigated by the Chief Constable of West Yorkshire.' But, Wyn Jones' status would remain unchanged. In other words he was still suspended. I could not understand why he wasn't reinstated, now that he seemed to be clear of the allegations that he had been involved in improper dealings with Asil Nadir.

Over the next few months there were suggestions in the press that Wyn Jones was embroiled in factional infighting at the top of the police service. He never returned to his job. Nor, despite the widespread feeling that he had been 'stitched up', was any public explanation ever given of what had happened to him. A tribunal was set up by the Home Office, and its investigations and decisions all took place behind closed doors over a period of five weeks. The Polly Peck links, which had started the inquiry, had been disproved very early on in the original police investigation. Instead the tribunal looked at a series of absurdly trivial allegations about Wyn Jones's use of his official car. At the end of it, Wyn Jones was out of the police force for good. It was tragic, and, as if he hadn't suffered enough, he was later to find himself dragged back into the Polly Peck saga yet again in the most bizarre circumstances.

The first news about the Wyn Jones allegations had come just a few days before Asil Nadir's arrest. He had been in Turkey and all his friends, including Aysegul, his ex-wife, had warned him not to come back. I arrived in Britain a few days before and spoke to him on the phone. I knew he had made his mind up about returning, and that nothing would change it. His attitude was that he had done nothing wrong, so what had he to fear? He could have stayed in Turkey, certainly in Northern Cyprus, without fear of extradition, and got on with the task of saving his extensive private business interests. He could have gone to Switzerland, where he now had residency. The Serious Fraud Office would then have had to explain to the Swiss why they wanted him before they had any hope of getting an extradition order. But, he chose to come home to certain arrest. He had arranged a meeting with the PPI administrators for Sunday, 16 December.

I feel the authorities didn't really want him back. It had been weeks since the SFO raid on PPI, and they hadn't even asked to interview him. His passport, which had been taken in the raid, was returned promptly soon thereafter, and there was never any suggestion that he should remain in the country. Most people who are under police suspicion are asked to stay in the UK, but he had been travelling freely in and out of the country since earlier in the autumn. He was getting warnings from Aysegul, who was well connected in London, that he'd be arrested on his return. Even the administrators said they were happy to go to Istanbul to see him, if he preferred that to a visit to London. But he was determined to come back.

The Polly Peck Jet Star left Istanbul on Saturday, 15 December. It was supposed to land at Stansted, but British air-traffic control directed it to Heathrow instead because of bad weather. On board the plane was the all-American crew, Captain David Dahl, his wife and the co-pilot. The passengers were Asil Nadir, his brother-in-law Fehim Nevzat and a Turkish Cypriot businessman. Captain Dahl asked for permission to land at Southampton because he knew Heathrow was not used by small business aeroplanes. His request was refused. That was when everyone on the plane realised what was happening.

As the jet landed, the pilot saw a few airport police appear beside the plane, who directed him to taxi to an area at one side. The warnings had been right, but when the captain asked Asil Nadir if he wanted to go up again, the answer was no. For half an hour the plane stayed on the tarmac, surrounded by airport security, who would not allow the doors to be opened. Then five police cars and two dog vans screeched to a halt alongside, having just rushed over to Heathrow from Stansted.

It was a reception fit for a Mafia godfather. Two armed policemen entered the plane and told everyone to remain seated – they were all under arrest. When the Turkish Cypriot businessman spoke Turkish to Mr Nadir, he was ordered to talk in English. One policemen identified the passengers: he mistook the businessman for Jason Davies, and asked Captain Dahl's wife, Jo Rae, if she was Elizabeth Forsyth. As my date with the SFO was only a couple of weeks away, they obviously thought I might be returning on the plane with Mr Nadir. The other policeman searched the plane with a gadget that looked like a Turkish hookah. It emitted a sound every time it touched metal and was presumably an arms detector. A third policeman came on board and informed Asil Nadir that he was being arrested for the theft of money from Polly Peck. Mr Nadir was escorted across the tarmac and driven to Holborn Police Station in London.

The police continued to search the aircraft and even brought in sniffer dogs. They seemed to think there were drugs on board, and they proceeded to rip the plane apart, causing thousands of pounds' worth of damage. Were they expecting to find some missing millions?

Or were they actually looking for narcotics? Allegations of drug-running had surfaced time and time again during the Polly Peck affair. Captain Dahl is convinced the police were led to believe that the plane was carrying narcotics.

All the other passengers and crew were taken to Holborn police station under armed guard and virtually strip-searched. Jo Rae Dahl was led to another room, where the police set about examining her jacket, in particular the shoulder pads. She was furious and told them that if they wanted to take her jacket apart they should split it at the seams so that it could be put together again. Eventually, everyone was allowed to leave the police station, except Mr Nadir, who awaited the arrival of his lawyers.

Fehim Nevzat was appalled by what was happening and returned home to Cyprus shortly afterwards. He told his wife Bilge that he feared no one would receive British justice in this affair – or, at least, not the British justice they had been used to in old colonial Cyprus, where his father had been a senior master at the British school in Nicosia. His words proved prophetic.

Peter Knight of Vizards turned up at Holborn around seven o'clock that evening, but Mr Nadir was not interviewed by the police and spent the night there in custody. The Sunday press had got wind of events on Saturday night and carried it in their later editions. I was devastated when I heard news of the arrest that evening and kept in touch with Peter Knight at Holborn. I had promised to take my grand-daughter Megan and her mother to the Christmas horse show at Olympia, and I didn't want to disappoint them. I kept disappearing to a phone box in the shopping centre nearby to call Peter Knight and also Hassan, Mr Nadir's chauffeur, who was waiting outside the police station.

Some time during the show my daughter Fiona said jokingly, 'The police are looking for you.' Two uniformed policemen were indeed walking up and down the aisles; pausing to search each row, they were obviously looking for someone. The arena at Olympia is huge, and they were still at the opposite side when I went downstairs to the shops and bought the only hat I could find – a Mexican sombrero – that would cover my fair hair. I didn't make any more calls and proceeded to watch the show huddled under my new hat, deep in my seat.

Mr Nadir was questioned all day on Sunday until six o'clock in the evening. The line of inquiry focused on transfers of money that had nothing to do with what he had been asked about in his Section 2 interview the day after the raid on SAM. Peter Knight was with him all day. When I phoned Peter later that evening, he told me that the SFO had to request a time extension to continue its interview. I was cheered by the thought that they were clearly having difficulty charging Mr Nadir.

Asil Nadir had already been in custody for nearly 24 hours, and the police were required to release him soon. With time running out, they charged him with 18 offences of theft and false accounting, amounting to £25 million, at 11 o'clock that Sunday night. His legal advisers were now aware for the first time what the police were looking for. They informed the police that there was an explanation for the transfers of money, but they would have to make inquiries on Mr Nadir's behalf and obtain the necessary information. Asil Nadir, meanwhile, was content to stay at Holborn Police Station, while instructions were sought from the SFO. The charges related to theft from the PPI holding company to the Cypriot and Turkish subsidiaries. The SFO had not been to Northern Cyprus or Turkey to investigate so I wondered how on earth they could have put the charges together.

Next morning we were all in for another shock when Asil Nadir appeared before Chief Metropolitan Magistrate, Sir David Hopkin, at Bow Street. His bail was set at a staggering £3.5 million – almost certainly the highest ever demanded – and the argument for its magnitude was that Mr Nadir was a citizen of Northern Cyprus, an unrecognised state with no extradition agreement with the UK. The family was stunned. To add insult to injury, a process server from the Enforcement Office of the Inland Revenue appeared while he was in the custody cells at Bow Street and served an order on him for unpaid tax.

The size of the sum demanded for the bail made it impossible for Asil Nadir's family and friends to find the money quickly. He spent the three following nights in custody in Wormwood Scrubs prison, while his family frantically tried to raise the cash. He sometimes talks about his time there, where he shared his cell with a young black boy, Anthony, who was about 17 or 18 – the same age as his own son Serhan. Anthony was accused, not convicted, of stealing a belt, and Asil Nadir was astonished that a child, as he saw him, could be imprisoned for something so minor. He and the Nadir family kept in touch with Anthony after Mr Nadir was released.

Asil Nadir suffered chest pains while he was in prison. His doctor, Alan Wootliffe, a longstanding friend, had great difficulty in persuading the prison authorities to let him in to see his patient. When he was eventually admitted, he found Asil Nadir in good spirits, although increasingly worried that he might have to spend Christmas in jail unless the bail money and sureties could be arranged before the courts closed for the holiday.

Mr Nadir's former wife, Aysegul, put up £500,000, and a Turkish Cypriot businessman, Ramadan Guney, came forward to pledge another £1 million. The rest of the £3.5 million came mainly from Turkish banks. He finally left prison on the Thursday after his arrest. Under the bail conditions his passport was handed in, and he had to report to Savile Row police station each day. Another bail condition barred him from contacting any of his or PPI's past or present employees, which theoretically outlawed most of his own family, as well as me. When he arrived back at his Mayfair home in Aldford Street, he found a posse of reporters standing in the rain on his doorstep. He offered them cups of tea and wished them a happy Christmas. He was relieved that he was not going to have to spend his own Christmas in prison, and so was I, but under those bail conditions I couldn't even contact him.

Asil Nadir had been charged with transfers of money from PPI to Unipac – the alleged offences had nothing to do with SAM at all. After months of speculation about insider dealing and share-support operations, the investigation was taking a completely different direction. Even the press, which seemed so well informed about the SFO's thoughts, appeared to have given up the hunt for mysterious Swiss 'letter-box' companies. More than ever I was convinced that the SFO knew they had made a massive mistake when they raided SAM and brought about the collapse of the Polly Peck shares. I wondered what on earth they were going to question me about.

6. Battles with the Serious Fraud Office

I DIDN'T FEEL particularly nervous about my interview with the SFO. I had been to many business meetings in my life and persuaded myself this was just another one. My solicitor Ludovic de Walden came with me. There were three SFO interrogators in the room, and a whole bundle of documents on the table.

Robert Wardle, colleague of SFO case controller Lorna Harris, told me they had charged Asil Nadir with theft and false-accounting offences. He was looking at dealings in PPI shares and the possible handling of stolen money. Ludo immediately jumped in and pointed out that, despite his repeated requests, we had not previously seen the documents on the table. All the men then argued. After a lengthy wrangle, I was given 15 minutes to look at them before questioning started.

Well, it wasn't really questioning. Initially, I was asked when and where I had met Asil Nadir, and I was encouraged to talk about my duties at South Audley Management and the Nadir family history. I was also asked about Birol Nadir and how Jason Davies came to be involved with SAM. They then handed me a list of companies, some of which I had never heard of, some of which I knew to be PPI subsidiaries that were nothing to do with SAM's operations. After about two hours of this, Ludo became irritated. How long was I expected to give lengthy narratives? Surely we were entitled to be asked some direct questions?

It was all a bit bizarre – there were bits of documents everywhere, and even the SFO didn't seem to know how they all gelled. As Ludo said, it would have been far more efficient to have provided us with a list of documents in the first place, before the interview. As far as I was concerned, the main objection to Section 2 questioning was not that it denied you the right to silence, but that it was such a complete waste of time – and taxpayers' money. Inevitably the question of share dealing came up and the by now familiar list of names. I could see how the investigating authorities had confused themselves. One stockbroker, whose contract notes were in the SFO bundle, had labelled every single trade for Restro and the other official family shareholding companies AN – Asil Nadir. The SFO clearly believed Asil Nadir had been buying the shares in his own name.

I pointed out that I would never have spotted this mistake, because I did not have access to internal documents of either brokers or banks. I also established that Mr Nadir bought very few shares apart from the declared family holding. When they showed me contract notes for shares registered in the name of Tristan, Safiye Nadir's company, bought through stockbrokers, which had been charged to AN's loan account, I told them that was incorrect. Shares would have been given as security to Citibank, who had lent money for Safiye Nadir's share purchases. I realised that the SFO had no documentation from Citibank, which would have shown conclusively that the large Tristan share purchases were indeed Safiye's and only purchased, not traded. It would be months before they would get that information from Switzerland.

The SFO interrogated me about exactly the same points that had been raised by Michael Allcock and Richard Cook during the tax investigation. They queried the contra cheque that had gone to A. J. Bekhor. They seemed to be concerned that this showed that PPI money had been diverted to Asil Nadir's private interests. I realised then why the Fax account at Bekhor's had attracted so much attention – they were hoping to show a flow of funds from PPI being 'washed' through the Rhone Finance companies. They had accused Asil Nadir of theft, but they didn't have any evidence that he had appropriated the money. When they questioned me about the botched card index from stockbrokers Douglas le Mare that muddled up Fax and Tristan, Ludo pointed out that the whole card had been crossed out. The stockbrokers had clearly realised they had made an administrative error. I spoke at length about the problems I had experienced with the faulty registration of Tristan shares that should have gone to Confidas against the loan at KOP.

At one point a Mr Morrison of the SFO showed me a document that seemed to come from the Stock Exchange, which he claimed 'demonstrates a very consistent pattern of dealing by a lot of companies'. I advised him that Tristan and Forum bought 7.9 million shares for Safiye Nadir and that there were only a few sales. That the share were all held, not dealt in, because they were pledged to the Citibank loan.

The SFO then claimed that I had met a stockbroker from CGS for lunch, along with Jason Davies, which was true. But they also maintained I had talked about dealing on behalf of Gateway and Riverbridge; that I was the person to whom the stockbrokers went for payment for these companies, something that I totally denied. It is clear to me now that the SFO were trying to establish a link between the Rhone Finance companies and SAM, which was what the Inland Revenue had previously tried to do.

The SFO said that A. J. Bekhor had eight accounts – Blade, Dilo, Equities, Fax, Forum, Gateway, Newbridge and Riverbridge – but none for Tristan. I pointed out that this was an administrative error; CGS certainly had an account for Tristan, which had, after all, bought 7.9 million shares, and it was clear from the correspondence I had exchanged with banks over missing share certificates that they had been bought for Tristan at A. J. Bekhor.

By now it was about 5.30 pm, and the questioning became personal. How much did I earn? Ludo grew increasingly exasperated. 'Can you tell me the purpose of these questions,' he asked Robert Wardle, then challenging him with, 'Can you identify one single charge in which Mrs Forsyth is thought to be remotely involved?'

Wardle replied, 'Not at the moment, no. If that had been clear I would have put it to Mrs Forsyth right at the start.'

Ludo asked for the SFO's assurance that the interview was going to be kept confidential. One newspaper had already phoned him that morning to ask about my attendance at Elm Street. When I left, however it came about, the press were there, and my presence was reported in the newspapers the next day. I left the SFO not only without being charged of any offence but also without a job and certainly without any credibility due to the huge amount of press coverage the previous summer and autumn. That was the last I heard from the SFO for 18 months. They only came back to me in the summer of 1992 when their case against Mr Nadir looked like collapsing. By that time I was in Cyprus.

Meanwhile Asil Nadir's case was dragging its way through the magistrates' court. Under the stringent terms of his bail conditions, I had to communicate with him through Aysegul, who was then still living in the UK. Most of the SFO's charges against him centred around internal company transfers from PPI, the holding company in the UK, to its Turkish Cypriot subsidiary, Unipac. But, no charges of theft from Unipac had been made against him. There was an extraordinary assumption that money sent out to the Cypriot subsidiaries was 'stolen', although it had just gone to another part of the PPI group.

It was hardly surprising that money flowed from PPI headquarters to Cyprus, where an important part of its business was located. The money wasn't needed in the UK, with Russell Hobbs the only significant manufacturing company. Unipac also operated what was effectively its foreign-exchange banking operation for Cypriots who wanted hard currency. As I understand it, payments due in Cyprus to contractors and suppliers of goods were frequently demanded in other currencies, and the Nadir family and other individuals used this facility. Asil Nadir had never denied any of this. His point was that the payments were matched in the Unipac books by receipts in Turkish lire at the Cyprus end. But the SFO had only seen cash going out of PPI, not coming in the other end. They had charged Mr Nadir without ever having been to Northern Cyprus to investigate, so how could they know if money was taken?

By now Asil Nadir had hired a leading silk, Anthony Scrivener QC, as his counsel; Peter Knight of Vizards remained as his solicitor. To speed things up, they decided to commission a report from an independent firm of accountants, Binder Hamlyn. The accountants looked at the transactions involved in the 18 charges against Mr Nadir. According to Anthony Scrivener, the results of the independent report were so dramatic that he decided to send it to the SFO in June 1991.

It was highly unusual for the defence to show its hand in this way at such an early stage in proceedings – the case was still in the magistrates' court. But, both Knight and Scrivener were conscious of the need for Asil Nadir to answer his charges as quickly as possible, so that he could help the administrators sort out the PPI companies. At this point the administrators were backing Mr Nadir's requests to have his passport returned to enable him to travel with them to Turkey and Cyprus. The Binder Hamlyn report concentrated just on the 18 charges of a £25-million theft from PPI. The transactions on which the charges were based were various transfers from PPI to Unipac. The report, which examined receipts deposited in Cyprus, demonstrated that payments were matched by receipts. This was authenticated by British forensic experts, who went to the TRNC to check that the documentation in Northern Cyprus was in order. As Anthony Scrivener was happy to tell the press at the time, the report showed that there was 'not a penny missing'.

The SFO's response was that they wished to satisfy themselves about the authenticity of the report by examining the Unipac documents with their own forensic experts. But they thought that the necessary forensic equipment was not available on the island. Although the independent forensic team had taken their own equipment to Northern Cyprus, the SFO for some reason could not do this. Instead they asked for the original documents of Unipac to be sent to them for examination in the UK. This was against TRNC company law, although the documents could be sent to Turkey, which was in the same jurisdiction, for examination by the SFO. The necessary equipment was also available in Turkey, and Vizards went to some trouble to track it down. The SFO did not pursue this option.

What was quite extraordinary was that no serious efforts had been made by the SFO to visit the TRNC, despite the fact that any theft alleged had actually happened there. The SFO had made several excuses for the delay in going, including the fact that the TRNC Government was not officially recognised by the UK.

Two weeks after it received the Binder Hamlyn report, the SFO told the Bow Street Magistrates' Court that it wanted more time before the case transferred to study 'new evidence' that as much as

£200 million could have been taken from PPI by Asil Nadir. Anthony Scrivener protested that this figure had never been mentioned before, and it was now seven months since Mr Nadir's arrest. In fact the charges against Mr Nadir were to change many times during his prosecution. He says that even when he left in 1993 he was still not certain quite which charges he would have to answer.

Finally Peter Knight wrote to Lorna Harris, inviting her to the TRNC. As he pointed out, 'Our client is anxious for you to see the original documentation, an invitation that was extended on 28 June and which so far you have declined to accept.' By the middle of July it looked as if the SFO were indeed going to go there. They told Vizards they wanted arrangements made for them to visit Unipac and the Industrial Bank of Kibris at the end of the month. Then the SFO changed its mind. Lorna Harris wrote to Mr Nadir's lawyers to cancel the visit, claiming that the TRNC Government was refusing to give the SFO access to the banking records of the Industrial Bank of Kibris. 'In view of the fact that we are being denied, at government level, access to those documents we cannot see any purpose at this stage in travelling to Northern Cyprus,' she wrote.

Asil Nadir was very disappointed, and his lawyers immediately contacted the TRNC Government's Foreign Affairs Department. The very same day it replied:

> I am advised to inform you that this information is not correct in substance. The SFO has made no proper application to the Government of the TRNC for such access to the record of the Industrial Bank of Kibris. No Commission Rogatoire or any legally valid application has been made for this purpose. The well known principles and formalities which apply in such cases under the rule of reciprocity have not been fulfilled. So the complaint that access has been denied is not true.

It was then pointed out that a Court Order was needed before access was obtained to any TRNC bank records and that the SFO were required to go through the recognised procedures to obtain it. This is not an unusual process at all and one that applies in most countries, including the United Kingdom, and many Cypriot lawyers are British trained. Lorna Harris claimed that in the past bank records had been able to be examined informally so as to bypass the official route. The inference was that Mr Nadir was blocking access.

Anthony Scrivener believes that the SFO were shaken by the Binder Hamlyn report and what it seemed to show. The lawyers realised that they had reached an impasse. The SFO had always claimed that it made determined efforts to go to Northern Cyprus and look for evidence, but they don't seem to have made any approach at all until July 1991, when they were put under pressure by the Binder Hamlyn findings. That much is indicated in a statement from David Madden, now British High Commissioner for Cyprus, but at that time a department head at the Foreign Office in London. His statement was sent to Michael Mates MP, when Mates later queried why the SFO had not gone to Cyprus. Madden said:

> Between July 1991 and January 1993 the High Commission have, as reported to the Foreign and Commonwealth Office, made informal requests on nine occasions for 'TRNC' cooperation in allowing officers of the Serious Fraud Office to investigate this case in Northern Cyprus. The 'TRNC' response has been throughout that Her Majesty's Government must make a formal approach through diplomatic channels by means of a 'commission rogatoire'. This is a means of communication between governments. As the TRNC is not a state we are not able to submit a 'commission rogatoire'. The Serious Fraud Office has therefore in effect been blocked from conducting investigations in Northern Cyprus.

But by whom? It appears that no commission rogatoire was necessary to inspect the books of Unipac. At the end of the day, the excuse seems to be that the TRNC was unrecognised, and that this justified the SFO's seeming reluctance to go and look for the evidence in Northern Cyprus – evidence that it did not even need to make a formal court application to inspect. It was a ridiculous situation.

By now Asil Nadir's lawyers were seriously alarmed at what was happening. At the time of the PPI raid, Peter Knight had realised the SFO had seized some of Mr Nadir's privileged papers, and they had appropriated others when they arrested him in December. It is a strict rule that these documents – which include correspondence between a defendant and his legal advisers – should not be in the hands of the prosecution, which is never entitled to have possession of them or look at them. That is an important part of the legal system.

Peter Knight had tackled the SFO over this after the October raid on PPI. At the end of 1990 he had been round to the SFO to inspect the documents. After a wrangle it was agreed that an independent barrister would be brought in to see what was, and was not, subject to legal privilege. Before that happened, however, Peter Knight realised that someone had tampered with the sealed bags. One privileged document had even been presented to a witness in the course of his interview in early 1991, despite the SFO's assurances that the contents of the bags would not be looked at. That was clear evidence that the prosecution team had obtained access to the privileged documents. In fact, as we were all to discover later, there had been extensive circulation of them to both the prosecution and the PPI administrators.

Peter Knight had become increasingly concerned about leaks to the press, which he thought could only have come from the SFO. He later complained to George Staple, Barbara Mills' successor at the SFO, that he was being phoned up by newspapers before magistrates' court hearings asking for comments on information given to them by the SFO. He was particularly surprised that the *Observer* newspaper seemed so peculiarly well informed, in advance, of what would happen in court. Later, when I returned to the UK in the autumn of 1994, this struck a chord with me. Even before I set foot on British soil the *Observer* had informed its readers of the precise charges against me.

Worse still, the SFO seemed to be delaying the transfer of Asil Nadir's case to the Crown Court. This, as I was to discover later when facing my own trial, is an important moment. A judge is assigned to the case at that point, and he (or she) should control the proceedings and get them moving as efficiently and fairly as possible. A judge has vastly more authority than a magistrate, which is important when it comes to dealing with something such as the Serious Fraud Office, which seems to delight in delaying tactics. Until a case actually transfers the SFO hasn't got to produce any of the documents to back up its charges, and I believe that the SFO was delaying Asil Nadir's transfer because they were waiting to get the Citibank documents from Switzerland. They hoped that these would show PPI or Unipac money funding massive share purchases. What they actually showed, of course, was that Safiye's company Tristan had bought PPI shares with a margin loan. The family had been increasing its shareholding. There were no illegal dealings in the shares bought by Tristan and later Forum.

In the months after my SFO interview I felt in limbo – only comfortable with my family and close friends. In retrospect I was in a state of shock, the way people are after having a nasty accident. In Cyprus people were very worried about their jobs. PPI was crucial to the economy: wives expecting babies had abortions so that they could take over as the main breadwinner; their husbands continued to work for PPI for greatly reduced salaries, or none at all, out of loyalty to Mr Nadir.

Everyone's credibility had been damaged by the affair. Aisling Daly, Asil Nadir's former personal assistant, had found it quite impossible to get a job. She was a most attractive and likeable woman, a soft-spoken Irish blonde, who had been to endless interviews without success.

I had not seen Aisling since I had gone on my fateful few days' holiday in September 1990. A year later we met for lunch. She had been forced to give up her flat because she was so short of cash, so she came and stayed with me, while continuing to look for work. It had been twelve months since the collapse of PPI, and the SFO had not contacted her or asked to interview her.

Within a week of her moving in with me, the SFO telephoned early one morning and asked to speak to her. She subsequently went along for an interview at Elm Street, and she got the tapes of it afterwards. We both sat and listened to them in my flat in front of the fire. They had asked her a lot of questions, but it seemed to us that the SFO was very keen to impress on her their version of events rather than discover what she thought had happened. At one stage an SFO interrogator said, 'Let me tell you what actually happened, Miss Daly. Mr Nadir transferred millions and millions of pounds from Polly Peck to Citibank in Switzerland so that Elizabeth Forsyth and Jason Davies could buy shares.'

I was transfixed by this. I knew that when the Serious Fraud Office received the documents from Switzerland – which they did in early 1992 – they would reveal that the 'stolen' money was, in fact, a perfectly legitimate loan that had been used to buy shares for Safiye Nadir's trust companies.

Asil Nadir had still not succeeded in getting his passport back to enable him to travel with the administrators. The SFO had come up with some bizarre arguments against relaxing his bail conditions. At one magistrates' court hearing, the policeman attached to the SFO had held up a Cypriot newspaper that he claimed showed that Asil Nadir had a gunboat on Cyprus. Anthony Scrivener nearly collapsed laughing. It turned out that the gunboat was a lifeboat that had been donated to a local Cypriot charity.

It was now September 1991, nine months since his arrest, and Asil Nadir was impatient to have his case transferred. On 14 September, the day before his next appearance at Bow Street, he was arrested and questioned by the SFO. The excuse was 'continuing police inquiries into additional matters'. When he appeared in court the next day, the SFO were granted another two weeks to examine transcripts of their latest interview. He was questioned again on 13 September, but no new charges emerged, and he was not given the tapes of his interview, which was unusual.

At the end of September, the transfer date was set for 7 November. But three weeks before this, Asil Nadir was arrested again and accused, along with the former Chief Accountant at PPI, John Turner, of another 58 theft offences. This now made a grand total of 76 charges, involving £130 million. Once again the SFO asked to delay the transfer, while inquiries were made about the new accusations. It was, according to Peter Knight, yet more of the same. The charges were based on transfers of money from PPI but demonstrated that the SFO hadn't any evidence of theft from PPI as a whole as it hadn't challenged the Binder Hamlyn report by presenting any evidence of theft from Unipac. It was difficult to see what the purpose was in bringing new charges, except to delay matters – and the SFO was already being widely criticised for its habit of bringing far more charges than necessary against defendants.

While the sums of money were now more impressive, the charges were still based on the same technical issue of inter-company transfers. Eventually a jury would have to decide whether there was a fraudulent intention, but how could a prosecution succeed without getting the evidence from the Unipac company in Cyprus?

In the meantime Asil Nadir was declared bankrupt, something he had managed to stave off for some time. One of his major financial problems stemmed from purchases of shares he had made just before the collapse of PPI – some £40 million worth – in an attempt to support the share price in the wake of the damaging newspaper articles. He owed money to several large stockbroking firms, including PPI's two former company brokers, but he had reached a settlement with them in February over the debts.

Ironically he had also received a letter from the Inland Revenue, which had concluded their investigations with a demand for £5 million in taxes – a far cry from the £22 million that had been previously suggested to our advisers. The letter included an inventory of the Nadir companies and trusts covered by the settlement. Tellingly, none of the Geneva Airport companies about which the Inland Revenue had been so concerned was mentioned in the long roll-call of family companies and trusts. Tristan and Forum were there but not the Rhone Finance operations, which the Inland Revenue had investigated so extensively.

With the settlement came the admission that there had been no offence on the part of Asil Nadir against the Inland Revenue. The implication was that the Revenue had accepted that Riverbridge, Gateway, Blade and so on had nothing to do with Mr Nadir. But it had been the investigation of these companies that had been the basis for the SFO raid on SAM, which had led to the collapse of Polly Peck.

The Inland Revenue had only itself to blame for not getting its money, and it now became a major creditor. Along with the brokers and some of the banks, it sought to have Asil Nadir jailed for contempt of court for alleged breaches of his financial agreements. He finally lost his fight against bankruptcy when Den Norske bank pulled the plug on a £1.4-million loan to a privately owned property company, after which other creditors joined them in the action. Once declared bankrupt Asil Nadir had to give up his remaining director-ships. He also had to apply for legal aid, and although he was able to retain his barrister, Anthony Scrivener, Vizards, his solicitors, were replaced by Pannone March Pearson.

At this point I began to get very worried about what was happening. Seeking advice, I went with Aisling Daly to the House of Lords to see Lord Ted Willis, whom I had met before at drinks parties. He had been a member of the Friends of Northern Cyprus cross-party parliamentary group that supported the Turkish community there. He was sympathetic to Mr Nadir's plight – but very, very cynical. 'The best thing he could do would be to take the next ferry to France,' said Ted. 'He won't get any justice here.' How right he was.

I think it was in the spring of 1991 that I contacted Christopher Morgan, a public-relations man whom I knew had good political contacts and whom I had first met in my banking days. Mr Nadir could not pay for help, I told him, but could he do something for him? Very kindly he did agree to help. Christopher's business partner, Mark Rogerson, lived in Hampshire, where he was a constituent and a friend of Michael Mates, then a back-bench Member of Parliament. Mates said that Asil Nadir's first port of call should be his own MP, Peter Brooke, who was indeed contacted.

Nevertheless Michael Mates agreed to meet Mr Nadir for lunch, during which he was horrified at what he heard about the behaviour of the SFO. He checked it all with Asil Nadir's lawyers and discovered that Anthony Scrivener, who was the chairman of the Bar Council, was extremely distressed about what was happening to his client. He decided to take up the case and was able to do so because Mark Rogerson was a constituent.

In September Michael Mates went to see the Attorney-General, Sir Patrick Mayhew, who asked him to put his concerns in writing. Mates raised the matter of the privileged papers, as well as its actions in opposing the return of Mr Nadir's passport. Mates also claimed that a few weeks earlier when Coopers & Lybrand had supported Asil Nadir's application, Lorna Harris had made it clear to Christopher Morris of the co-administrators, Touche Ross, that he would be cross-examined by the SFO if he backed Mr Nadir's bail variation. Mates also queried the KOP bank documents that had been presented to Asil Nadir by the SFO at his first interview, which Mr Nadir's advisers believed, wrongly, it seems, had come from the Inland Revenue. He also sent Mayhew a section of Peter Knight's note of his encounter with the Inland Revenue the day after the raid on SAM, which was one of the privileged documents seized from PPI by the SFO. He concluded his lengthy letter by asking why the SFO had not been to Northern Cyprus to look for evidence.

Three weeks later he received a reply from the Attorney-General. Mayhew admitted that two of the bags containing privileged documents had been opened owing to a misunderstanding on the part of police officers, with no improper motive and no examination of the other documents in those bags. He denied that the SFO had given advance warning to the press about Asil Nadir's first interview at Elm Street, the day of the Polly Peck share collapse, or the raid on PPI headquarters the following month. He informed Mates that the documents from KOP had been acquired by the SFO following a Section 2 notice served on the bank the day before the raid on SAM. They had not come from the Inland Revenue as Mr Nadir's lawyers claimed.

The SFO acquired copies of KOP documents from the bank itself on 18 September – the day before the raid – yet that left them just 48 hours to digest them before they interviewed Asil Nadir. In addition, how did they know for which documents to ask? And which might be relevant to their investigation?

Mayhew was seemingly unperturbed by the contents of Peter Knight's note, which he said, rather intriguingly, that he had seen before:

> I observe that it contains, first, a recollection of a recollection of a telephone conversation between an official of the Inland Revenue and an official of the SFO at a time (21 August 1990) when the SFO were considering whether or not to investigate the affairs of Polly Peck International, and secondly a recollection of opinions of two officials of the Inland Revenue as to the actions of the SFO.

According to Mayhew's reply to Mates, the SFO were only considering whether to investigate Polly Peck at the time of the telephone conversation between Michael Chance, then the SFO's Deputy Director, and Dennis Parrott of Special Office 2 of the Inland Revenue. So just when, in fact, did the investigation into PPI start? The affidavit sworn by Lorna Harris to obtain the warrant to raid SAM claims the investigation had been started on 28 August. But, in her affidavit sworn a few weeks later to obtain a warrant to raid PPI, she says the investigation was begun on 20 August – the day before Chance phoned Parrott. If this is correct, then the Inland Revenue was being asked to chair a meeting once the investigation was in process. Clearly their input was considered to be very crucial by the SFO. Why otherwise should it have asked the Inland Revenue along to preside over the proceedings?

Finally Mayhew stated that the Commissions Rogatoires procedure could not be used to obtain evidence from Northern Cyprus, because 'Her Majesty's Government does not recognise the "Turkish Republic of Northern Cyprus" as a state and consequently had no official dealings with its organs of government.' He suggested that Asil Nadir could himself maybe help the situation by getting the Unipac documents sent to the UK, which he claimed was not in contravention of local laws.

I had no idea this correspondence was going on. I was just grateful that Christopher Morgan was trying to help Asil Nadir. It was now January 1992, and I had heard nothing from the SFO since my interview a year before. Then I saw an interesting article in the *Financial Times*, which revealed that the Swiss authorities had sent the documents requested by the SFO to London. I realised that they would soon know that the 'missing millions' that they had suggested to Aisling Daly had gone to Citibank in Switzerland was a figment of their imagination. They would discover that the shares had been purchased with a loan instead. Each purchase had been made with a combination of the loan money and Safiye Nadir's own funds from Cyprus. If it had been a huge swindle, why would there have been a loan?

I came to the conclusion that the SFO would now be under considerable pressure to justify the charges against Asil Nadir. If they were to drop the case against him, how on earth would they substantiate the raid on SAM and the collapse of the PPI shares? By now I had a healthy mistrust of the SFO.

I left England at the end of January 1992 with two suitcases for what I thought would be a short holiday in Cyprus. I was to be away for two and a half years. The following month Aisling was again contacted by the SFO, asking her to talk to them on a more 'informal' basis. She met Detective Superintendent James Davies in the coffee bar of the Meridien Hotel in London's Piccadilly. It was a friendly encounter, apparently, and the atmosphere was very relaxed. At one stage Aisling asked what Davies considered would be the eventual outcome of the PPI case. He replied that he thought Asil Nadir was a very nice chap and that they had experienced a great deal of difficulty during their interviews in finding anyone to say anything bad about him.

My intuition that the tax authorities would return to me proved correct. In March 1992 I received a strange letter from Richard Cook, asking me to attend an interview to discuss my tax affairs and those of companies connected to Asil Nadir and his family. I had received no notification from my own tax office that there was any query over my affairs.

I knew that the Inland Revenue had closed their investigation of Asil Nadir a year before, when they had agreed a settlement. It was also odd that Cook had written to me at my London address, when the one my own tax inspector used was in Grantham. My London phone number was ex-directory, so they could not have found the address that way. I telephoned Cook and left a message on his answering machine that I was in Northern Cyprus and did not consider the request important enough for me to return to the UK to meet him.

On 11 February 1992 Asil Nadir and his co-defendant, John Turner, were finally committed for trial at the Old Bailey. It had been 14 months since Nadir's arrest, and the trial was not expected to start until spring 1993. George Staple, a City solicitor, took over from Barbara Mills as Director of the Serious Fraud Office in 1992. There had been mounting criticism of the organisation following the collapse of two of the Guinness prosecutions and stern comments made by the trial judge, Mr Justice Henry, about the length and complexity of the cases initiated by the SFO. Asil Nadir's trial judge had clearly taken all this on board. At his first pre-trial hearing Mr Justice Tucker told the court that Mr Nadir's trial should be straightforward and short and that it should be centred on no more than ten charges. He pointed out that if the SFO could not get a conviction on ten they could not get a conviction on twenty. The next pre-trial hearing was at Stafford Crown Court, where everyone trundled up for a hearing, and the case was adjourned until the beginning of June.

On 8 June, Judge Tucker dramatically dismissed 46 of Asil Nadir's charges, involving theft of £120 million, after an application by his lawyers. This, according to Anthony Scrivener, rested on an interpretation of the Theft Act 1968. A recent case, which was due to be heard by the Lords, had brought into focus the fact that there had to be evidence of appropriation if charges were to go ahead. Scrivener argued that Asil Nadir's charges under the Theft Act involved the transfer of money from PPI to Unipac's bank accounts – something that Mr Nadir was authorised to do. Scrivener said:

> there was no doubt that Mr Nadir was authorised by PPI to make transfers. However, the question was, whether this authorisation was subject to the proviso that transfers had to be for the legitimate business purposes of PPI? The fundamental question was whether the element of appropriation had to consist of an unauthorised act?

It was a purely technical point, with no relevance to Nadir's defence, but Scrivener could see a way of getting the bulk of his client's charges thrown out at this stage. When the prosecution alleged that Asil Nadir had no authority to transfer assets other than for legitimate business purposes and that the transfers were therefore fraudulent, Mr Justice Tucker disagreed.

The prosecution's argument entailed the proposition that if the defendant had changed his mind after transferring the assets to Unipac and had applied them for the company's proper purposes, he would still, his initial dishonest intention having been proved, have been guilty of theft. That, Mr Justice Tucker decided, could simply not be right.

That left the SFO with 16 charges relating to money transferred from Unipac, but it appeared they still had not been to Cyprus to look at evidence. How were they going to substantiate these allegations? Judge Tucker had earlier called for a drastic reduction in charges, but it was clear that the SFO intended to rely on the transfers from PPI to Unipac to prove their case. The Serious Fraud Office was absolutely furious. According to those in court that day, Lorna Harris, the SFO case controller, was practically breathing fire when she heard Judge Tucker's decision. It was a dreadful blow for the prosecution.

Meanwhile the marathon SFO Blue Arrow case had brought the organisation into the headlines again. The affair dated back to 1987, when, as a fast-expanding recruitment agency, Blue Arrow took over a much larger American rival, Manpower. An attempt to support the Blue Arrow price after a failed rights issue led to charges of fraudulent conspiracy against ten representatives of some of the City's best-known banking and brokering houses, all of whom were eventually cleared. The acquittal of the last four defendants by the Court of Appeal in July 1992, following a case that had lasted a year and had cost an estimated £40 million, was the worst disaster so far for the SFO, which was now perceived to be sagging under the weight of prosecuting three major cases – Asil Nadir, the Maxwell brothers and BCCI.

The Blue Arrow débâcle, and the dismissal of Asil Nadir's charges, brought the SFO's future once more sharply into focus. There were criticisms that the organisation relied on 'scattergun' charges – the sheer numbers of which resulted in chaos for the court and the jury. For its part the SFO let it be known that it would like an extension of its already draconian Section 2 powers. Statements gleaned under these interrogations could not be used in court – unless they contradicted testimony that was later given in court. Now there were rumblings that life would be so much easier for the SFO if only they could use Section 2 evidence routinely in court cases. They had already been given huge powers to attack fraudsters and had made a mess of it. Now they wanted an extension of their authority, and they were unlikely to get it.

The SFO's new broom, George Staple, swept into the director's chair and proposed a complete change in the handling of complex fraud trials. The Roskill Commission, which had launched the idea of the Serious Fraud Office back in 1986, had recommended trial by tribunal instead of jury. This was not an option favoured by Staple, who preferred something more on the lines of the American system of plea-bargaining, allowing defendants to cooperate with the prosecuting authorities in return for a lighter sentence. He also wanted the accused to be made to disclose details of their defence at an earlier stage in the proceedings. This, in fact, Asil Nadir's lawyers had already done, when they revealed the Binder Hamlyn report to the SFO.

There were promises of major changes at the SFO, but nothing could disguise the fact that it had proved a mighty disappointment to everyone. By now Barbara Mills, its second boss, was Director of Public Prosecutions, a post its previous incumbent had resigned after he had been discovered kerb-crawling. All in all, it was not a happy time for Britain's crime fighters. *Private Eye*'s Slicker column, always a good barometer of the emotional temperature at SFO's Elm Street headquarters, informed its readers that the fraudbusters were now in deep gloom over Mr Nadir's prosecution: 'Failure to get a result on Nadir could be a fatal blow, worse than Blue Arrow to the short lived brave new world of fraud prosecution,' it moaned.

As I had always believed they would, the SFO came back to me. On 27 July Lorna Harris wrote to my lawyer, Ludo de Walden, informing him that I was now wanted for handling stolen goods. It had been eighteen months since my interview. The SFO was in crisis – it was desperate. But help was at hand. On 29 July 1992, when the UK newspapers were awash with condemnatory headlines about Blue Arrow and the SFO was reeling from the attacks on its operations, a man called Michael Francis, using the alias Trevor Howard, phoned the Serious Fraud Office from Zurich. He offered them information about Asil Nadir.

Administration of the Polly Peck company was running into the sand, much to Asil Nadir's frustration. He had, at the beginning, established friendly relations with the top accountants who had been appointed in October 1990 to run and hopefully revive the company. But he was now disgusted at the way they had gone about their business. In the summer of 1992 the two senior Coopers & Lybrand partners appointed as administrators to Polly Peck International even found themselves hauled up before a tribunal of the Institute of Chartered Accountants, their professional governing body. Michael Jordan and Richard Stone were charged with breaching ICA rules in accepting the administration of PPI two years earlier.

When the court had appointed them in October 1990, it was known that Coopers had done work for both PPI and Asil Nadir. They had advised on the tax investigation, among other things, which was why Touche Ross, in the portly form of Christopher Morris, another top UK accountant, had been appointed as joint administrators. Jordan and Stone were there to rescue PPI as a commercial operation. Morris had the task of investigating what legal action, if any, should be taken against any directors and auditors of PPI, which might, of course, lead to action against Asil Nadir, Coopers' former client.

The ICA tribunal eventually decided that there was a clear potential conflict of interest from the outset: Coopers should not have accepted the PPI administration. Its decision was not surprising. As well as handling Mr Nadir's tax affairs for many years, Coopers had been called in to advise the PPI board on the treatment of foreign currency in the company's accounts, which had been a controversial topic in the wake of the collapse. It had also given consultancy advice on some PPI subsidiaries and had acted as auditors to others. Coopers' Jersey branch had formed and managed one of the Nadir family companies that was now investigated by co-administrators Touche Ross, which ironically interviewed Coopers' own Jersey representative in the course of their inquiries.

When I met Michael Jordan in Cyprus in the winter of 1992 he was at pains to tell me he had not been aware, when they took on the administration, that other departments of Coopers had been so involved with PPI or Mr Nadir. The ICA clearly took the view that he should have been and fined the Coopers' duo £1000, amid grumbling from the ICA's humbler members that the 'Big Six' accounting firms were getting away with a light rap over the knuckles for what was considered to be a serious breach of the profession's ethical guidelines.

Quite apart from this rather sordid little episode, the joint administration of PPI was running into real problems by mid-1992 – and into costs of tens of millions of pounds. In August the administrators sold Del Monte, PPI's most prestigious company, for £260 million to Grupo Cabal of Florida. This was well below the price paid for the banana and pineapple producer by PPI back in 1989. The deal was something of a setback for Michael Jordan, who had been telling shareholders and creditors that Del Monte would not be sold but become instead the centrepiece of his reconstruction of PPI.

Nearing 60 when he took on PPI, Jordan clearly saw it as his big chance, maybe his last, to demonstrate how the relatively new and untried process of administration could, in the hands of a skilled practitioner such as himself, succeed in achieving a genuine reconstruction of a fallen company. Five months into the administration he told the London *Evening Standard* that the exercise would be a landmark event in UK corporate history. 'Never before has a major company been pulled back from administration,' he chirruped confidently.

Jordan had made his reputation as a liquidator, heading up Cork Gully, the UK's best-known firm of corporate undertakers. He had huge experience, working for years as second-in-command to Sir Kenneth Cork, the specialist firm's flamboyant founder, who thought nothing of turning up at a bust company in his Rolls-Royce, smoking a fat cigar, to sack the workforce. Jordan scored his first major public success in the mid-1970s, cleaning up the financial mess left in the wake of the spectacular secondary banking and property collapse. Later he was co-receiver of Barlow Clowes, the investment company that collapsed in 1987, leaving thousands of its clients destitute.

When Jordan took over as co-administrator of PPI, he reckoned on retaining Del Monte and reconstructing the PPI group. His partner, Richard Stone, was not a liquidator but a corporate expert, which heightened expectations that PPI would indeed be the first company to demonstrate how administration, a much more expensive process than liquidation, could work to save a company rather than just break it up and sell off its subsidiaries. Although envied and admired for his prowess as a liquidator, Jordan saw that a successful administration of PPI would give him credibility as a company saviour too.

The administration process was roughly based on the American system of Chapter 11, whereby a beleaguered company seeks protection from its creditors, but with one important difference: in the UK management control was transferred to court-appointed accountants rather than leaving the company in the hands of the existing directors, as happened in the USA. But, it enabled a firm to take a breathing space and receive protection from the demands of its creditors while its business was reorganised, and there might even be something at the end for shareholders.

The downside of administration is that creditors have to wait for their money, which might or might not be more than they would get from a straightforward liquidation. Equally the costs of employing the administrators – highly paid professionals with fleets of accountants and lawyers in attendance – can be very high. By the time over 1000 PPI creditors and shareholders met in May 1991 to approve the administrators' plans for reconstruction, the costs so far, in administration and legal fees, were already £5.5 million.

There were some minor disposals in the early months: Russell Hobbs, the consumer electricals group, was sold; and the antiques and works of art that graced PPI's Berkeley Square headquarters were auctioned at Phillips in a well-publicised sale. Aysegul Nadir, never one to miss a photo opportunity, went along and informed reporters that, No, she wasn't sad about it. It was after all, only the office furniture.

By the beginning of 1991 the administrators had made little headway with PPI's Turkish and Cypriot assets. The PPI businesses were the electronics lifeblood of the Turkish community, and in Northern Cyprus a group of fruit growers got an injunction against the administrators. In the early stages of administration the Cypriots had panicked at the sound of the name Cork Gully, which they knew was a firm of liquidators. Although Cork Gully had joined up with the much larger Coopers, Jordan had been keen to maintain its separate identity.

The administrators had initially fired the Cypriot directors on the board of Voyager, the holding company for some of the Cypriot subsidiaries. Few in the TRNC believed that they wanted to enhance the value of the Cypriot assets rather than sell them (possibly to the Greek Cypriots), despite all the assurances. At one stage Jordan and Stone wanted Asil Nadir to run the Eastern Mediterranean companies, a sensible suggestion that was strongly opposed by Christopher Morris, the co-administrator from Touche Ross.

There were, it seemed, plenty of potential buyers for Del Monte. In the early part of 1991 the US Chiquita Brands made it known they would be prepared to pay some £513 million for Del Monte in conjunction with an unnamed partner. Banana group Geest also said it was interested in buying it. Later Fyffes, the Irish-based fruit group, was a keen purchaser. The administrators, however, said they were not interested in selling Del Monte, for which they were seeking a trade partner to expand its business for the benefit of PPI creditors.

If they had sold Polly Peck's 'Jewel in the Crown', it would have effectively undermined the rationale of their administration. As the dark night of recession threatened to end the days of easy consultancy fees for the major accountancy firms, administration was gratifyingly lucrative. In an interview with the *Daily Express*, Michael Jordan expressed deep sorrow about the fees. In the old days the liquidator would get a percentage of the assets sold, he explained: 'Nowadays it's all done on time sheets and computerised, and the fees end up out of all proportion.' In the case of the PPI administration, this would prove to be all too true.

In September 1991, Union Capital Partners, a US venture-capital consortium, revealed that it was prepared to pay £365 million for Del Monte. The bidders were even ready to increase their offer if inspection of the books justified a higher price. By this time Michael Jordan was talking about floating part of Del Monte on the New York Stock Exchange, although an increasing number of creditors wanted a trade sale instead. The Del Monte situation was complicated by the fact that some $300 million of its debt was ring-fenced and had to be paid out to creditors whose money had financed the original purchase. But, even after paying these debtors, there would be a substantial amount of money for PPI group creditors – around 25p in the £1. So far they had received nothing, except suggestions from the administrators that they might get twice that if, and when, part of Del Monte was floated.

By the time creditors met the following month to agree the Del Monte float, the administration bill for Coopers alone was £5.8 million, while Touche Ross was due £2.5 million. Meanwhile Fyffes was reported to be willing to offer as much as £400 million for the US fruit group. Part of PPI's share stake in Sansui, the Japanese electronic group, which needed refinancing, was sold to a Hong Kong company for a nominal sum.

By the end of October 1991 any hopes of a reconstruction involving the hotels, packaging plant and fruit interests in Cyprus were effectively over. While Jordan and Stone had adopted a softly-softly approach in the TRNC to try and get access to the local companies, Christopher Morris of Touche launched a £1 billion claim against Asil Nadir and members of his family, freezing the assets of scores of private companies. Also named in the writ was the Central Bank of Northern Cyprus, which held most of the TRNC's sterling reserves in London. To the Turkish Cypriots, this was the equivalent of freezing the assets of the Bank of England. Taking action like this against a central bank was unprecedented, but Christopher Morris assumed that he could do it because the British Government didn't recognise the TRNC as a legitimate government.

Few things were more calculated to infuriate the Turkish Cypriots. There were political upheavals in Turkey, and President Denktas was resisting American pressure for a Cyprus settlement. Now it looked as though the British were conspiring to squeeze the

TRNC economically in order to get them to the negotiating table. Understandably, it doesn't take much for Turkish Cypriot paranoia to surface, and the economic threat was certainly real. Touche Ross was claiming some £39 million, which would make a nasty dent in the estimated £50 million the Central Bank held in the UK and in the TRNC's total foreign-currency reserves of around £100 million.

Even those in the TRNC who had been ambivalent about Asil Nadir since the collapse of the company a year before could rally to the cause now over a matter of principle. TRNC Prime Minister Dervis Eroglu backed out of talks with Richard Stone of Coopers. How could there be any sensible negotiations when the co-administrators Touche Ross were holding the tiny TRNC's economy to ransom?

The Central Bank case proved a turning-point in the administration and an expensive mistake for Touche – or rather the hapless PPI creditors on whose behalf Morris was acting. Five months later Touche's decision to freeze Central Bank's £39 million was overturned in the Court of Appeal. Lord Justice Scott said the injunction brought by Morris could cause irreparable harm to the bank, while the claim against it was no more than speculative. It was unfair, he said, to impose a freezing order, interfering with the defendant's normal course of business, before liability was established.

It caused a public rift, too, in the ranks of the co-administrators. Stone and Jordan of Coopers issued a press release in the TRNC, distancing themselves from Touche's action against the Central Bank and regretting the fact that in court Morris had described the Turkish intervention in 1974 as an 'invasion'. This remark had brought feeling against the administrators to boiling point in the TRNC. Having won its court battle against the injunction the Central Bank now sued for damages.

By the summer of 1992 the PPI administration was in a mess. Somewhere along the line Coopers abandoned its plans for a flotation of Del Monte – the cyclical banana market appeared to have taken a downturn – and sold it. There had been a split in the ranks over the Central Bank action and hopes of reorganising the company round the Turkish and Cypriot interests were fast receding. The costs of administration, paid to the accountants before creditors got a penny, were mounting daily.

Asil Nadir was furious at what was happening to his company. He was already contemplating the day when he could buy back the Turkish and Cypriot assets himself and eventually offer PPI shareholders equity in a new company. With the dropping of his 46 charges, he was looking forward to his trial – scheduled for the following March – and clearing his name.

However, with the strange phone call from Zurich to the Serious Fraud Office at the end of July, Asil Nadir's prosecution was about to enter a new and bizarre phase. It would start with the extraordinary allegation that there was a plot to bribe his trial judge and end with his own flight back to Northern Cyprus.

7. A Plot to Bribe the Judge?

I WAS ENJOYING supper with a friend at Niazi's restaurant just opposite the Dome Hotel in Kyrenia when I first saw Wendy Welsher. She was there having dinner with Safiye Nadir. It must have been early summer 1992, because it was warm enough to sit outside in the evening. I enquired about the visitor and discovered she was a British businesswoman, who was interested in setting up a holiday village on the island, maybe in partnership with the Nadirs. I thought no more of it, but the next time I encountered Wendy Welsher it was in the most bizarre circumstances.

In September 1993 Mr Nadir asked me to go into the office in Nicosia to transcribe some important video recordings and taped telephone conversations. I knew that some evidence vital to his case had been recently unearthed, and everyone was very excited. Earlier that summer, a month or two after he had arrived back in Cyprus, Asil Nadir had told me that someone had been trying to contact him with information. He hadn't at first paid much attention, but then he had received evidence about a painting, owned by Aysegul Nadir, which seemed to back up some of the informant's claims. The painting was *Sisters* by the nineteenth-century artist Frederic Leighton, which appeared to have made its way from London to Northern Cyprus.

'I am going to have my photograph taken with that painting one day and send it to the SFO,' he told me. I had no real idea what this all meant.

Weeks later, sitting in a locked room with a bodyguard manning the door, I started to transcribe the video. I could hardly believe what I saw and heard: there was Wendy Welsher, the fair-haired business-woman I had seen down at the harbour that night a year and a half ago, recounting on video tape how she and an accomplice had tried to entrap the Nadir family into paying £3.5 million for the return of Asil Nadir's passport. Her accomplice was a man called Michael Francis, whom she first knew as Michael Adams.

In fact he appears to have used a string of aliases – Michael Francis and David Kent among others – and he has a criminal record as long as your arm, including convictions for violent crimes. He also claims, with some credibility, to be a long-time police informant. I had trouble understanding what he was trying to say on video due to his strong cockney accent. Wendy Welsher had to come into the office to help me work out what Michael was saying.

According to Wendy, the idea was to make it appear that Asil Nadir was planning to bribe the trial judge for the return of his passport. As I transcribed the tapes, I realised that they were explaining what had happened nearly a year before, when Mr Nadir's case was thrown into complete disarray by extraordinary allegations that he had tried to bribe Judge Tucker. It was one of the most bizarre events in the history of the criminal-justice system. Not only was Judge Tucker intimidated, but Asil Nadir's counsel, Anthony Scrivener, was also named in the allegation.

The matter had first surfaced in public when former government minister Michael Mates accused the Serious Fraud Office of concocting the bribe allegation to undermine Asil Nadir's trial, during his resignation speech in the House of Commons in June 1993. This had been swiftly denied by the Attorney-General, Sir Nicholas Lyell, and SFO boss, George Staple. But, for months before he left England, the allegations that he was behind a plot to bribe Judge Tucker had dominated Asil Nadir's pre-trial hearings. More than anything else it convinced him that he was not going to get a fair trial. He returned to Northern Cyprus in May 1993, furious at the way these accusations had been used by the SFO prosecutors to upset the trial. He argued that it was they, not him, who had tried to pervert the course of justice. But, it wasn't until later that summer, when two police informants, Wendy Welsher and Michael Francis, turned up on the island, that he discovered what lay behind the allegation.

Wendy told an astonishing tale. She had been approached by a friend she knew as Michael Adams, who told her that he was working with the British police. He had chosen her because she knew Turkey and the holiday business. Her task was to approach the Nadirs, under the guise of proposing a business joint venture, and suggest that Mr Nadir's passport could be returned if he paid £3.5 million. He would then be free to go in and out of the UK, able to visit Northern Cyprus with his lawyers to get important evidence. I could hardly believe my ears when she gave details of alleged meetings she had attended with the police, who, she said, confirmed to her that Michael Adams was indeed working with them.

Wendy had managed, through a Turkish acquaintance, to make contact with the Nadirs. She had met Safiye Nadir in Northern Cyprus and following that had several meetings with Mr Nadir's sister Bilge Nevzat in London to discuss setting up the time-share business in Northern Cyprus, mainland Turkey and Spain. She hadn't raised the matter of the passport with the Nadirs but told the police that she had managed to interest them in a business contract which was, in fact, true. She claimed that she was trying to obtain a financial-transaction document with Mr Nadir's signature on it – something she never succeeded in getting since she was dealing with his mother and his sister rather than Asil Nadir himself.

As the months wore on, Wendy continued with the scheme of getting the Nadirs to sign off on some £100,000 towards funding the holiday project. It was finally realised when Bilge handed the money in cash to Wendy in Paris on behalf of her mother. Wendy had insisted on meeting there, telling Bilge that she wanted the financial transactions to be out of the country for tax reasons. They also opened a bank account in Switzerland.

Bilge says that she herself was initially suspicious of Wendy, but her mother, Safiye, who provided the money, had taken a liking to her – Wendy had been sympathetic about her son's predicament when they had first met in Cyprus. Safiye insisted the time-share deal should go ahead – the family must keep going in business for the sake of Asil Nadir. At some point Wendy persuaded Bilge that they needed to put up some security against a loan for the time-share development, and it was then that Aysegul Nadir signed over as surety one of her paintings – *Sisters*, which had been a gift from her ex-husband. Wendy collected this in London.

A few months later, in July 1992, Wendy took the work of art to Bonhams in Knightsbridge, where it was to be valued prior to auction. The auctioneers gave it a value of £400,000. She says she was aware that something was wrong when she received a phone call from Michael Adams, telling her to collect the painting from Bonhams and deliver it to him in Paris. Hower, she drove to France with the painting in the boot of her car and handed it over.

As Wendy was to discover later, Robson Rhodes, the trustees for Asil Nadir's bankruptcy, who were trying to claim any of Nadir's personal assets they could, had put *Sisters* on the Stolen Arts Register in August 1992. She was interviewed about *Sisters* by lawyers acting for the administrators of Asil Nadir's personal bankruptcy in October 1992, and they prepared an affidavit that she then refused to sign. When Neil Cooper of Robson Rhodes swore an affidavit in the High Court on 15 April 1994, he confirmed that Wendy Welsher had indeed been interviewed and that she had refused to sign her affidavit: 'She said she was only prepared to sign the same on the basis that she would append a note that she was being pressurised into making the affidavit,' he said in court, verifying at least that part of Wendy's story. The police have confirmed that by this time they were investigating Michael Francis's allegations that Asil Nadir was involved in a plot to bribe Judge Tucker.

On another occasion she asserted that she had helped concoct evidence with her accomplice that Asil Nadir had a 750 million DM account in Lichtenstein. At this point a couple of other people came into the story, who were supposed to have been asked to organise the transfer of the money and were also interviewed by the police. Wendy became increasingly worried because she had not put the passport proposition to the Nadirs as Michael Francis was expecting her to do. Finally, in October 1992, Wendy claims she received an anonymous phone call threatening her and her baby daughter's life unless she carried on with the scam.

By now it was clear to her that she would be the main police witness backing allegations that Asil Nadir was attempting to bribe Judge Tucker. She went to Cyprus to warn Safiye about what had been going on. Safiye, whose command of the English language is not perfect, either didn't understand what she was saying or did not believe her. She turned her away. Wendy left a note for Bilge warning her that she and her brother Asil might be arrested. There is a copy of her letter written on Jasmine Court Hotel notepaper. That was Wendy's story. But how much of it could be believed? Or proved?

I used to phone Bilge from Cyprus each time Asil Nadir went to court to find out what had happened. When I contacted her at the beginning of October 1992 she told me a very strange story. Mr Nadir had gone to his pre-trial hearing at London's Old Bailey on 2 October. His legal team had put in a request that his bail restrictions should be varied so that he could visit Northern Cyprus with them to collect evidence vital to his case. The prosecution had known for a week about the application for the return of his passport.

But the Judge had not turned up in court, although he was actually in his room in chambers. Anthony Scrivener got his clerk to phone, and the Judge took the call himself. No one seemed to know what had happened. It simply emerged that Judge Tucker had been advised not to appear in court, and another judge was brought in to replace him.

Asil Nadir did not pursue his bail application that day because the case was so convoluted that the temporary judge would have had difficulty grasping its complexities. A new date was set for the following month – the sixth of November. The day before the hearing both Asil Nadir and his sister Bilge were arrested and questioned by the police. Their homes and offices were also raided. On the morning of the 6th, when everyone met in court, Robert Owen QC, prosecuting counsel for the SFO, told the court that once again the hearing had to be postponed.

But, this time Judge Tucker was there, having received what he described as 'an astonishing document and astonishing suggestion' from the Serious Fraud Office the day before; he was determined to know more. The document was a photocopy of a business agreement signed by Safiye Nadir and her daughter Bilge for the payment of £3.5 million to a David Kent. In handwritten block capitals, above the signatures, were the words: 'WE THE ABOVE NAMED PERSONS SIGN ON BEHALF AND FOR MR ASIL NADIR.'

The suggestion referred to by Judge Tucker was an allegation contained in a separate document, that there was evidence of a conspiracy to bribe His Lordship to relax Asil Nadir's bail conditions. No details were given of from where the allegations had come, except that the Director of the Serious Fraud Office had been informed about the document signed by the Nadirs on 1 October, the day before the last, cancelled hearing, when Lord Chief Justice Taylor had been informed.

This had all been faxed through to Judge Tucker on the morning of 5 November, but the defence hadn't received it until very late that same afternoon, on the instructions of the Attorney-General Sir Nicholas Lyell. Anthony Scrivener, Asil Nadir's QC, had then passed it on to his client. A friend, who went round to see Asil Nadir after he had been released by the police, found him baffled by the whole business and completely shocked by the allegation that he was planning to bribe his trial judge.

Now High Court judges come in for criticism when they hand down bizarre judgements, but never have there been any suggestions that the British judiciary was corrupt. Scrivener told his distraught client that the last occasion a judge had been accused of corruption was several centuries ago. Astonishingly no evidence was given of a link between the business document and the Judge, apart from the SFO's own claim. In court the next day, however, Robert Owen told Judge Tucker: 'The current view of the prosecution is that there are no very substantial grounds to invite your Lordship to discharge yourself from trying this matter.'

'I see no reason to,' said the Judge, who no doubt felt he was in a rather better position than prosecuting counsel to know whether there was any substance in the allegation that he was being bribed. But, having first raised the possibility of the Judge standing down, Robert Owen was determined that everyone should be aware of just how seriously the police were taking the allegations.

'It is only right that I should mention that those responsible for the investigation instruct those instructing me that there is a probability that officers involved in that investigation would wish to interview your Lordship.' This, he said, 'may be relevant to the question of your Lordship's view of continuing to preside over the matter.' These were weasel words, once more confirming the most astonishing suggestion of all – that Judge Tucker might feel he could no longer preside over the case. He had been told that the allegations were of sufficient strength that he, a High Court Judge, might be interviewed by the police. At least that was what it sounded like.

Anthony Scrivener was furious. He believed that the Judge had been put in an intolerable position, and on the basis of no evidence at all. He rushed back to his office and wrote an angry letter to Sir Nicholas Lyell, stating his main point bluntly:

> It means that a Judge who finds against the SFO on some matter (the Judge in this case found that over 40 counts on the indictment were bad in law) would be vulnerable to such an allegation and have to withdraw from trying a case. It seemed to us that Mr Justice Tucker was very conscious of this.

Very much at the forefront of his mind was the fact that Judge Tucker had recently ordered the SFO to drop 46 of the charges against his client. Scrivener had also been about to apply for variations in Asil Nadir's bail, something scheduled to be discussed at the 2 October hearing, which was abandoned. The SFO's bombshell threatened to pre-empt the bail application and derail his client's trial. And maybe, if the judge did indeed stand down because of the problems caused by the allegations, delay it for months, if not years.

I hadn't heard the full details of all this until I saw Bilge in Cyprus that Christmas, when she arrived back on the island in a terrible state. The day before the 6 November hearing she had been arrested and interrogated by the police. Amazingly, in view of what was said in court the next day, she was never asked any questions about the bribery allegation. The documents that were faxed to Judge Tucker that morning were not revealed to Asil Nadir's defence until much later that day.

Bilge was kept in police custody all day and had the feeling that the police were waiting for something. Asil Nadir was arrested and questioned later that day, again with no mention of the bribery allegation. Both of them were devastated by what had happened. At one point Mr Nadir had caught a glimpse of his sister sitting miserable and frightened in the police cells as he himself came in for questioning, which was the first time he knew that Bilge had been arrested too. It was yet another pressure on him.

Bilge never returned to England after that Christmas. Asil Nadir believed that his sister would be constantly harassed by the police, as he had been, if she remained in the UK. She felt upset at having to leave her three children in Britain, where the youngest had just started university. She was also desperately worried about leaving her brother. But in the end she felt she had to go back to Cyprus, where she could stay near her mother, Safiye, who was not well. After her arrest and the extraordinary courtroom revelations, Bilge thought that anything could happen.

At the next court hearing on 15 December 1992 proceedings were again interrupted by the bribery allegation. There were already reporting restrictions, and none of the pre-trial hearings could be covered by the press. Each time the court turned its attention to the bribery issue, anyone in the public gallery, including the Nadir family and the press, were told to leave.

At this hearing it became clear that the Metropolitan Police, who were investigating the allegations, were finding it hard to produce any evidence. When questioned by Robert Owen, Chief Superintendent Thomas Glendenning confirmed that inquiries were hampered, 'by virtue of the absence of the source of information', which would indeed be something of a handicap. The business agreement signed by Safiye Nadir and Bilge Nevzat was the main evidence behind the allegation, but there was also evidence that 'funds and property' were being moved on behalf of Mr Nadir, then, of course, a bankrupt whose assets belonged to his creditors.

Cross-examined by Anthony Scrivener, Glendenning said: 'It has been perhaps indicated that it may be in the form of paintings, but I can't confirm that.' Glendenning then told the court that he had as yet no evidence whatsoever to support the allegations that there was a plot to bribe the judge, as outlined in the SFO's original missive to Judge Tucker. 'We have indications that substantial sums of money have been moved, but we can only speculate as to what the purpose of that money was for and to what use it would be put,' he said. As the hearing went on, Glendenning seemed concerned to distance himself and his inquiries from the actions of the SFO, admitting under questioning that it was the SFO rather than his own Metropolitan Police that had obtained the search warrant for the raid on Asil Nadir and Bilge Nevzat on 5 November. Moreover, he admitted, 'I do not believe that anything relevant to this inquiry was found.'

The SFO had sent the Judge notice of the bribery allegations the day before the last hearing, where Judge Tucker had been told that he might even be interviewed. Now Glendenning was telling the court, in effect, that the SFO had jumped the gun. It emerged that Glendenning had not even seen the original document on which the allegations were based, just a photocopy of it. And the police themselves seemed by no means convinced that there was a plot afoot to bribe anybody, let alone a High Court judge. Finally, Scrivener went in for the kill. He asked Glendenning, 'Was it ever your intention to interview the person named in the highlighted section of that report?' By this he meant Judge Tucker.

Glendenning replied, 'I never had evidence that would justify such a course of action.' Quite why the SFO's prosecuting counsel had jumped in at the earlier hearing on 6 November with the outrageous, and it appears presumptuous, suggestion that the Judge might be interviewed was never examined by the court.

The Metropolitan Police were investigating the allegations on an 'arm's length' basis, yet the November raids on the homes and offices of Asil Nadir and his sister had been conducted on the strength of an SFO search warrant obtained under the Bankruptcy and Insolvency Acts, following suspicions that Asil Nadir had been moving assets around. According to Glendenning, the document outlining the bribe allegation had been prepared by the SFO, not those responsible for the investigation. Was it simply over-enthusiasm on the part of the SFO?

The SFO has another explanation. According to Assistant Director Robert Wardle, who wrote to my solicitor in October 1995, Mr Owen QC had been told that it was 'the professional view of one of the senior SO6 officers assisting that investigation that the police would need to interview the Judge if only to obtain a negative witness statement'. But Mr Owen had not said anything about a negative witness statement – he had said the police might interview the Judge. Why had Detective Chief Superintendent Glendenning then suggested that there was no reason to interview Judge Tucker? The SFO had an answer for that, too. Glendenning had taken over the inquiry on behalf of the Metropolitan Police on 10 November, a few days after the hearing, and that was the view he had formed.

According to the SFO, 'At most this point reflects different professional judgements by different officers at different times on what was an operational police matter.' But the fact was that the suggestion that he might be interviewed alarmed Judge Tucker and no wonder. Were those who had instructed Robert Owen QC genuinely expecting something – as Bilge Nevzat felt they were on that horrible day she spent in the police cells – that would justify bringing the allegation up in court? It was only months later, when Wendy Welsher and her accomplice turned up in Northern Cyprus to give their version of events, that the reasons behind these extraordinary court-room scenes became clear. The police, who had obtained the business agreement signed by Safiye Nadir and Bilge Nevzat, had been led to believe that they would be supplied with additional evidence – in the form of incriminating tape recordings.

The SFO have confirmed that they were indeed told about the existence of some incriminating tapes, and it was at this point that Wendy Welsher's accomplice played a crucial role. Michael Francis says that it was he who was one of the informants mentioned in the court hearings, a statement that is confirmed by the police.

On 22 August 1992 Michael Francis had been arrested at Gatwick Airport. He claims that while he was in custody the police were encouraging him to produce evidence against Asil Nadir. The police claim that it was Francis who offered the evidence in the first place. Francis seems to have led the police a merry dance. On 20 October 1992, while on bail, he was taken to Zurich by Detective Superintendent James Davies to get documents and tape recordings that would back up allegations about Mr Nadir and Judge Tucker. By the time he and Davies left Zurich to fly home, Francis had produced nothing to back up the bribery allegations that had clearly excited the police.

On 30 October, this time accompanied by Detective Constable Andy Barnes, Davies again took Francis to Zurich in an effort to get the promised tapes and papers. Francis was once more allowed to disappear on his own to collect them. Amazingly, the two policemen left him in Zurich and returned to London, following a promise from Francis that he would return the following week with the 'evidence'.

On 5 November 1992, Asil Nadir and Bilge Nevzat were arrested, despite the fact that Francis had not returned to London as promised. Far from having any evidence, as Robert Owen so confidently intimated in court the following day, the police had nothing except the business document, or rather a photocopy of it, with the vital handwritten link to Asil Nadir. They had no proof that the Judge was being bribed, and only the hope that their two informants had succeeded in entrapping the Nadirs. They had also been promised incriminating tape recordings that they had not received, and their informant had not turned up as promised. All of this ought to have cast doubt on the whole basis of Francis's allegations and evidence.

It is reasonable to expect the police to have realised, on 5 November if not before, that there had to be a very good chance that they had been hoodwinked. Yet counsel for the SFO had been instructed to go into court the following day and make suggestions calculated to unsettle the Judge, regardless of the fact that their investigation, far from progressing, was displaying every sign of being a hoax. Why were they so certain that they would shortly have something that indicated the existence of a plot to bribe Judge Tucker? Why were they so ready to take the word of a known villain? The police have always maintained that they first heard of the bribery allegation in October 1992 and had to investigate it to see where it led.

If the police were indeed approached by Michael Francis with his hoax story, they demonstrated extraordinary patience and a naive credulity, as their informants failed to provide any solid evidence to back their story. What is not in dispute is that the police and SFO had extensive dealings with Francis in the summer and autumn of 1992. The SFO claim he first made contact with them when he phoned from Zurich at the end of July calling himself Trevor Howard.

Mr 'Howard' wanted to give the SFO information about Asil Nadir. He seemed very well informed about Mr Nadir's case and the recent dismissal of 46 of his charges. Those initial phone calls at the end of July 1992 seem to have led to nothing. On 22 August Francis was arrested at Gatwick for the use of a false passport and driving licence. He was then held under the Prevention of Terrorism Act (PTA), following the discovery of brochures and documents relating to the sale of arms in his briefcase, and Special Branch was alerted.

Rather surprisingly the PTA restraint was lifted the next day, but he remained in custody as other 'serious offences' were being investigated. There was an arrest warrant outstanding for possession of a stun gun, and he was also wanted by police in Boston, Lincolnshire, for jumping bail. These offences would, if proved, be enough to put him in jail.

Francis claims that he was desperately worried about a possible prosecution under the Prevention of Terrorism Act. The police version is that Michael Francis informed them about his dealings with Mr Nadir after he was arrested in August 1992. What is certain is that following the surprisingly swift end of the PTA investigations, Francis had a series of meetings with officers from the Serious Fraud Office during the weeks he was in custody. The solicitor handling his case was asked by Francis to contact the Director of Public Prosecutions, then Barbara Mills. Francis told his solicitor that he had vital information about Asil Nadir. That phone call to Barbara Mills' office led to at least three visits from senior officers from the SFO and Metropolitan Police.

When Francis applied for bail over the passport and driving-licence offences, he had been in custody since the end of August and was wanted elsewhere for other offences. The records at Crawley Magistrates' Court show that the clerk made the following note:

> Defendant's first application for bail, no previous record of absconding, can live with family, no intention to leave this country, already in custody since August 1992. Did assist Serious Fraud Office to provide information in high profile cases.

When the solicitor briefed the defence barrister for Michael Francis on the passport and driving licence charges he wrote:

> Mr Francis has through Instructing Solicitors been able to assist the Serious Fraud Office in the investigation of a very serious matter and whilst these matters were being pursued, instructing solicitors were assured by David Kyle, who is head of general casework at the DPP's office, that no active matter was outstanding against him apart from these matters currently at Crawley Magistrates' Court. There was also a discussion as to whether these matters were to be proceeded with and if so whether the DPP would provide a letter of comfort to be produced to Crawley Magistrates' Court in the event of a conviction and for the purposes of sentencing.

In other words he was an important witness in a high-profile case who was cooperating with the police. At the end of October he was fined £800, after pleading guilty to the false passport and driving-licence offences.

It could be that the bribery allegation was invented by Michael Francis, who had involved Wendy in a business transaction with the Nadir family. Realising that he faced a jail sentence over serious offences, he may have seen the opportunity to do a mitigation deal. When his solicitors first approached the DPP in September, Francis was claiming that he could provide proof of hidden assets and tape recordings, which would supply evidence on the existing charges against Mr Nadir.

The Serious Fraud Office is very clear on this point. But on 1 October, according to the SFO, Francis produced a document that he claimed was evidence of a deal to ensure the return of Asil Nadir's passport and claimed for the first time that Judge Tucker was party to the plan. Francis had been in custody since 22 August. All of a sudden – and the day before 2 October court hearing, when Mr Nadir was going to ask for his bail variation – he produces a document and claims Judge Tucker is party to the conspiracy to get back Mr Nadir's passport.

The crucial part of the police interview on 1 October, in which Francis first made the claim concerning Judge Tucker, was not tape-recorded. Francis apparently insisted that one of the two policemen interrogating him should leave the room before he talked about the £3.5 million bribery conspiracy for the return of Mr Nadir's passport. Francis offered the police no evidence of his allegations to back up his own account, except promising them an incriminating tape recording of Asil Nadir.

But it is clear that the passport issue must have surfaced before then. The attendance note of Francis's solicitor, dated 11 September, records his conversations with an SFO police officer.

> An officer will be sent to Crawley Magistrates' Court to see Francis on the 16th September to see what, if anything, needs to be done. The trial date is fixed for March 1993. They have Robert Owen Q.C. and David Calvert-Smith Q.C. acting for the Prosecution and he was aware of the possibility of Asil Nadir going for a bail variation for his passport although he hadn't been notified of any such application to date.

138

If Francis were only, at that stage, assisting police with evidence about Mr Nadir's existing theft charges, as the SFO claims, why was the passport issue already being discussed in anticipation of Mr Nadir's application for it? The SFO document, sent out on 5 November outlining the bribery allegation, states clearly:

> The matters to which it relates will be relied upon by the Crown in any application relating to the bail of the defendant Asil Nadir.

On 8 October, Michael Francis had his own application for bail turned down – he was still in custody. The Prosecutor Ann Toynbee then said that granting bail at that point might hinder other enquiries. On 14 October, according to the SFO, Francis informed the police that Anthony Scrivener QC and Assistant Commissioner Wyn Jones were involved in the 'conspiracy'. Again this crucial allegation appears to have been made in a conversation with only one policeman present, after the other one who had been interviewing Francis as well had left the room.

On 15 October, the bail application at Crawley Magistrates' Court was successful, when the prosecution simply withdrew their objections to Francis having bail. Michael Francis had been in prison since the end of August.

What is incredible is that the SFO took Michael Francis's allegations so seriously. Francis was a hardened criminal, desperate by now to get out of a tight corner. Yet, on his say-so and nothing else, Robert Owen QC had apparently been instructed to bring the bribery allegation to the attention of the court. On the day after, Francis had failed to deliver the evidence that he had duped the investigating police into believing he held.

By 6 November the police had every reason to suspect that they had been conned when Francis failed to turn up. He had led them up the garden path – even getting them to take him to Switzerland twice. He had managed to get a deal over his charges, and he was out of the country. In the weeks that followed the police tried to contact Francis without success. One can understand that they felt angry and disappointed.

What is inexplicable is that prosecuting counsel Robert Owen was instructed to inform Judge Tucker that he might be interviewed. By whom? Owen was instructed by the SFO, since he was their prosecuting counsel. He might have meant that they in turn had been instructed by the investigating team from the Metropolitan Police.

But, officers attached to the SFO's Nadir inquiry had been among those who had interviewed Michael Francis and had taken him to Switzerland on their failed mission to get the evidence to back up his allegations that there was a conspiracy to bribe Judge Tucker. It had been those officers who had returned empty handed – it appears without the tapes or their informant.

Those instructing Robert Owen, the SFO, certainly knew the real state of the 'bribery' inquiry at first hand, for at the beginning of November 1992, the bribery investigation was being conducted by a SFO police officer, who had been involved in the PPI prosecution from the start. This is confirmed by one of the letters written by the Attorney-General, Sir Nicholas Lyell, to Michael Mates, then Minister for Northern Ireland, in February 1993. Mates had queried why it appeared to be the case that the SFO had obtained the warrant for the 5 November raids on the homes and offices of Mr Nadir and his sister, if the bribe allegations were supposed to be handled separately from the PPI case itself?

Sir Nicholas Lyell replied:

> The warrant was sought by the police and not, as your letter implies, by the SFO. The fact that Det Supt Davies is described in the warrant as being attached to the SFO does not detract from the fact that on this particular inquiry he was working under the command of senior offices of SO1 Division.

Equally convoluted is the explanation given to my lawyer in October 1995. Assistant SFO Director Robert Wardle wrote:

> The SFO has no power to investigate offences other than those involving serious or complex fraud. Accordingly it was decided that this fresh investigation should be the responsibility of SO1 Branch of the Metropolitan Police. The investigation was initially carried out by an SO6 officer attached to the Serious Fraud Office working directly to the Commander SO1. Responsibility for the investigation was taken over by SO1 officers on November 10 who were assisted for a short period by the original investigating officers.

No one can seriously believe that the SFO did not know the real status of the bribe allegation on 6 November when Mr Owen went into court and told Judge Tucker he might be interviewed? Chief Superintendent Glendenning appeared to be playing down the amount of evidence unearthed when he appeared in court later, just before Christmas 1992. But it was distracting to have a major allegation such as this hanging around. Not for nothing did Anthony Scrivener pointedly ask Glendenning, 'Was your action on the day before the bail application was being made anything at all to do with the bail application?' Glendenning was not sure 'the particular timing was relevant'.

But, in May 1995, two years after Asil Nadir had left Britain, Ramadan Guney, the Turkish Cypriot businessman who had stood bail for Mr Nadir, applied for leave to go to the House of Lords about his loss, claiming that he should not forfeit his surety. At that hearing there was no doubt in the mind of Sir Thomas Bingham, Master of the Rolls, that the two matters were linked. He outlined what had happened in court on 6 November.

> The judge was told by Mr Owen that those responsible for investigating this plot would probably wish to interview him. The Crown's intention was, it seems, to rely on these allegations on any application relating to Mr Nadir's bail conditions.

He also commented:

> The outlandish notion that Tucker J would in any way have lent himself to any plot can of course be dismissed without a second's hesitation.

But it wasn't.

After the December disclosures one might have expected the authorities to become a little more circumspect about the whole affair as the pre-trial hearings continued. But not a bit of it. A few weeks later, on 8 March, Judge Tucker's courtroom was again thrown into confusion when Alun Jones QC, representing the Director of Public Prosecutions, Barbara Mills, appeared in court and declared that Anthony Scrivener QC and Assistant Commissioner Wyn Jones had also been implicated along with His Lordship in the allegations. 'Is there anyone else you are going to include?' commented an astonished Judge Tucker. Apparently not. Two minutes before the hearing Alun Jones had informed Scrivener that his name was now in the frame – he was about to be named along with the Judge in the bribery allegations. Scrivener just laughed, convinced that the SFO was finally heading round the bend.

'I had dinner with the Archbishop of Canterbury the other evening,' he informed Jones. 'Is he now under threat?'

But, just in case anyone else was inclined to a fit of the giggles at this point Mr Jones informed the court:

> The police and I know more about the details of the allegations than I can disclose in court. My Lord, it is right to say that the police are pursuing inquiries and the police have got to the stage from which it is reasonable to conclude that this allegation is not a hoax or a prank.

It looked as if the police investigation had moved on to a higher plane of credibility and was getting very near the point where investigations would yield charges. That was certainly the impression conveyed by Alun Jones QC as he said, 'I am submitting that on behalf of the Director of Public Prosecutions, there are serious problems foreseeable and dangers in your Lordship presiding over the trial, of the kind that I have mentioned.'

The matter, he said, was so 'operationally sensitive' that he could not tell the Judge anything he knew (and he claimed that he did know) about the informants, 'who are entitled to be frightened', or what the alleged connection was supposed to be between His Lordship, Asil Nadir, Anthony Scrivener and Assistant Commissioner Wyn Jones. They were not, he continued, even certain about the object of the supposed conspiracy. Mr Nadir might be trying to destabilise his trial by concocting the bribe allegation himself and arranging for it to be discovered. Or his enemies might be doing it to try and embarrass him. The point that Alun Jones QC made time and time again in court was that whichever way you looked at it Judge Tucker had been put in a very difficult position, and he must consider what might happen if he continued with the trial.

Jones opened up a veritable Pandora's box of judicial horrors for the embattled Judge to contemplate. He expected the police inquiries to take two months, but even then there was 'a serious possibility that the inquiry would be simply concluded as not being substantiated, neither proved, nor disproved against any or all of the parties'. In other words the Judge and leading defence counsel might not be in the clear by the time the main trial started. So much for the later claim that Judge Tucker was only going to be interviewed so that he could confirm that no approach had been made to him.

The Judge might then be faced, he went on, with a problem about ruling on the disclosure of evidence. The defence would want to know the identities of the informants, whereas the prosecution might argue for anonymity.

> Your Lordship could then be in a position of having to look at material to decide whether that material ought to be disclosed to the defence, and your Lordship would be looking at material setting out allegations against your Lordship, and indeed my learned friend, and deciding in the balancing exercise how that ought to come down, in favour of prosecution or defence.

Once again the Judge is told that there may be allegations against him. The 'learned friend', of course, was Anthony Scrivener QC, the defence counsel and a former chairman of the Bar Council. So Judge Tucker might find himself deciding on the disclosure of evidence to the defence – evidence that linked him and one of the UK's leading criminal lawyers to a conspiracy. Moreover the attempt to destabilise the trial might be 'only the first episode'. Whoever was trying to upset his Lordship might try something else. And what if the press got to hear of it?

Robert Owen was worried about that too: 'One cannot rule out the possibility, if this attempt is to destabilise the trial, of this coming into the public domain through the press,' he declared.

'Where is this going to end?' exclaimed Judge Tucker, who pointed out that the unknown plotters could well try the same tricks on any judge that replaced him. Would a second judge have to remove himself in turn as well, if similar allegations were made against him? 'I thought there was the assumption that Her Majesty's judges were incorruptible?'

As Judge Tucker pointed out, no one had yet been to interview him. Nor for that matter were Anthony Scrivener or Wyn Jones ever questioned. The police and prosecution never produced a shred of evidence that there was ever an allegation of a link between the three of them and the defendant. Since Anthony Scrivener had already put in an application to vary Mr Nadir's bail, why was he being bribed? And what on earth had Assistant Commissioner Wyn Jones to do with the case? What was he supposed to have done for his share of the alleged £3.5m bribe?

In March 1993 the Assistant Commissioner was still suspended, although cleared of the allegations about his relationship with Asil Nadir in 1990, criticised only for trivial infractions over the use of his official car by a disciplinary tribunal, and planning to seek a judicial review of his case. He knew nothing about the bribe allegations involving Judge Tucker until Michael Mates made his dramatic resignation speech in the House of Commons. At no point in the police investigation had he been interviewed or asked for his comments. Neither was he informed officially about the investigations or the basis of the allegations. He had never met any of his alleged co-conspirators. It was extraordinary, and the only link between them all appears to be the furious letter Anthony Scrivener wrote to Sir Nicholas Lyell on 6 November 1992 about the prosecution's handling of his client's case.

One of the 'bizarre events' about which Scrivener complained was the fact that the Wyn Jones affair in 1990 had surfaced in the press just days before his client Asil Nadir's first arrest. Little did Scrivener know that in a few weeks something more bizarre would happen – and this time he himself would be involved. For weeks Scrivener had been having an angry exchange of letters with not just the Attorney-General but also with the Director of the Serious Fraud Office, George Staple, about the handling of Mr Nadir's case, and he did not pull his punches: 'The papers in this case are voluminous,' he had told Staple, who had just written back to say he was 'entirely satisfied' with the way things were going in the Nadir case. 'After nine months most of us have not been able yet to read them all. I can only congratulate you on being able to be satisfied with the manner of the investigation after what must have been a matter of a few days.' Clearly a lot of extra evidence had been unearthed between mid-December 1992, when Glendenning had said they had nothing, and the beginning of March 1993 when the DPP's counsel, no less, was taking it more seriously than ever.

One fact is clear. The police have neither disclosed what new evidence they discovered during those months that prompted the appearance of Alun Jones QC in court in March 1993 nor justified their claims about the advanced state of the investigation. Even when they later found themselves under pressure from all sides to justify their actions. By the time the court reassembled a few days later Mr Nadir had been arrested and questioned yet again, further proof for Mr Alun Jones QC that the allegation was not a hoax or a prank. 'It is reasonable to suppose that is not the case because of what the police are investigating. They have been looking at this matter now since October,' he said, returning to his favourite theme.

But, if the police had obtained any new evidence or any evidence at all, Mr Nadir was not confronted with it following this latest arrest. He was simply told he was being arrested for conspiracy to pervert the course of justice. He then started asking about Judge Tucker, Anthony Scrivener and Wyn Jones. Had they been arrested, or even questioned? Surely the police should be questioning all the parties to the alleged conspiracy? Didn't it take more than one person to conspire? Was Judge Tucker also under arrest, and if not, why not? The police interview with Asil Nadir was terminated after this barrage of questions.

Judge Tucker had been resolute in his determination to carry on with the case, declaring 'I have not the slightest idea what is going on, and I am completely unaware of any approach, attempt, of anything at all.' As he pointed out, there was no reason for him to step down. By doing so, in fact, he might give some credence to the allegations, details of which he was not permitted even to hear. But Mr Nadir had, by now, reached the end of his patience and decided, reluctantly, that the only way forward was to ask that Judge Tucker should be discharged from the trial. The allegation of bribery and conspiracy now completely dominated the case, threatening to disrupt the main trial at any point when it went ahead. Police investigations were continuing, apparently. What might they turn up next?

The prosecution and DPP lawyers had between them created an impossible situation, with their lengthy discourses on the difficulties of Judge Tucker's situation. They had conjured up a conspiratorial scenario, with their references to frightened witnesses and evidence and on-going investigations, all shrouded in secrecy. Yet they were themselves reluctant to apply for the discharge, even though they brought the attention of the Judge to the possibility time and time again.

The SFO says it was aware that Asil Nadir was going to ask Judge

Tucker to stand down and was anxious that the court was fully informed about the progress of the investigations, which was why the allegations about Scrivener and Wyn Jones were revealed at this point. Asil Nadir resented that he had been put in the invidious position of actually having to ask for the discharge himself. The SFO claim that Alun Jones was there 'to ensure that the court had available to it up to date factual information about the progress of the investigation'.

Two and a half years later, when Sir Thomas Bingham MR outlined the affair during the Ramadan Guney case, the real situation in that courtroom was certainly clear to him.

> On March 8th 1993 leading counsel for Mr Nadir applied to Tucker J to discharge himself from further conduct of the trial. This application was in effect supported by leading counsel instructed by the DPP who informed the judge that the police were pursuing inquiries into the alleged plot.

That is an interesting, unbiased view of a very senior judge. Although Mr Nadir and his advisers felt the prosecution could go on forever raising the spectre of the allegations at any point it suited them, at the same time it was potentially very damaging for the defence to be asking the Judge to stand down. But they had no option. In the event the SFO were forced to show their hand when Judge Tucker resisted the application that he should resign, and a few weeks later the matter went to the Court of Appeal.

Anthony Scrivener had asked the Judge to stand down because Mr Nadir had become so unhappy about the situation following months of courtroom revelations. But Scrivener himself did not actually want the Judge to go. It meant months of delay while a new judge acquainted himself with the case, and keeping Judge Tucker was a form of insurance. If by some chance the case went wrong, what had happened to the Judge would have made an obvious ground for appeal. But to ensure he could use that later if he needed it, Scrivener had to go through the motions of appealing against Judge Tucker's decision to stay.

The three Appeal judges rejected Mr Nadir's application. Anthony Scrivener made a particularly mellifluous speech thanking their Lordships for their decision. Even Mr Nadir was taken aback by it. Having reluctantly decided to ask Tucker to go, he was astonished to find his lawyer so happy in defeat and was prodding Scrivener in the back furiously as he was waffling elegantly to Their Lordships. But, the reason for Scrivener's joy soon became clear, when the Serious Fraud Office, which had supported Judge Tucker's decision not to stand down, suddenly changed its mind. Having given the SFO something for which it had argued, the judges were baffled that the SFO now sought leave to appeal to the House of Lords that Judge Tucker should be removed after all.

The SFO's application was turned down. Who knows what had been going through their minds? As Anthony Scrivener originally felt when he wrote to the Attorney-General the day the bribery allegation first came up in court, 'I simply say that I do not believe the information available would justify interviewing anyone let alone a High Court Judge.' The SFO possibly understood that in their haste to bring allegations into court before they had any evidence, they had handed the defence a powerful weapon. What was to prevent Mr Nadir's counsel from calling Judge Tucker as a witness in the main trial, in front of the jury? As Anthony Scrivener left the court he reminded the prosecuting lawyers of the date: it was 1 April – April Fool's Day.

None the less the police were reluctant to admit they had been misled. Once Mr Nadir had left the country, and Michael Mates had raised the matter in the House of Commons, the press felt itself free to speculate on the affair. At that stage the Nadirs only knew that someone must have been trying to set them up, but they had no idea what had been happening. Bilge was very unhappy that it had been the document she and her mother had signed that had been produced as 'evidence'. The press had clearly been told that there was indeed a plot to bribe the judge.

In July the *Sunday Times* Insight team reported: 'Asil Nadir, the disgraced boss of Polly Peck, was behind a £3.5 million conspiracy to bribe Mr Justice Tucker, the Old Bailey judge handling Nadir's fraud trial.' According to Insight, Scotland Yard had evidence to support the allegation plus detailed statements from two key witnesses who had been put under police protection 'because of fears of reprisals from those loyal to Nadir'. Not a hint of the fact that the police had been gulled.

Wendy Welsher claims that at this stage she was far more frightened of the police, who were keeping a close eye on her, despite the fact that she had been given a letter promising immunity from prosecution. When a reporter from *Today* managed to track her down in August, she told him: 'I can't say a thing. Don't you know what that man [Nadir] will do to me? My life is in grave danger.'

Today gave a colourful account of what had happened. 'Her story has provided a unique insight into the shadowy ways in which the former Polly Peck boss used his vast army of agents, who only had the briefest contact with each other,' it burbled, as it detailed Wendy's role in handing over the picture to Bonhams the summer before. But Wendy, despite her public utterances, was only too happy to go to Northern Cyprus with her little daughter within weeks of making them and seek the help of Mr Nadir.

On 7 November 1993, when her presence in Cyprus had become known, the *Sunday Times* faithfully reported that Scotland Yard were still pursuing their inquiries into allegations to pervert the course of justice, despite the rather awkward fact that their two witnesses appeared to have changed their minds.

It was now a year since Michael Francis had failed to turn up with the alleged incriminating evidence against Mr Nadir. No evidence of a plot to bribe Judge Tucker, or anyone else, has ever surfaced. If indeed the police had evidence, one might suppose that it would eventually have emerged as justification for what had gone on in court the previous March and for many months before. Sir Nicholas Lyell, the Attorney-General, on whose instructions the 'astonishing suggestion' was sent to Judge Tucker on the morning of 5 November, managed to fend off calls for a public inquiry, from, among others, the former Law Lord, Lord Scarman. His Lordship told the *Financial Times*: 'Nothing that has been revealed so far gives any guidance to the truth. The only thing that has emerged is the necessity for a public inquiry.'

Eventually, in February 1994, members of parliament attending the Home Affairs Select Committee hearing on the Serious Fraud Office managed to extract an apology from SFO director George Staple for bringing the uncorroborated allegation against Judge Tucker into court. Staple explained limply, 'I feel there was nothing else that we could have done in the circumstances.'

The fact was that the bribery allegation had been brought into court by the SFO before the police had sufficient evidence to back it up. Furthermore, counsel for the Director of Public Prosecutions went into court to tell the Judge what a difficult position he was in. Anthony Scrivener QC and former Assistant Commissioner Wyn Jones had been included in the plot on the say-so of a known villain, a claim to which the DPP's counsel had given credence as well. Mr Nadir's trial had been wrecked. He despaired of getting justice.

In the end Judge Tucker at least was able to extract his revenge. In a court hearing to lift reporting restrictions on the bribery allegations in December 1993, many months after Mr Nadir had left the country, David Calvert-Smith, counsel for the SFO, made a grovelling apology to the Judge for the 'spurious and groundless allegations' made against him in November 1992, adding, 'Mr Nadir is no longer a suspected party to the allegations.' There was no credible evidence, he admitted.

That was not enough for Judge Tucker. 'I don't like "credible". There is no evidence.' Needless to say few details of this hearing ever surfaced in the press. There are those who still prefer to believe that Asil Nadir tried to destabilise his own trial by concocting the bribery allegations himself.

By Easter 1993 Mr Nadir was certainly convinced that he was never going to get a fair hearing in the UK. Over in Cyprus, Bilge was becoming desperate that their mother, Safiye, by then over 70, would die before she saw her son again. A formidable business-woman in her own right, Safiye Nadir had aged considerably under the strain; Bilge herself was not well, and I could see she was deeply depressed. It was tragic. In the spring of 1993, as the weather warmed up and the mountains behind Kyrenia began to bloom with wild flowers, I heard whispers that 'Mama was preparing the barbecue' for Asil Nadir's return.

8. The Flight to Cyprus

IN THE STILL dark early morning hours of 5 May 1993, Aisling Daly burst into my bedroom to tell me that Asil Nadir had arrived in Northern Cyprus. She had just got a call from the editor of *Kibris*, his daily newspaper, that a plane with Mr Nadir on board had arrived at Ercan airport sometime after midnight. That was all she knew, and it sounded unbelievable. We sat drinking endless cups of coffee as we waited for more details, both in complete shock, not knowing whether to laugh or cry. We had been in limbo out there in Cyprus, cut off from what had been going on in London. I was getting desperate for Mr Nadir to clear his name, but in any event I was already considering coming home. His trial seemed to be taking for ever to come to court.

We had sensed, through Safiye and Bilge, that Mr Nadir had been losing heart in the past few weeks, but his decision to leave Britain, after fighting for so long to prove his innocence, still came as a shock. There were often rumours on the island that he was about to come home, and I had learnt not to take them too seriously. But, now it had happened. When the news broke in the British press about his audacious flight, it was assumed that he had jumped bail rather than stand trial. In fact he was worried whether the authorities would ever let him go to trial and answer the allegations. It seemed to him that the authorities' handling of 'the plot to bribe the judge' accusations demonstrated their willingness to meddle in the proceedings and cause delay. He felt he was under attack from all sides and no wonder.

Since the previous autumn, when the absurd allegations that he was planning to bribe the trial judge first surfaced, Asil Nadir believed that Robson Rhodes, the trustees in charge of his personal bankruptcy, were seeking to have him jailed for contempt of court. It was quite clear that the police were in constant communication with them. Thomas Glendenning had admitted as much in court. The police informers had been trying to get 'evidence' that Mr Nadir was moving assets around, and this allegation had cropped up several times in his pre-trial hearings. The solicitors to the trustees in bankruptcy claimed they had a right to his defence papers, because they might reveal the whereabouts of assets they were claiming on behalf of creditors.

He felt that he was being squeezed in a pincer movement – and that the consequence might be that he would be jailed for contempt of court. The trustees had been enquiring into the situation of Ramadan Guney, the Turkish Cypriot businessman who had stood surety for Mr Nadir. He was involved in a business transaction concerning properties owned by the Nadir family. They had also sent Asil Nadir a lengthy list of questions about his assets.

Among other demands, the trustees wanted details of every gift Asil Nadir had made over the value of £5000 between 1980 and 1991, when he had been made bankrupt. It was a quite impossible request to fulfil in the short time allocated. Mr Nadir had been a very wealthy man; he had twice married and divorced the same woman, who was the mother of his two elder sons; he had serious relation-ships with several girlfriends and two more sons by one of them. He was generous with them all, so how could he possibly remember what gifts he had made over the past decade, or how much each had cost? It was quite ridiculous. His bankruptcy had been extraordinarily complicated. There was even a legal battle going on over whether Robson Rhodes, the trustees in bankruptcy, had been properly appointed. There were arguments with the trustees over art works that he had given to his former wife, Aysegul, and over some of the Turkish and Cypriot family businesses, which belonged to Mr Nadir's family.

Since he had been made bankrupt, Asil Nadir's Eaton Square flat had been raided regularly, as had his office. Not only had his personal possessions been taken but his defence papers as well had been seized – some by the police in SFO raids, others by solicitors acting for the trustees. He lost count of the number of times his home had been invaded and searched and by whom. His mail was also intercepted.

Just before Christmas 1992, Michael Mates had attended a meeting with the Attorney-General, Sir Nicholas Lyell. Mates had raised a whole series of concerns about the progress of Asil Nadir's prosecution. He had already brought up the matter of the bribery allegations, as he had discussed the matter of the privileged documents earlier with the previous Attorney-General, Sir Patrick Mayhew. Mates was still unhappy about all this and the conduct of the SFO. He raised the possibility that there might be some political motivation behind the extraordinary happenings in the Nadir case.

According to the note of this meeting, the Attorney-General said that the allegations concerning the possible plot to bribe Mr Justice Tucker were most unusual, and it was profoundly improbable that the judge was personally involved. However, as the matter was in itself very serious, it was something for the Metropolitan Police to investigate under the direction of the Director of Public Prosecutions. There were various possible explanations, depending upon which way it was viewed, and each had to be explored carefully.

By Christmas 1992, the Attorney-General himself thought that the plot allegations were highly improbable, and presumably he or his staff had done some research into them. In one of his communications to the Attorney-General, Michael Mates had advised him of a forthcoming *Panorama* documentary about the Polly Peck affair. *Panorama* had been looking at the saga for months, and, according to Mates, they had acquired proof that the Greek Cypriots had plotted with the British and Americans to bring down Asil Nadir. No such production of *Panorama* has ever been screened, however.

The strain of his court case and the bizarre plot allegations had taken its toll on Asil Nadir, and his QC, Anthony Scrivener, was concerned about the health of his client. He suffered chronic back pain and was walking with a stick some of the time. He had also given up smoking and had put on a lot of weight. Anthony Scrivener was amazed by what was happening, declaring it the weirdest case in which he had ever been involved and feeling continually that someone, somewhere, was pulling the strings. But, he was more amused than concerned when he noticed his refuse being collected by gentlemen in suits with a rather smart car. He put a Christmas card out for them saying how sorry he was that they had such a beastly job.

Another judge, with whom he had never got on, had even suggested to him that he should 'look to his own situation'. In other words he should consider whether he should go on with the case. There was never any question of him taking the hint, though, and he was a great emotional support for his client.

There were some good days that reminded Asil Nadir that not all the world was against him. During one of his pre-trial hearings at the Old Bailey in December 1992, he went with some friends and family for lunch at a restaurant opposite the Central Criminal Courts. It was near Christmas; the place was full, and there were no tables. As they began to leave, a waitress came after them to say that a gentleman who had a table booked for one o'clock would be honoured if Mr Nadir and his party would take it instead.

Mr Nadir's lovely young Turkish girlfriend, Abide Gonultas, whom he had met some years earlier when she had joined Polly Peck, had been a great support to him. Now she was having difficulty with immigration officials in London, who were refusing to renew her visa. She didn't dare return to Turkey to see her family, because she was by no means certain that she would be allowed back in to the UK. Her father had died without her seeing him, but she had felt she could not leave Mr Nadir. Christmas 1992 had been utterly miserable. They had hardly any money, and Bilge had gone back to Cyprus, so there was no family celebration. It was absolutely grim. Mr Nadir is a proud man, and he did not like to appear defeated, but there were many friends who would have welcomed him that Christmas, and who only discovered afterwards what a miserable time it was for him.

The final raid on Asil Nadir's Eaton Square flat took place in early April 1993. Solicitors acting for Robson Rhodes arrived with a removal firm to confiscate furniture, including the dining-room table and chairs. They were there for several hours, as the removal men stripped Mr Nadir's home, and they searched it from top to bottom. After they had finished, Asil Nadir saw one of the solicitors to the door and extended his hand in farewell. Noticing the Blancpain watch on Mr Nadir's wrist, the solicitor asked for that as well.

Friends who visited Asil Nadir and Abide Gonultas that evening were shocked by the story. By the time they arrived for dinner, a table and chairs had been acquired, and they ate by candlelight, which disguised the large patches on the dining-room walls, where paintings and mirrors had once been. After dinner Mr Nadir and one of his guests sat on a sofa flicking through a book on the flowers of Northern Cyprus. Now was a wonderful time of year on the island, he told her, describing how the wild flowers bloomed everywhere there. Considering his ordeal that day, he was amazingly calm, perhaps too calm. He talked about his boyhood in Cyprus, how he had been brought up to respect the British; how the Turkish Cypriots may have made a fundamental mistake in siding with them against EOKA all those years ago. There was a tinge of real bitterness that his friend had never heard before, despite all that had happened. For the first time she had the feeling that he might just give up and go.

Asil Nadir's pre-trial hearing on 20 April was probably the turning-point. His lawyers had objected to the seizure of their client's defence papers – on which he needed to work for his trial. They had been taken by the trustees in bankruptcy, who had raided his flat and offices earlier in the month, accompanied by the police. Only when I was working on my own, did I realise just how much paperwork was involved. To have your defence papers taken is a real injustice and almost certainly illegal. By the time he left the country, Asil Nadir had left only a few of his defence papers, to which he had been told he could have access by appointment.

Judge Tucker was sympathetic when Asil Nadir's lawyers raised the issue in court and clearly angry at what had happened. It seemed to him extraordinary

> that a trustee in bankruptcy or his minions should see fit to take papers relating to your client's defence in relation to a criminal trial. I do not know because no one has told me and I am not criticising what the powers of the trustee are in this connection. It simply surprises me as a common lawyer brought up in the criminal law, as some of you have been, to hear that a man's personal papers relating to his criminal defence can be seized by anyone and once they have been identified as falling into that category they have not been immediately returned.

But despite his scathing remarks, Judge Tucker felt unable to order their return, saying he had no jurisdiction. Asil Nadir was bitterly disappointed. He felt that the Judge should have full control of the case, but he suspected that he had been unnerved by the extraordinary revelations about the alleged 'conspiracy' to bribe him, particularly when he remarked that he needed to be careful about what he said. At this point Mr Nadir despaired. If the Judge were not in control of the case – and worried about speaking his mind – how could he ever get a fair hearing?

There were other factors that convinced him he should leave the UK. He was worried about his family's businesses in Cyprus, believing that old rivals on the island were trying to gain an advantage from his own incarceration in London. He was also concerned that the London-based Turkish Cypriot businessman who had put up over £1 million surety might withdraw it. Then in mid-April his old friend Turgut Ozal, the President of Turkey, had died. He had felt let down by Ozal in many ways, but his death was still a blow.

He wondered what the Serious Fraud Office would do next. Looking back, the plot to bribe Judge Tucker looks like a farce, but at the time Mr Nadir and his friends were very worried that he might be arrested again and jailed – he had been arrested and interviewed over the allegations for the second time in March. Furthermore, the SFO were under extreme pressure. The previous month had seen the acquittal of the American lawyer Thomas Ward, the final defendant in the tortuous Guinness case, which had taken seven years to go through the courts.

The first four accused had indeed been found guilty, although, ironically, they were prosecuted before the SFO came into existence. But the rest of the Guinness prosecution had been an unmitigated disaster for the SFO, while the second Guinness trial against Lord Spens and merchant banker, Roger Seelig, had been brought to a halt because of Seelig's health – the strain of trying to defend himself proved unbearable. The prosecution against David Mayhew of Cazenove, the top London stockbroking firm, had also been dropped. Ward's acquittal opened the floodgates of criticism for the Serious Fraud Office.

Leading lawyers, including Anthony Scrivener, lined up to point out that cases such as Ward's should never have been the subject of criminal prosecution. The judge in Ward's case called for changes in the conduct of serious fraud trials. One of his suggestions was that documents and evidence held by the defence should be shown to the prosecution to shorten the whole process. This was, of course, what Scrivener and Peter Knight had tried to do in initiating the Binder Hamlyn report on the Polly Peck cash transfers but to no avail.

The SFO faced a wholesale shake-up of its mandate. It had lost Blue Arrow and the second Guinness trial at enormous public expense and earned a reputation for an extraordinary combination of ineptitude and ruthlessness. The trials of George Walker and the Maxwell brothers loomed; all three were eventually acquitted. Trying the two Maxwell boys had become a bit like a production of *Hamlet* without the Prince. The SFO was determined to win the case against Asil Nadir, whatever.

The thought of being imprisoned was a real fear for Mr Nadir, and in the end it haunted him night and day. His few days spent in jail while his family had raised the enormous sum demanded for bail had made a huge impression on him. He was not going there again. Never.

On 24 April, a few days after his last hearing, he went to a cocktail party given by Lesley Ellwood, the mother of his two younger sons, Giles and Eren. Lesley was desperately worried about Asil Nadir by this stage. Although they had not lived together for some years, they kept in close contact, and in the end she was one of the few people he felt he could trust. At the party he met up with an old friend, Hopie Dimond, an attractive woman in her early forties, whom Asil Nadir had known since the early 1970s. Hopie had then been involved with a Turkish man, who introduced her to Asil around the time he had met Lesley.

For years Hopie Dimond had known them as a couple, and Lesley and Hopie became close friends with children roughly the same age. The gathering at Lesley's house that night was a sales party for Cabouchon jewellery, which both she and Hopie sold. Hopie had arranged for her husband, Peter, to come. Peter's great love in life was planes.

'How good a pilot is your husband?' Asil Nadir asked Hopie when he arrived at the party.

'You'll have to ask my husband that,' she replied.

Peter Dimond did not know Asil Nadir very well, although he had met him a few times over the years. Like everyone else he had followed the Polly Peck saga but didn't know much about the detail of what had been going on in court for the last few months. After chatting to the other guests for a few minutes, both men went into the garden. What Peter Dimond quickly realised was that Asil Nadir had finally reached breaking-point. He no longer felt that he could get a fair hearing. It was hard for Peter to follow Asil Nadir's explanation of all the events that had led to his present predicament.

It was a long and complicated story, but Peter understood enough of it to be convinced that there was something very wrong with the way the case against Asil Nadir was being prosecuted. Here was someone who needed help – and he would give it. As they talked, he asked Asil Nadir directly if he wanted to leave the country, to which Asil Nadir replied: Did he have any friends he could trust to help? Peter deliberated for a moment and said he needed a bit of time to work out a plan. He would phone him tomorrow.

Only when he was on his way home to Petersfield did Peter realise what might be involved. He had flown across the Channel to France, but that had been in a single-engined aircraft from a known airfield with other people on hand to assist. This would have to be organised quickly and in complete secrecy, and Asil Nadir wanted to leave as soon as possible – within a week, he had said. As he raced home with Hopie in the car he was thinking of all the problems. What if the weather were bad? How could he leave the country without going through the normal customs procedures? He didn't have a plane of his own – so he needed to find one – but he did not want to implicate anyone else in what he was doing. He had already decided that he needed a twin-engined aircraft, equipped with the necessary navigational aids for safety and bad weather. He had committed himself, and now he had to make sure that the flight was a success. There could be no mistakes.

When Peter Dimond's part in Asil Nadir's escape became known, there was a lot of cynical sneering that he had done it for money, which is absolutely untrue. Peter acted from the best of motives, and despite all the problems and frustrations that he has faced since then, he has never regretted what he did. I got to know Peter Dimond very well when I was in Cyprus. He is intensely honest – something of an idealist really – prepared to stick his neck out when he believes in something, and I admire that. He has paid a heavy price, however, for his decision to help Mr Nadir. His two children have become teenagers while he has been away, and he has only seen them when they have been able to go to Northern Cyprus. He has also lost his home and, should he return, faces possible arrest for helping Mr Nadir.

Peter Dimond knew he needed help – and a plane – but he didn't want to cause trouble for anyone else. He had a good friend who owned an airfield at Compton Abbas in Dorset, whose name was Clive Hughes. A charming, larger-than-life character with whom he often went flying, Hughes was his own HMS Customs agent, as owner of the airfield, which was small and out of the way. The more Peter thought about it, the more Clive Hughes was the ideal person. But how could he manage to involve him without implicating his friend?

Peter phoned Clive the next day and asked if he could fly him, together with a friend, who would remain nameless, to France the following weekend. Peter would return, but the friend would not. Clive was hosting an airshow that Bank Holiday weekend, and he suggested the following Tuesday, the 4th of May. Peter managed to get a coded message to Asil Nadir. The date was fine. They would meet at the Zen restaurant in Covent Garden the next day to finalise arrangements.

By the time they met Peter Dimond had worked out a plan to get Asil Nadir out of Britain as quickly and quietly as possible. Mr Nadir was very nervous about flying, and he hated small aircraft, but this was hardly an issue now. He was just delighted that Peter was organising the first leg of his journey home. The aircraft would be a Piper Seneca twin-engined six-seater machine capable of flying in bad weather. Ideally Le Bourget in Paris would have been first choice, but it was a very busy airport. Peter instead decided that Beauvais, a smaller airfield further north of Paris, used by a lot of private planes, would be better.

Meanwhile, Mr Nadir had arranged the second leg of the journey, from Paris home to Ercan in Northern Cyprus. A friend, David Hamilton, who was a pilot and had an air-leasing business, would fly the day before from Hatfield in Hertfordshire to another airport in northern France and meet up with them in Beauvais. He would take a Cessna jet that could, if necessary, land on grass. The full flight plan did not have to be registered before they left England, and Asil Nadir could not travel in the Cessna from England. It could only fly from a larger airfield where he would have to have gone through some kind of control, and the route would be too easy to track. The way it was planned, there was nothing to connect the two flights. Peter and David did not even know each other. They were not leaving the same day. And they were going initially to different airfields. Until Peter actually arrived in France, mid-morning on 4 May, he did not know anything beyond the fact that a connection had been arranged to take Asil Nadir on to Cyprus. That way Asil Nadir hoped to protect his helpers and confuse the authorities.

Getting Asil Nadir out of Britain was the crucial first stage, and Peter Dimond worked out the timings to the minute. It would take him one and a half hours to reach Compton Abbas from his Petersfield home – he had tested the journey several times. The flight to Beauvais would then take about an hour and a quarter. It was important that there should be nothing to alert the authorities until the second leg of the journey had been completed.

Only later, when he had arrived back in Northern Cyprus, did Mr Nadir discover that the British authorities had been warned several times that he might try to leave the country. They cannot have taken the warnings too seriously. Asil Nadir checked in at Savile Row police station on Bank Holiday Monday, 3 May – under his bail conditions he had to report there once a week. Abide had left the country a few days earlier. Friends who phoned the Eaton Square flat to wish Mr Nadir a happy birthday that weekend were told that she was not very well. Mr Nadir seemed in good spirits, but one friend who phoned got the distinct impression that something had changed – that something was happening. In the middle of their conversation – Mr Nadir was explaining why he and Abide could not take up their invitation to a birthday lunch – he suddenly started thanking her, in a very formal manner, for all her support over the last couple of years. It was like a goodbye.

Anthony Scrivener had phoned Michael Mates a few days earlier to tell him how concerned he was about his client. Following the latest raid, Mates had been along to Asil Nadir's office to help him compile a chronology of events. Mr Nadir had been upset and angry. Mates was horrified to see rows of empty shelves in the office – the last time he had been there the place had been chock-a-block with Asil Nadir's defence documents. Now, after the raids, there was absolutely nothing, and all the papers had gone. When Asil Nadir had told him about the raid – and the final indignity of having his watch taken – Mates felt really sorry for him and suggested to Scrivener that they should take him out to dinner that Friday to celebrate his birthday.

They arranged it secretly with Abide, who told Asil Nadir that they had to go out that night because the boy who helped in the flat was having some time off. Mr Nadir was on the balcony when he saw Michael Mates come round the corner of the street. Scrivener and his wife joined them, and they all went out to eat at the Chinese Inn of Happiness. It was, Michael Mates recalls, a wonderful party. He had wondered what to give Mr Nadir as a birthday present, and he had hit on the idea of a watch, inscribed DON'T LET THE BUGGERS GET YOU DOWN. It was just a fun gift, and everybody laughed.

No one at that party, apart from Asil Nadir and Abide Gonultas, had an inkling of what was to happen. On the morning of the 4th, Mr Nadir drove from Eaton Square to Peter Dimond's house near Petersfield in Hampshire. Once in the car with Peter, he started smoking through sheer nerves – it had been months since he had lit a cigarette. At one point Peter thought he was losing time and speeded up, breaking the speed limit. Suddenly he spotted a police motorcyclist in his rearview mirror – but breathed again when it took a different direction at the roundabout.

Ten minutes from the airfield, Peter phoned to make sure every-thing was ready for take-off. Clive Hughes was at the controls, and he never saw his passenger. With Peter next to him, and Asil Nadir behind him, they were off. At midday they reached Beauvais, where the Cessna and crew had already arrived. Peter had expected to take a car to another airport, but the two planes met there at Beauvais. Mr Nadir made a quick telephone call, and within half an hour they were off again. Clive Hughes flew back to Compton Abbas.

The Cessna made one refuelling stop at Vienna and then flew on to Istanbul. It had all gone very smoothly, with a sense of urgency but no panic. The weather was beautiful as they flew across Europe, arriving in Turkey at dusk.

Now they were more relaxed. At Istanbul Airport half a dozen of Mr Nadir's friends boarded the plane, although he had wanted to disembark, because there were quite a lot of people there to welcome him. He was advised to stay on board, however, for security reasons. The flight plan had only gone as far as Istanbul and they had to get permission to fly on to Ercan. They opened the champagne when finally they took off again with Abide on board for the last stage of their journey to Northern Cyprus.

Bilge had been receiving various messages for a while that her brother would be coming home soon. But, she did not know when he would arrive and was in Kyrenia on the evening of the 4th when she got a message from Istanbul Airport to go to Ercan to meet his plane. When she got there, no one seemed to know anything about it: they were not expecting a private jet to land that evening. In fact, the Cessna had not been in communication with Ercan because of a huge thunderstorm over Northern Cyprus that night, and the plane had not been picked up on the radar. It was almost over Ercan by the time they managed to contact the traffic-control tower and request permission to land. Abide was talking to the control tower in Turkish, and Mr Nadir was worried that they might land in Greek Cyprus by accident, as the two airfields on each side of the border were actually very close to each other.

At the airport Bilge had managed to find air-traffic control. As she was standing in the control tower, wondering what had happened, the voice of the pilot of the private jet came on air. The traffic controller was a bit mystified and inclined to refuse permission to land, until Bilge reassured him that it was all right – she was expecting a friend in a private plane that night. She quickly sought out the officer in charge of the airport and whispered to him, 'You must let the plane land. It's my brother.' As the aircraft touched down, she ran across the tarmac to greet her brother, with her long dark hair, usually elegantly rolled back, flying around her face. Only a small number of people at the airport realised what had happened that night.

The first thing Mr Nadir did on landing was to go and visit his mother, who lived in Nicosia, only a short drive from the airport. They hadn't seen each other for over two years. When Bilge and her husband, Fehim, knocked on the door, Safiye answered it. As the porch light shone on her, Asil Nadir emerged from the shadows behind them. Her only son had come home.

Back in the UK, the lunchtime edition of the *Evening Standard* carried the front-page news that Asil Nadir had jumped bail, but it was several days before the authorities found out how he had managed to escape. There were various reports: he had flown from Scotland; he had gone to France on a hovercraft; he had crossed the Channel by hiding on a lorry on a ferry. Clive Hughes was watching the television news when he heard about the escape. Beside him his wife was doing the ironing – more and more slowly, increasingly distracted as the truth dawned on both of them: 'It was you, Clive, wasn't it?' she said.

'I've got an awful feeling it might have been,' her husband replied.

Peter Dimond had been expecting to return home from Cyprus within a few weeks, once all the fuss had died down. But, somehow, Reuters managed to find out the names of the crew and passengers who had arrived in the Cessna on the night of 4 May, and from then on the game was up. The police found Peter's car at Compton Abbas airfield, and eventually discovered the whole story. In the end Peter admitted that he had organised the first leg of the journey, without telling Clive what was really going on. The police were interviewing Clive, and it looked as though he might be charged, which would have been unfair because he had not known who his passenger was – Asil Nadir had adopted a wig and glasses on Peter's instruction to disguise himself – and, in fact, nothing came of it.

But Peter could not do much to help his own family. His wife, Hopie, was interviewed by Serious Fraud Officers over the next few days. 'They were obviously looking for some big fish who had masterminded Asil's escape,' she told me. 'They seemed convinced that there had to be more behind it.' During her second interview, the police asked her if she knew Asil Nadir – they hadn't asked her that before, which demonstrates a certain level of incompetence. Yes, she'd said, she had known Asil Nadir for a long time. He was a family friend.

The police officer was clearly shocked that their search for a Mr Big was over and had ended with a nice normal family living in a pleasant but ordinary country village who had just wanted to help out an old friend. It was as simple as that, and a far cry from the specu-lations of some newspapers, which informed their readers that the escape had been planned for months by the best criminal minds. If the police had looked more carefully the first time they had visited Hopie, they would have seen a birthday cake, decorated with the name GILES, that Hopie had prepared for Asil Nadir's son who boarded at a nearby school. But, as ever, they were on the hunt for something much more sinister.

Quite extraordinary stories were concocted by the press in the wake of Asil Nadir's departure: he had taken to building sandcastles in his Eaton Square flat; he had surrounded himself with images of panthers; he had become completely paranoid. It was clear that by the time he left the UK he was not a well man, who dwelt on the injustices of his prosecution at length. This was hardly surprising – being accused of bribing a High Court judge was a pretty serious allegation. But, he was not paranoid, just angry and frustrated, and he certainly wasn't playing with sandcastles. His friends were in fact amazed at how rational he was, considering everything that had happened to him.

But there was another target at which the press could aim: the Serious Fraud Office itself. A couple of days after his arrival in Cyprus, the SFO was admitting that it had been tipped off about Asil Nadir's plan to leave Britain over the spring Bank Holiday weekend. They had issued a standard warning to all ports and airports but had not actually placed him under surveillance. When he had turned up as usual on the Bank Holiday Monday at the police station, the SFO had relaxed. But, it emerged that Ramadan Guney had been in Cyprus the week before Asil Nadir's arrival there. Guney's advisers had faxed to the Central Criminal Courts an application for a hearing to have his surety withdrawn – something he had found out while in Cyprus had worried him. Eventually, he withdrew his application, calling it a 'misunderstanding', but he suffered a heart attack just a few days after Asil Nadir's departure.

Many months after he went back to Cyprus, Asil Nadir was brought a copy of the 6 May Central Criminal Courts list by a well-wisher. According to this list, Mr Justice MacPherson was due to take a hearing in Court 8, where the defendant was Asil Nadir himself. It was set for 10 o'clock and expected to last half an hour. Was this the bail withdrawal? Or was it the trustees in bankruptcy whose patience had run out? Asil Nadir has always said that he went when he did because he feared an attempt to jail him.

The SFO defended its seemingly dilatory behaviour in the face of their tip-offs by pointing out that it had always opposed bail for Asil Nadir from the start. This remark stirred Sir David Hopkin, the former Chief Magistrate who had set Asil Nadir's stratospheric bail, out of his retirement. As he told one newspaper who asked him about Mr Nadir: 'He has been here for two years since I granted bail, which doesn't exactly show he had an immediate intention to bugger off, does it?'

Marcel Berlins, who writes an astute legal column in the *Guardian,* summed up how he believed the SFO saw things:

> Nadir's trial was going to be an absolute nightmare for the prosecution. It would have lasted ages, some of the evidence against him was not altogether watertight, and there was a real risk of an acquittal, or, just as bad, a messy conviction resulting in a successful appeal. The Serious Fraud Office cannot afford another failure in a high profile trial. It is therefore in the interests of British justice that Nadir does not stand trial. This way his name gets blackened anyway, he can't return, taxpayers' money is saved, and the embarrassment of letting him get away is still far less than the embarrassment of a bungled trial.

As the implications of Mr Nadir's arrival back in Cyprus sank in, this is exactly how I regarded the situation. From that moment it was inevitable that I would return and call the SFO's bluff. There was no other way that the SFO would ever be confronted with what they had done. My return was only a matter of time.

The next few days were not without their comic side. No sooner had Asil Nadir arrived to a hero's welcome than it was discovered that Barbara Mills, Director of Public Prosecutions, George Staple, her successor as director of the SFO, and Lord Mackay, the Lord Chancellor, were enjoying the sunshine of Greek Cyprus at a Commonwealth lawyers conference in Nicosia a few miles away.

It was really very funny – and even more amusing when Lord Mackay actually crossed the Green Line that divides the two communities to ask President Denktas to return the fugitive. Here was the Lord Chancellor, popping over the border for an informal chat to try and see if he could get Mr Nadir back. Denktas took the view that since the British government refused to recognise the TRNC he had no obligation to hand over Asil Nadir. Indeed it would have been illegal for him to do so. What was extraordinary was that the Lord Chancellor was prepared to go to Northern Cyprus at all, following the series of excuses the SFO had made about not being able to get there and look at evidence because the TRNC was unrecognised. They had refused to go through the official procedures, arguing that the TRNC had no diplomatic relations with Britain. But the Lord Chancellor clearly had no such qualms. He earned a rebuke for his pains. Not just from Denktas but also from British MPs, who were appalled at his behaviour. It was all farcical and stank of hypocrisy, particularly when, a few weeks later, at the end of July, Lorna Harris and Robert Wardle of the SFO went to the TRNC themselves, something they had omitted to do before then.

Asil Nadir himself had already sent a handwritten fax to Douglas Hurd, the Foreign Secretary, saying that he would come back, provided he was guaranteed a fair trial and the freedom of his passport; his reply confirmed that it was a matter for the British courts, not the Government. Meanwhile Tristan Garel Jones, a Foreign Office minister, had been exploring the possibility of Turkey bringing some pressure to bear on the TRNC, suggesting that they wouldn't want to be seen as a 'refuge for fugitives'.

By Wednesday 5 May the press corps had arrived in Northern Cyprus, from Turkey as well as the UK. Asil Nadir's house in Lapta was ringed by reporters and television camera crews. For several days the villagers there sat in their cafés, bemused by car loads of journalists who took up residence outside Asil Nadir's house. The locals watched the endless comings and goings, their heads turning from side to side, like spectators at a Wimbledon tennis final.

It certainly put Northern Cyprus on the tourist map. Some people had never heard of it before, and certainly never seen such an unwitting promotion of its unspoilt delights. The Greek Cypriots enjoyed a thriving tourist industry in the South and showed no compunction in threatening to boycott UK travel agents who tried to market the Northern coast to holidaymakers. Bilge Nevzat encountered a lot of difficulties when she set up her own travel business in the UK, and travel editors on the national newspapers used to receive endless complaints from the Greek Cypriots if they published articles on Northern Cyprus. But now we were getting lots of coverage, and hotel bookings did remarkably well that summer.

Asil Nadir went out briefly to meet reporters, at what must have been the most filmed front door on the planet. A journalist who got in round the back for an interview informed Mr Nadir that his colleagues at the front of the house would have to stay there all day in the boiling sun on the orders of their editors. If he were to promise them a fixed time for a press conference, they could all go off and enjoy themselves for a while and return in much better humour.

I was told to keep out of the way and stay indoors, but I could see all the action from the window of my flat, just opposite the Jasmine Court, where the press were in residence. At the end of the week Mr Nadir gave a press conference there. It was a bit of a disaster but not without its amusing moments. Roasting a whole sheep in someone's honour is an old Turkish custom, and many of the poor animals were roasted in Northern Cyprus during these first few days. One had a lucky escape. The staff of the Jasmine Court were seen by some reporters to be preparing it for slaughter, when the man from the *Sun* stepped in and offered to buy it. The staff suddenly realised what would happen if they went ahead and slaughtered the sheep. Jumping bail was one thing – many people found the story amusing and thought the SFO had got what it deserved – but killing an animal in full view of *Sun* readers would probably damn Asil Nadir in their eyes for ever.

At the press conference Mr Nadir gave a lengthy speech, revealing the allegations that he was attempting to bribe Judge Tucker and strongly criticising the SFO. He did not get a very sympathetic reception. The whole prosecution had been very complicated, and none of the pre-trial hearings had been reported because of press restrictions. He had lived with the whole business for so long that he didn't realise how difficult it would be for his listeners to take in what he was telling them.

When reporters started asking him, 'Are you a crook, Mr Nadir?' and calling him chicken, he decided to leave – and I can't say I blamed him. Time after time, Asil Nadir has been presented as some kind of media manipulator. The truth is that his public relations have always been a disaster area – he has rarely taken competent advice even when he has received it – and the idea that he has a huge PR machine is not true. At that first press conference, when he tried to give his side of the story, he was genuinely hurt and amazed that none of the press seemed to want to listen. Why had they bothered to come at all? He hadn't invited them in any case.

Several days later, when things had calmed down a little, I had a meeting with Mr Nadir at Loch Manor, his other home on the island. It is a beautiful place, and quite different in character from the house in Lapta. The garden there is wonderful. Planted originally by an English owner, Lady Loch, it extends over several acres of wooded walkways and rose gardens. I hadn't seen him for two years, because his bail restrictions meant that officially we were not supposed to speak, even by phone.

It was an emotional meeting, at which he told me, 'I used to get up every morning at 6 am and dress as if I was going to the office, just in case I received any unexpected visitors. I won't have to do that any more . . . I had so many early calls from the police that I could almost recognise which policeman it was by the way he rang the doorbell.'

At that point I had hopes that his flight might bring the Polly Peck story under some kind of proper scrutiny. I gave some interviews to the UK press. They were actually very nice to me, which I found surprising, given the kind of articles they had been writing about Mr Nadir. *The Times* published a very long feature, which highlighted the role of the Inland Revenue in bringing down Polly Peck International. I was allowed to put my side of the story, and it was accurately reported. Likewise the *Daily Telegraph*, which had been openly hostile to Asil Nadir, granted me a very fair hearing. The *Daily Telegraph* article opened with the following: 'Mrs Elizabeth Forsyth makes an unlikely looking fugitive. She is a highly intelligent, privately educated, twice married mother of two, with a refined Home Counties accent, and immaculately styled blonde hair.' They didn't call *me* a crook – even though the SFO was saying it wanted me for questioning. There was, and remains, a large element of xenophobia in the media's treatment of Mr Nadir, and they vilified him in a way that was shameful.

9. The Honourable Member

MICHAEL MATES HAD been shocked when Asil Nadir left the country. He was shaving when he first heard the news and immediately phoned Anthony Scrivener. Scrivener himself had already been contacted by a journalist, who informed him that his client had gone. The following week Mates had another meeting with the Attorney-General, Sir Nicholas Lyell, to whom he said that he found the recent events 'appalling but not surprising'. He raised several issues, including the removal of Asil Nadir's defence papers and the role of the Inland Revenue in the Polly Peck affair. He also told the Attorney-General he had been advised that the secret services had become involved in the case, and he named Lord Erskine of Rerrick as the emissary. Mates had known Erskine well, because of their common army background, long before the eccentric Earl had gone to live in Northern Cyprus. He was aware that Erskine had been used on occasion by the secret services.

I had actually met Lord Erskine myself when I was in Northern Cyprus. He had wanted an introduction to Asil Nadir, who was then in London. The two men did eventually meet, although I have no idea what they discussed. At one point Lord Erskine was supposed to be helping Michael Jordan, the senior administrator to PPI; on another occasion he was said to have asked Mr Nadir if he would sue

168

when the case against him failed. I got the impression that Erskine was in dire financial straits. He had endured a prolonged battle over trusts allegedly left by his father in the control of the Royal Bank of Scotland, to whom Erskine left his testicles in his will: 'To the Royal Bank of Scotland I leave my balls as they appear to have none of their own.' My view is that Lord Erskine's main interests in life were financial survival and meeting interesting people. Michael Mates had correctly picked up on many of the oppressive features of Mr Nadir's prosecution, but I feel that Erskine was a bit of a red herring.

When details of Asil Nadir's flight emerged, it was something of a shock for Michael Mates to read that Peter Dimond was involved. He was barely acquainted with Peter, who lived in his constituency, but he knew Hopie Dimond's family. Her parents had even invited him to Hopie's and Peter's wedding years before. It was all an extraordinary coincidence. But nothing prepared him for what happened in the last weekend of May 1993, when the *Mail On Sunday* splashed with a sensational and detailed story of how the Security Minister for Northern Ireland had given Asil Nadir an inscribed watch, just days before his flight.

The newspaper had phoned 10 Downing Street, and Michael Heseltine, who was known to be a friend of Michael Mates, was also alerted. Heseltine was aware that Michael Mates had written to the Attorney-General about Asil Nadir's prosecution; now he was on the phone to Mates, completely baffled by the newspaper's story. 'You didn't give him anything, did you?' he asked. When Mates told him about the watch, both men groaned.

Michael Mates believes, though quite erroneously, that the story of the watch was leaked to the press by Peter Dimond. I know that is not correct and that Asil Nadir never mentioned this to Peter. At the time the tale emerged, Peter in fact, knew nothing at all about it. I, however, do know how the story came out, and how the journalist concerned came to hear about it.

But, while the watch episode might have been left unreported, it was pretty inevitable that Michael Mates's intervention with the Attorney-General would become public knowledge. Copies of his letters were among the defence papers taken from Asil Nadir's home and office, and several ministers knew his position. In any case Mr Mates himself felt that he had nothing to hide. He had first approached the Attorney-General, then Sir Patrick Mayhew, in

1991, when he was a back-bencher. When he became a minister in April 1992, he realised his position was now substantially different. When the bizarre affair of the conspiracy involving Judge Tucker surfaced, he took advice privately from a very senior minister, who indicated that it was perfectly proper for Mates to continue his inquiries with the new Attorney-General. So as far as Michael Mates was concerned, he had done absolutely nothing wrong, except for the minor indiscretion – and human gesture – of giving Asil Nadir a watch for his birthday.

Michael Mates still seems stunned when he recalls the drama that engulfed him. The story of the watch completely swept aside the more serious aspects of his involvement – the fact that he had challenged the behaviour of the Serious Fraud Office and its treatment of Mr Nadir. He knew about the bizarre allegations of the plot to bribe the judge, but at that point it would have constituted contempt of court to talk publicly about this.

Meanwhile, it emerged that Michael Mates was not the only senior Conservative Party figure to have been approached by Asil Nadir. The press produced names like rabbits out of a hat. Peter Brooke, the then Heritage Minister, had been Mr Nadir's MP and had passed on his complaints to the Attorney-General. But, there was far more fuss over the news that Michael Heseltine, the President of the Board of Trade, had also raised the matter with the Attorney-General, following a conversation with Christopher Morgan, the public-relations man I had persuaded to help Mr Nadir. Morgan knew Heseltine from the time of the Westland crisis, when he had been a press adviser to one of the banks.

Heseltine was a known friend of Michael Mates, and the Whitehall gossip factory was working overtime. Gerald Malone, another top Conservative, was momentarily confused when his name was thrown into the ring. Had he seen Mr Nadir or not? He finally decided that he had, although he hadn't actually made any representations on his behalf. Abide Gonultas still remembers Mr Malone's fondness for champagne and caviar, which she recalls him enjoying at the Eaton Square flat.

Overhanging all the speculation were two key issues. Firstly, the behaviour of ministers had become a hot political issue. David Mellor and Norman Lamont had both recently resigned, and John Major, as Prime Minister, had been accused of lacking firmness in his dealings with them. 'They were looking for a third victim,' Mates remarks philosophically.

Secondly, there was a lot of debate about political-party funding, and the House of Commons Home Affairs Select Committee was already investigating the issue. The revelations about Michael Mates gave a nervous edge to its inquiries with the inference that Mr Nadir had managed to get top Conservatives to speak up on his behalf because he had given a lot of money to their party. It was one more issue that deflected attention from the serious nature of Michael Mates's concerns over the SFO's mishandling of the case. By now this had been completely drowned by the press feeding-frenzy and political backbiting. The media was on a roll and hunting for blood.

The Conservative Party had been criticised for accepting donations from overseas businessmen who benefited from tax concessions. Asil Nadir was known to have given the party over £400,000, and now the Opposition made the most of it. Apparently Mr Nadir had wanted a knighthood – although, if so, it was very strange that he had been planning to move to Switzerland before the collapse of PPI. Mr Nadir had also made 'secret' donations from 'stolen' funds – well, the donations had been paid, in fact, by the Cyprus subsidiary, Unipac. But there was no reason why they had to be shown in the PPI accounts, and the Unipac board had sanctioned the payment. It was all quite legal and never clear to me why Asil Nadir became a political football, kicked from side to side as both parties aired their differences over funding in public.

Like many other successful entrepreneurs and tycoons, Asil Nadir had been assiduously courted by the Conservative Party. He had been invited to lunches arranged by the Conservative Industrial Fund to meet other businessmen, and there was usually at least one minister there. After the lunch, someone used to go round to PPI headquarters to collect a cheque, which seemed to be standard Tory fund-raising procedure. Now his donations had become a major political issue, Conservative Party chairman, Sir Norman Fowler, told the Select Committee that if the donations proved to be stolen money they would be returned.

The row over political donations proved an enormous strain on the Conservative Party, not helped when its former chief fund-raiser, Alistair McAlpine, claimed that Asil Nadir had visited him early on in his prosecution to try and persuade the party into helping him.

Aysegul Nadir had known McAlpine and had bought a good number of antiques from him. Asil Nadir had met him socially too. Now the former Conservative Party Treasurer didn't want to help him.

Asil Nadir's political contributions were not the only talking-point. The hills were alive with allegations of Tory 'sleaze'. There were firmly denied stories about Saudi Government money swilling into the Conservative Party coffers. Dramatically, just hours before he was due to appear before the Select Committee to round off the Government's argument over party-political funding, Michael Heseltine had a heart attack in Venice. Mr Nadir got blamed for that, too. DID NADIR CAUSE HEART ATTACK? was the banner headline in the *Sun*. Lord McAlpine, who was in Venice at the time, put them right. 'Why go to a beautiful place like Venice and discuss a sleazy fellow like Mr Nadir?' he quipped when reporters speculated on what Mr Heseltine and Lord McAlpine might have been discussing.

Two days after the watch revelations became known, John Major had said in Parliament that Michael Mates could only be criticised for a 'misjudgement'. The giving of the watch was not a 'hanging offence'. On 7 June 1993, a week after the watch revelations, Mates wrote a two-page note from the Northern Ireland Office to the Prime Minister. It detailed his relationship with Asil Nadir from September 1991, when he had been first approached by Mark Rogerson, Christopher Morgan's public-relations partner, to 10 May 1993, when he had had a final meeting with the Attorney-General over some of the issues raised by Asil Nadir's case.

As far as Michael Mates was concerned, this was the end of the matter. His job as Minister for Northern Ireland seemed secure, and he had acted properly. There was no question of that. If that note and the relevant correspondence had been published there and then, it would have cleared the air and opened the way for a public examination of the issues involved. As it was, the press was left to speculate on the reasons for his concern. Mates himself, it seems, would have much preferred to speak out, if only to demonstrate the honesty of his intentions. He said that throughout his dealings with Mr Nadir, he had no idea that Asil had made contributions to the Conservative Party.

Then a newspaper published an allegation that Mates had

borrowed a car for his estranged wife from Mark Rogerson. Up to this moment there was no question that Michael Mates had acted out of genuine concern for the way Asil Nadir's prosecution had been handled. At worst it was accepted that he had been unwise in making the kindly gesture of the watch. Now, in the atmosphere of sleaze allegations that surrounded the question of political funding, the story of the car was blown up out of all proportion.

It was, says Mates, a thoroughly stupid story. He had found a Volvo for his estranged wife, but she had wanted one with a bigger engine, for which she would have had to wait a week or two. It was coming up to half-term, and she needed something to transport her daughter, Arabella, to Pony Club. His constituent Mark Rogerson, who was also a friend, was looking for a car as well, so Mates told him about the one he had originally found but not bought. Rogerson was grateful. He bought the car himself and lent it to Michael Mates' estranged wife, just for the half-term at the end of May.

When this tale hit the headlines, Michael Mates knew he was in trouble again, and this time he had embarrassed his Government. It was the timing that was crucial, just as the fuss over political donations was on the boil. He claims that ever since the watch revelations, journalists had been snooping around his Hampshire constituency and elsewhere for evidence of financial links between himself and Asil Nadir. It was thoroughly unpleasant, but the car episode was all they could find.

By the last week of June it was being widely reported that Michael Mates would be forced to resign. There were allegations that the powerful back-bench MPs on the 1992 Committee executive were baying for his blood, but in truth it was the media that wanted to show its strength and get the scalp of another minister. Nevertheless Mates believes that he would have survived even this.

Then the *Daily Mail* published a recent letter he had written to the Attorney-General, Sir Nicholas Lyell, about Mr Nadir's case. Mates had queried the fact that Metropolitan police officers appeared to have gone to Northern Cyprus to investigate Asil Nadir, and yet the Serious Fraud Office had never officially been there. The correspondence made it clear that Mates had been pursuing the matter since 1991 with two successive Attorney-Generals. He asked why Sir Nicholas Lyell had suggested that the SFO had made repeated attempts to visit Northern Cyprus when he had been told by Lyell's predecessor, Sir Patrick Mayhew, that no formal approaches had been made, because the TRNC was unrecognised.

The letter itself would not make much sense to anyone who had not followed the twists and turns of this particular argument. Nor indeed would it have been obvious that when Mates referred to 'the bizarre events of the past weeks' he meant the extraordinary court-room scenes in early March 1993 that had taken place just a few days before he wrote the letter. That was when Anthony Scrivener and Wyn Jones had been included along with Judge Tucker in the 'bribe' allegations, all of which was still shrouded in secrecy.

But, fascinatingly, the *Daily Mail* report that accompanied the letter dwelt at length on the penultimate paragraph – a short reference querying the role of the Inland Revenue. That would have made no sense at all to anyone who had not appreciated its involvement in the investigation of Asil Nadir. Mates had promised the Attorney-General further evidence of the Revenue's involvement but gave no details. But the *Daily Mail* chose to highlight this aspect of the letter, claiming that Revenue investigators were hot on the trail of up to £100 million of tax due from Mr Nadir's offshore companies, 'mainly in Switzerland', as the article predictably stated.

In fact the Inland Revenue had already put in a claim for its modest £5 million tax demand over two years before. But, according to the *Daily Mail*, Asil Nadir had made his political contributions so that he could keep his favoured tax status, and it was this, it said, that the Inland Revenue had been trying to get him to relinquish. I knew this was absolutely untrue and unsubstantiated.

The focus of the accompanying article did not ring any bells with Michael Mates at the time. He knew there were only a few people who had copies of his correspondence with the Attorney-General. He phoned Anthony Scrivener and checked with him. Then he got in touch with Christopher Morgan on his car phone and told him he wanted to see him. Christopher was on his way to the Reform Club for dinner, and Mates joined him there. Their presence together was reported in the newspaper – and it sealed his fate. It connected him once again with Asil Nadir, and the Government could not take any more embarrassment. Michael Mates resigned.

But from where had the letter come? It had been shown to Mates by the *Daily Mail*'s highly respected political editor, Gordon Greig, who had it faxed to him by one of the newspaper's reporters.

According to Mates, it must have been leaked by someone at the Serious Fraud Office after the SFO had been required to answer the Attorney-General's questions about the conduct of its inquiry. Copies of the correspondence may also have been taken in raids on Mr Nadir's home and office.

Particularly galling for Michael Mates was the fact that two weeks earlier he had asked the Attorney-General to publish all the correspondence. He had wanted to prove that he had nothing to hide. Lyell had refused to reveal what he called 'his correspondence', even though Mates had pointed out 'half of it is mine'. Mates had been forced to sit tight. Lyell seemed to have no intention of exposing any of the awkward facts of Mr Nadir's prosecution. He had been answering Michael Mates' queries for months, suggesting that nothing was wrong.

Mates had already given the facts to John Major. Cabinet Secretary Sir Robin Butler had also looked at the correspondence. Yet, when he was forced to resign, it was made abundantly clear to him by one of the Tory Whips that the leaked letter had been 'the last straw'. Looking back, it all smacks of humbug. Particularly when John Major revealed in the indiscreet tape recording of a supposedly off-air chat with TV interviewer Michael Brunson that Sir Robin Butler believed that getting rid of Mates was an act of 'gross injustice'.

Michael Mates had been a back-bencher, albeit an important one, for years. He had also worked as Michael Heseltine's campaign manager. The job of Northern Ireland Minister was one he relished. He was approaching 60 when he was appointed, which is late in the day, and knew he would probably not get another chance. When he rose to his feet to make his sensational resignation speech to the House of Commons on 29 June – nearly two months after Asil Nadir had left the country – he had clearly decided, however, that he had absolutely nothing to lose by speaking his mind.

Over in Cyprus everyone had become quite excited at the prospect of what he might say. We were deeply disappointed by the way the facts of Mr Nadir's case appeared to have been swept under the carpet during all the huffing and puffing over political donations and Tory sleaze. The day before Mates was due to make his resignation speech, Asil Nadir warned me that he might run into trouble with the Whips or the Speaker if he decided to tell the whole story. Even so the event, when it happened, was even more spectacular than I had imagined.

It all started off calmly enough, with an outline of how he had initially become involved. He stressed that he was not making judgements about guilt or innocence – that was for the courts to decide – but that concern over certain aspects of Asil Nadir's case had led him to write to the Attorney-General. He then launched into a full-scale attack on the Serious Fraud Office, condemning their habitual leaking of sensitive information to the press and accusing them of 'trial by media'. He questioned the refusal of the SFO to go to Northern Cyprus, and their inconsistency over the matter of whether they could or could not go. He raised the issue of how the investigation against Mr Nadir began, pointing out that the tax officer concerned had admitted that he had passed information on to the Stock Exchange.

By this time Speaker Betty Boothroyd was getting worried. She reminded Michael Mates that his comments might prejudice Mr Nadir's trial. Mates replied that a very senior lawyer had looked at his speech with that in mind, while Ms Boothroyd countered that the House had its own rules about what was and was not *sub judice*. By now Michael Mates was plunging into deep waters as he brought up the matter of the privileged documents that had been seized in the raid on PPI.

Betty Boothroyd interrupted him again. She was, she said, reluctant to let him continue. Mates pointed out that he was not talking about the trial but about the handling of the case by the authorities. This was an important distinction, and the Honourable Member was not to be deflected. Mates' point was that the Attorney-General had written to him about the matter, and he was entitled to communicate the contents to the House.

So Mates went on to explain how the sealed bags containing privileged documents had been opened and some of the contents had ended up with the administrators. He called for an inquiry into this and the circumstances in which Mr Nadir's defence papers had been removed. He raised a huge laugh when he talked about the removal of 'various personal effects – one of which I was later to replace in inscribed form'.

Then he turned to what he described as the most serious aspect
of the affair, telling the House that 'quite improper pressure has
apparently been exercised by the SFO on the trial judge Mr Justice
Tucker.' There were gasps of astonishment. The Speaker was
furious. According to several press reports, the Commons' clerks,
who were being signalled at by Sir Nicholas Lyell, the only person
who actually knew what Mates might be going to say, were encouraging her in turn to stop Michael Mates. She ordered Mates to sit
down, and at this stage it looked as though he might do so – until he
quickly reasserted himself and appealed to his fellow MPs. If one
couldn't speak in this way in the House, not about innocence or guilt
but about what has gone wrong with the system, then what was the
point of being there?

That was the turning-point, and although Betty Boothroyd made
one last attempt to tell him that the information should be given at
the trial, not in the House, she had lost the argument. The other MPs
clearly agreed with Mr Mates that the House was indeed a proper
forum – and by now they were all fascinated to know more.

He related the story of how the trial judge had been told it might
be necessary to interview him, following the allegation that there was
a conspiracy to bribe him. He pointed out that later a senior police
officer had said that there had never been any evidence to justify
interviewing the judge. 'The only conclusion,' said Mates, 'is that the
SFO misled the judge about the intentions of the police.'

He went on – uninterrupted now – to disclose how the conspiracy
allegations had widened to include Wyn Jones and Anthony
Scrivener QC, pointing out that neither they nor the Judge had ever
been interviewed by the police, although Mr Nadir had been arrested
and questioned. He said that he had raised the matter with the
Attorney-General, who assured him that he had got it wrong, that the
alleged conspiracy was against the Judge rather than involving him.
This was a crucial point. A reading of the transcripts makes it clear
that Judge Tucker was given the impression that it was believed he
might be involved in the plot.

Mates finished his speech by calling for an independent inquiry
into the matters he had raised, saying that he hoped he would have
the courage to do the same thing again. He reminded all the MPs:
'Surely we are here, either as front or back-benchers, to take up
questions of apparent injustice, and if we should ever flinch from

such a duty, then the reasons for our existence as MPs would be much diminished.' It was the most extraordinary occurrence I had ever known of in the House of Commons. In Cyprus we all felt relieved and hopeful that the behaviour of the SFO would now be investigated.

The immediate reaction from the Government was to state that all Michael Mates' allegations had already been looked at carefully. George Staple took a similar line and defended the SFO from any accusations of misbehaviour. But the Attorney-General had to return to the House the next day to state that there was no evidence that Judge Tucker had been involved in any conspiracy. This was just the information that Mates had been trying to extract for months.

Now the pressure was on to release the letters and other documents that had passed between Michael Mates and the Attorney-General's office during the preceding months. A couple of days later Sir Nicholas Lyell rejected Michael Mates' call for an independent inquiry, but even as he did so, other proof that something was seriously wrong at the SFO had come to light.

The day after Michael Mates' speech, Sir Nicholas Lyell found himself challenged in the House of Commons over an extraordinary hoax letter that had been forged by an SFO officer in the name of the well-liked MP, Sir David Steel, who now emerged to back Michael Mates' call for an inquiry into the SFO. The story Sir David had to tell was predictably bizarre.

In early 1992 he had taken up certain aspects of the SFO's handling of the case of an Asian businessman, Nazmu Virani, with the Attorney-General. Like Mates, he had written several times to the AG. When Virani was arrested, the SFO objected to bail – an anonymous informant had told them Virani was attempting to move millions of company money out of the country. Before his appeal hearing on the bail, the SFO lawyer had shown Virani's solicitor a letter, purporting to come from Sir David Steel, saying he intended to attend the bail hearing himself. It was a forgery, calculated, presumably, to embarrass Steel, who had been inquiring into the treatment of Virani. When Sir David Steel took the matter up with the Attorney-General, the AG had described the forgery as a 'thoroughly misguided April Fool's joke'.

Not surprisingly Sir David Steel felt the Attorney-General's reaction was somewhat inadequate – the officer was, after all, still working for the SFO. This underlined the demand from Michael Mates that the SFO needed an independent investigation, a point also made by Sir John Nott, the former Department of Trade Minister, in a *Times* article the following week. He concluded:

The behaviour of the SFO and the present law and procedure relating to the pursuit of fraud should now be investigated by an independent judge, not by the Director of Public Prosecutions or the Attorney-General's office. Why? Barbara Mills, the head of the SFO when many of the alleged abuses were perpetrated, is now the DPP, and the Attorney-General's office includes former officers of the SFO. How can natural justice be served if these people investigate themselves?

But it was months before Michael Mates was finally vindicated in his outspoken attack on the SFO. Many commentators took their cue from the fact that the Attorney-General had rebuffed most of the claims. The inference was that Mates had been deceived by Asil Nadir. Immediately after Mates' statement it had been made clear that there was no question of Judge Tucker's implication in the bribery allegation. Extraordinarily it emerged that the Lord Chancellor had known nothing about the affair. As Michael Mates pointed out to me, this meant that Judge Tucker had been dispensing justice for nine months after he was told that he might be interviewed by the police, and no one thought it mattered.

But the embarrassed and belated assurances about the Judge did nothing to remove the taint of corruption from Asil Nadir and his family. Several newspaper articles insinuated that Mr Nadir had indeed been involved in some dastardly plot. It was all very distressing, particularly for his sister Bilge. Once over the excitement and joy of her brother's return she sank into a deep depression. The arrival of Michael Francis and Wendy Welsher only made matters worse. Although she now possessed answers to the questions that had caused her so much anguish, she found it hard to come to terms with the fact that anyone could have done something like this to either her or her brother.

By the end of September Asil Nadir's Nicosia office was busy trying to verify Wendy Welsher's and Michael Francis's stories. Everyone had grown so suspicious. Was this just another attempt to set them up in some way? Asil Nadir's lawyer, Dr Ali Reza Gorgon, was attempting to find hard evidence of this incredible tale. He phoned airlines and ferry companies to check travel dates and passenger lists. He recorded conversations between Michael Francis and his police contacts. There was no doubt that Michael Francis was a well-known informant. The conversations with these policemen at least confirmed that.

Finally, in November, the *Independent* published a front page about the attempt to entrap the Nadirs in the bribery allegation. Now the Crown Prosecution Service admitted that the police had uncovered no evidence of any conspiracy to bribe Judge Tucker. It was a mealy-mouthed response. For months the police had claimed that they were investigating a conspiracy. It had hung over Asil Nadir's pre-trial hearings. He had left the UK because of it. Now they admitted there had never been any evidence.

Both Michael Mates and Anthony Scrivener QC renewed their calls for an inquiry and received a bland response from Sir Nicholas Lyell, the Attorney-General. It was deeply depressing for those of us in Northern Cyprus. Peter Dimond and I had hoped that this extraordinary episode might force some kind of review of Asil Nadir's prosecution. I myself began to think very seriously about returning to the UK. At the end of September the SFO had abandoned its prosecution of John Turner, the chief PPI accountant who had been accused of false accounting, saying it could not try him without Asil Nadir. This was all very convenient for the SFO, but my position was different. It went to the root of the issue – the raid on SAM, my company. If Asil Nadir were not able to bring his case into focus, I would go home and challenge the SFO myself.

Meanwhile the Attorney-General was forced to eat his own words in the House of Commons over the matter of the mishandling of Asil Nadir's privileged papers. Peter Knight of Vizards had been pursuing this for months with a terrier-like zeal – long after he had stopped acting for Asil Nadir. In dispute were the documents taken not only in the raid on PPI but also when Mr Nadir was arrested. They were in sealed bags, and the SFO had agreed not to open them. Peter Knight knew they had been opened and that the SFO was therefore in breach of the rules and its undertakings to him. This was one of the first issues Michael Mates had taken up with the Attorney-General, then Sir Patrick Mayhew, in the autumn of 1991, and

Mayhew had said that the opening of two of the bags was a misunderstanding. Sir Nicholas Lyell had repeated this assurance to the House of Commons after Michael Mates' resignation speech.

But Peter Knight believed that several more bags had been opened, and that two Attorney-Generals had been given the wrong information. In the wake of Michael Mates' speech, Knight had watched in amazement as George Staple appeared on BBC's *Newsnight*, brandishing one of the privileged documents. It was Knight's own note of his bizarre encounter with the Inland Revenue officials the day after the PPI share-price collapse some three years earlier. Knight then wrote to Staple pointing out that other bags had been opened, despite what the Attorney-General had told the House of Commons. Scathingly, Knight suggested to Staple that the inordinate problems he had encountered over the last eighteen months in trying to sort out the issue of the privileged papers was due to the fact that 'no workable system existed in your office and that either the problem has now been remedied or will be remedied.'

In December we discovered that the truth was worse than even Peter Knight had suspected. It was now admitted that privileged documents had been circulated to the prosecution team and to the administrators. More than two sealed bags had indeed been opened.

Michael Mates consequently put down a Commons' question for the Attorney-General. Did he have anything to add to the statement he had made to the House at the end of June? Then he had fobbed off Mates' claims that there had been a far more serious mishandling of privileged papers than anyone had admitted. Now Sir Nicholas Lyell had to state that he had mistakenly misled the House.

> I regret that the fact that copies of privileged documents had been circulated was not acknowledged by the then case controller to Mr Nadir's solicitors. And that no decisive attempt was made to retrieve them until December 1991. Despite Vizards' frequently expressed concern about the matter and the fact that the then case controller appears to have recognised, at least by January 1991, that copies of potentially privileged documents had been circulated.

This was extraordinary. Someone had realised that a mistake had been made as far back as January 1991 – months before Michael Mates started his inquiries and two Attorney-Generals had been given the wrong information. How had that happened? Had anyone really bothered to inquire? Had someone lied? And, if so, who – and why? In the light of this revelation Peter Knight's suggestion that the SFO was disorganised seems a remarkably charitable criticism.

Lyell's admission suggested that there was more than just incompetence and careless paper shuffling at the root of the privileged-papers saga. Predictably he still did not see any reason for an inquiry into the handling of the Nadir prosecution.

The Attorney-General's statement in December 1993 rounded off a truly rotten year for the SFO. There had been enormous public anger when financier Roger Levitt – whose investment-management company had crashed, owing investors millions of pounds – was sentenced to 180 hours of community service, following what appeared to be a bungling attempt at plea bargaining. Asil Nadir's flight had been the biggest débâcle of all, and the subsequent revelations had brought sharply into focus the many serious flaws in the SFO's operations. It had raised question marks over the integrity of a High Court Judge on the basis of no evidence at all. It had misled two Attorney-Generals. By the end of 1993 its credibility was practically at zero. The SFO had only been in existence for five years. It had been given huge powers but had become a byword for incompetence, and a wide-ranging review of its operations was already in progress.

But none of this was much help to us over in Northern Cyprus. No one was asking the obvious question: how could so many things go wrong with one prosecution? I had long since given up believing that what had happened to Mr Nadir was a series of unfortunate coincidences. It was all designed to justify the fact that PPI was destroyed when the SFO raided SAM. The effort to get a public inquiry peaked in the wake of Michael Mates' resignation. He had been proved right on many of the important issues he had raised. But it had resulted in nothing but limp apologies. My return to the UK was inevitable.

10. Back in the Firing Line

I EVENTUALLY RETURNED to England on 19 September 1994, four years to the day on which the SFO had raided South Audley Management. I was accompanied by a charming young journalist, John Mullin from the *Guardian*, whom I'd met a year before when he had come out to Northern Cyprus for a story on the Nadir case. We had got talking at Rita on the Rocks, a restaurant up the coast from Kyrenia, which is a home from home for visiting British press teams. Its owner, Rita, is an English woman married to a Turkish Cypriot, a larger-than-life character with a heart of gold. The following May, the first anniversary of Asil Nadir's arrival back in Northern Cyprus, John had returned to do a feature on 'the fugitives'. I told him I was going back to the UK as soon as all the media pressure had subsided. John made me promise to tell him when I was returning. He wanted to fly out and write a piece on my homecoming.

During my stay on Cyprus, people had been very kind, but this was no substitute for home, a job and, most important of all, my family – especially my little granddaughter, Megan, who was growing up so fast. There really wasn't much for me to do on the island. Before Mr Nadir returned, I had grown so desperate to do something useful that I asked Safiye Nadir if I could check over the antique oak furniture in his two homes. I was worried it wasn't being looked after properly. Safiye obviously thought I was mad to be worrying about that. 'We are preserving people at this moment, Elizabeth, not furniture,' she told me.

When I first arrived on Cyprus, I stayed at the Olive Tree holiday village until I could organise my own apartment. It is a delightful place, owned by Bilge Nevzat and tucked quietly into the foothills of the Kyrenia range a few miles from the town. That winter was exceptionally cold, with the only snow the island had seen in twenty years, so I have some unusual photos of the Olive Tree in a snowstorm. Eventually I moved to a house, the best that could be found at the time, where I froze without central heating, trying to cope with a temperamental immersion heater, an intermittent telephone line and constant power cuts.

I made some good friends on the island, where there is a large community of some 20,000 British expatriates. Many of them had served in colonial Cyprus during the troubles of the fifties and early sixties, fallen in love with the island and eventually retired there. The main event of the week was Sunday morning service at the local Presbyterian Church of St Andrew in Kyrenia. Inevitably, there were lots of bridge parties.

But, within a few months of Asil Nadir's return, I had decided I must go home. By the beginning of 1994 it was clear that there was not going to be any public inquiry into Mr Nadir's prosecution, and I knew why. The Serious Fraud Office had raided South Audley Management and brought about the collapse of the company – they had been justifying that error ever since. Unless I went back to England and challenged the authorities, it would all be swept under the carpet.

Asil Nadir was busy trying to get the PPI businesses on the island going again. There were the two hotels, the Jasmine Court in Kyrenia and the Palm Beach at Famagusta, plus the Crystal Cove, which was still unfinished when the company had collapsed in 1990. In addition there were the citrus and packaging interests. Some of these owed the TRNC Government substantial sums in taxes and social-security payments built up over the three years Mr Nadir had been in London. The administrators had been refused access to these businesses by court injunctions in Northern Cyprus.

By 1994 the administration was effectively over, with the three administrators, Richard Stone, Michael Jordan and Christopher Morris, facing criminal charges in Turkey. At the end of 1993, when in Istanbul on PPI business, Michael Jordan had been visited by the police in his hotel and taken for questioning by one of the City's senior prosecutors, following complaints made by Mr Nadir about the handling of the administration. It was an extraordinary state of affairs.

It emerged that Asil Nadir had got hold of a Coopers & Lybrand memorandum detailing the possible sale of a Turkish printing company, AN Graphics, at which the administrators had a purchaser for some of its machinery. In the memo reference was made to 'other customs handling costs and bribes' that would have to be paid. This was hugely embarrassing for Coopers, who admitted that the memo was genuine but strongly denied that the firm had made any illegal payments. It was, Coopers explained, just a bit of 'loose wording' used in an internal communication. But, it sparked off an investigation by the Turkish police and eventual charges against the administrators over sales of assets, which are still being pursued. It also meant that Jordan, Stone and Morris could no longer go to Turkey, where they now faced arrest. But it was another blow for PPI creditors and shareholders. By June 1994 the administrators' bill, including legal costs, was over £33 million.

Christopher Barlow, another Coopers man, took over as administrator, announcing that the survival of PPI could no longer be achieved and that all efforts would be made to realise the remaining assets. When a new Coalition Government came to power in the TRNC at the beginning of 1994, he was hopeful they might get access to the Northern Cypriot assets. Although the new Government, or elements of it, was hostile to Asil Nadir – the new Deputy Prime Minister of the TRNC was no fan of his, it emerged – and they were pressing for tax payments, Barlow saw that he might yet do a deal.

There was another major political upheaval, however, when in the summer of 1994 the European Community ruled that no citrus should be imported from the TRNC because its Government was not recognised as legitimate. The Greeks, now EC members, were jubilant, as was the *Daily Telegraph* in London, which informed its baffled readers that the banning of Cypriot fruit was designed to put the squeeze on Asil Nadir. The fact that tens of thousands of other Turkish Cypriots might be impoverished by this vicious edict, which would make a huge impact on the TRNC's shaky economy, did not seem to matter.

Some of the TRNC politicians blamed Asil Nadir for the EC embargo on the Republic. Even worse, he was blamed when one

Coopers' accountant in Istanbul was beaten up and another shot in the legs during two separate incidents. Journalists got the idea that these horrific incidents were something to do with Mr Nadir. There was no proof, but the incidents were faithfully recounted in the administrators' report to creditors.

Asil Nadir's financial problems meant that it might be some time before he could bring an abuse of process case against the authorities in London. I had already decided to go home and open up the case myself by challenging the SFO. I knew I needed legal representation, but I could not afford to retain Ludovic de Walden, my original lawyer. In the spring of 1993 I met Peter Krivinskas, Asil Nadir's solicitor, who had a practice in Manchester. I liked him a lot, and he seemed to grasp the complexities of the situation. He agreed to represent me.

I wanted to give the SFO three months' notice of my return and asked Peter Krivinskas to arrange an appointment for 19 September. Shortly afterwards I was dining with some friends when I met the well-known television journalist and writer Sandy Gall and his wife, who were in Cyprus on holiday. I told him I was returning to England. The very next day Jonathan Rugman, Turkish correspondent of the *Guardian*, materialised out of the blue and interviewed me. Then John Mullin phoned, hot on the line from London, to remind me about my promise to let him accompany me home. I knew I needed media support. I also realised that many journalists were now far more questioning about the Polly Peck affair. Although Asil Nadir didn't want me to leave, he accepted my decision, but I don't think he really believed that I would go until I set foot on the plane.

I returned to England via Paris. If I was to be arrested on arrival, I thought I might as well get a decent night's sleep beforehand. I reached Holborn Police Station a minute before my noon appointment, accompanied by Peter Krivinskas. The press and television cameras were there, and the subsequent *Guardian* feature was very funny. The front page of the tabloid section showed a photo of me with the headline: BRITAIN'S MOST WANTED GRANNY.

Being arrested was an experience I'll never forget. Over the next five days I was interviewed for 36 hours, and in the end I lost my voice. On the second day the SFO tried to dismiss my solicitor, Peter Krivinskas, on the grounds that he was Asil Nadir's legal adviser, too. As far as we were concerned, there was no conflict of interest, and Peter stayed put. It was all quite dreadful, particularly after the tranquillity of Cyprus. At one point my three interrogators – two policemen and an SFO accountant – were all shouting at me at once and had to be told by Peter to ask their questions one at a time. 'Am I allowed to speak or are you going to speak for the rest of the tape?' I asked them.

On the final day, they put me in the cells at Holborn Police Station for two hours while they had a lunch break. I hadn't been charged, and their excuse was that they had to collect some documentation that I had requested. Peter Krivinskas stayed with me, and we shared a sandwich. The cell was awful – just a thin mattress on the floor and a wooden bench. But at the end of it all, I still wasn't charged, and the police asked me to return eight days later, on 5 October. It wasn't clear either to me or Peter Krivinskas what would happen then.

When I returned to Holborn Police Station just over a week later, however, I was charged with two new offences of knowingly handling a total of £400,000 of stolen money in October 1989. The two charges read:

1. Between the 16th and 22nd days of October 1989 you dishonestly undertook or assisted in the retention, removal, disposal or realisation of certain stolen goods, namely £88,050 in monies belonging to Polly Peck International plc by or for the benefit of another, or dishonestly arranged to do so, knowing or believing the same to be stolen goods. Contrary to Section 22(1) Theft Act 1968.

2. Between the 16th and 22nd days of October 1989 you dishonestly undertook or assisted in the retention, removal, disposal or realisation of certain goods, namely property to the value of £307,000 belonging to Polly Peck International plc by or for the benefit of another, or dishonestly arranged to do so, knowing or believing the same to be stolen goods.

So, back in 1989, before there had been any police interest in PPI, I was supposed to have known that money was being stolen, although Mr Nadir had not stood trial, let alone been found guilty of any theft. More to the point, the actual £400,000 that I was accused of handling had not even been included in any of his charges – and what had happened to the allegations of illegal share dealing? Four years before, this, and my alleged role in it, had been at the centre of the suspicions regarding SAM and Asil Nadir.

I had my fingerprints taken by Wendy Russell-Rayner, the policewoman who had ransacked my desk at South Audley Management in September 1990. My photograph was also taken. I was surrounded by police as if I were some kind of violent criminal, but it was as if I were watching all this happening to someone else. I remember murmuring that I had never appeared in court before – not even for a driving offence. I was driven by the SFO in a private car to Bow Street Magistrates' Court, where I was again put in a cell to await my appearance in court. The SFO asked for my passport to be withheld, and they wanted the bail set at £100,000 – a huge amount of money in relation to the size and seriousness of my charges. They didn't get it. The bail was fixed at £20,000 until the middle of November.

The SFO asked the magistrate for three months' delay before transferring my case to the Crown Court. They wanted to make further investigations in Switzerland, apparently to follow up inquiries that they had already had four years to pursue. In any case, I phoned my mother, who went along and surrendered my passport at Great Dunmow Police Station, although I was more worried about her than anything else. In her late eighties, she now had to go and arrange the surety for me; she is, however, a feisty Scot and has proved a great support to me.

Just after noon, I was escorted to a large white police prison lorry, however, which was to take me to Holloway while the surety was organised. The journey took two hours since the driver stopped at the Elephant and Castle in south London to have his lunch break. I was locked in another cell there for two hours and eventually reached Holloway at about 2.30 pm. By now confirmation on the surety had arrived at Bow Street. As I left the prison, the journalists were waiting for me – along with a representative from PPI's administrators, I discovered later. A man had barred my way as I opened the car door and chucked something on to the back seat. In the confusion I had ignored it as we were being hotly pursued by a press photographer on a motorbike, who drew alongside us at every set of traffic lights.

Later that afternoon I talked to Mr Nadir about the charges. 'Better the SFO had done nothing than do this,' he told me. 'They will live to regret the day.' He was surprised at how the press had reacted to my return, although I wasn't. It was obvious to many of the journalists that the PPI affair had been poorly handled by the SFO, and they were rightly suspicious. As Peter Krivinskas told *The Times*, the SFO had never managed to justify its raid on SAM and the collapse of the PPI shares. Many of the PPI shareholders had lost far more than the £400,000 that I was now accused of mishandling.

Meanwhile I had to think about my defence and gain some insight into the workings of the SFO. Through a mutual friend, I met Patrick, Lord Spens, who had himself been prosecuted in the second Guinness trial, which had collapsed. Although he was acquitted, Patrick was still furious at the way the SFO had conducted their business in his own and many other prosecutions. I went for lunch with him at the House of Lords, where I found him very sympathetic and full of useful advice. He told me that the people whom the SFO feared most were the press, and one essential protection for me was to make sure that reporting restrictions were lifted. He told me that the SFO would try and impose them – and he turned out to be absolutely right. In my ignorance I had assumed that those restrictions were somehow or other for my benefit, but now I realised that I could have them removed if I asked – I had nothing to hide, after all.

I had been told that it wasn't necessary for me to go to the 16 November hearing at Bow Street, but I wanted to make sure the reporting restrictions were indeed lifted. There were about twenty members of the media in court, and sure enough, the SFO opposed my solicitor's request for lifting press restrictions. Peter Krivinskas stuck to his guns, however, and won that round. Predictably the SFO had nothing to report from Switzerland, and they were now given to the end of December to complete their investigations.

Then, out of the blue, the question of my bail was raised once more. Apparently the surety given in October had to be done all over again. My mother had 'signed on' at Great Dunmow rather than at Bow Street itself, so it had to be renewed. No one had advised me of this, and the SFO had even said that I needn't be in court that day. I was in a panic, and it was enough to give my mother a heart attack as I could see myself being taken to Holloway again. Fortunately, a friend, who was in court, stood temporary surety for the £20,000.

Meanwhile I had decided that if the SFO had been given all this time to find their evidence in Switzerland, I was going to ask for the return of my passport so that I could go there myself with my solicitor. I had collected the £400,000 in October 1989 from Warburg's, one of the Nadir family bankers, so I needed to go and see them. I made an appointment for January. At the hearing on 29 December, the SFO told the magistrate that they had still not obtained the necessary information from Switzerland, and they vigorously opposed the temporary return of my passport so that I could go and research my defence. We won, however.

Peter Krivinskas and I had a very successful trip to Switzerland, where one thing we discovered was that Christopher Morris, the Touche Ross administrator, was taking action against Warburg's, alleging that the £400,000 that had been handed to me was the property of PPI. They were trying to recover the money on behalf of PPI's creditors. It wasn't long before Warburg's realised that they were in a peculiar position: no theft had been proved, yet the administrators were threatening to sue them. I also discovered that the money had only arrived at Warburg's Geneva branch after I had collected the funds in question. I wondered how they could accuse me of handling 'stolen' PPI money.

The strange document that had been thrown into my car as I left Holloway had been a summons from the administrators. Touche Ross wanted to interview me under oath in the High Court at the beginning of February. There was also another hearing at Bow Street scheduled for a couple of days later. I felt it was outrageous that the administrators, who were suing Warburg's, were able to pull me in and question me in the middle of criminal proceedings, before any theft, let alone my knowledge of it, had been proved. I felt that an important point of principle was involved here. The administrators had not served their notice correctly in any case, but more to the point I was feeling the strain. I cancelled the interview with the administrators on health grounds.

That didn't stop them harassing my mother, who was dismayed, at 88 years of age, to find a process server, sent by the administrators, ringing her door bell and shouting through the letter box one evening when I was out. The next day a friend came round to visit. As I opened the door to let her in, the process server jumped out from behind a wall and shouted, 'Elizabeth, you will be arrested if you don't attend the court on Monday.' I closed the door, leaving my friend outside to see him off. The process server then posted £50 through the letter box to pay my 'expenses' for the journey to court. Christopher Morris of Touche Ross had spent a great deal of money trying to take legal action against various people and had failed. Now £50 of PPI money had landed on my doormat. I had to laugh.

The SFO then tried to delay the next magistrates' court hearing. The day before the hearing Peter Krivinskas had been amazed to receive a phone call from the SFO Director George Staple himself, who was asking to postpone everything for a couple of weeks because the case handler, Peter Kiernan, was indisposed. In October the SFO had said they needed three months to complete their investigations, but they had already had four years. Now they were trying to delay the transfer of my case. Peter refused.

The next day in court I was sitting next to one of the journalists covering the case. It was clear that they all knew now about what had gone on behind closed doors in the Asil Nadir affair. There was no way, with the reporting restrictions lifted, that they could postpone proceedings, the journalist told me. I mentally gave thanks to Patrick Spens for his advice as the case was transferred to the Crown Court.

Patrick had also told me that I needed a very forthright, non-establishment Queen's Counsel for my defence, someone who would not be intimidated by the SFO. Asil Nadir was not a popular cause, and my case was inextricably linked to his. I also wanted someone who could see the larger picture here. I had come back to prove that the SFO had made a huge mistake when they raided SAM and collapsed PPI. I was not worried about my own charges, but I wanted to fight my case in a way that would highlight what had happened to PPI and its shareholders. I couldn't instruct Anthony Scrivener, who really understood the case in his capacity as Mr Nadir's QC. So who could I approach? Patrick, ever cynical about lawyers, had no one he could recommend.

One weekend I opened my *Sunday Times* and read an article about an impending court case following the publication of photographs of the Princess of Wales exercising at a gym. The defendant's QC was Geoffrey Robertson, who, it was reported, was prepared to put the National Treasure in the witness box should the case go ahead. Mr Robertson, according to the article, was noted for his 'dogged interrogation, fearless oratory and anti-Establishment views'. I felt this was the QC for me.

I phoned a journalist friend of mine to ask about him, and she explained that he was the lawyer who had acted for the Matrix Churchill directors. Over in Cyprus I had heard nothing of this *cause célèbre* – or of how it had led to the Scott investigation into the arms to Iraq scandal. My friend had met him many years ago. He was an Aussie originally and enjoyed a fight. He was, she told me, one of the best ideas I was ever going to have in my life, and I was to get on the phone first thing Monday morning. A few weeks later we had a conference at his Doughty Street chambers, and I met him. Actually I saw his tie before I saw him. It was a dazzlingly bright orange with yellow flowers.

My case was due to transfer, and a judge was appointed. I now got a real shock: Judge Tucker was to be the trial judge. I just did not know what to make of this. Judge Tucker, I felt, must be heartily sick of the whole PPI affair, considering what had happened in his courtroom two years previously. I could hardly believe that he would now relish a return to the PPI case.

What, I wondered, had he made of the bizarre events in his courtroom when proceedings had been disrupted by allegations that there was a conspiracy to bribe him for the return of Asil Nadir's passport? He had been told that he might be interviewed by the police. He had eventually received an apology. But there had been no investigation into how this bribery allegation had come about. For all I knew he might believe that Asil Nadir had concocted it. If so, what would be his attitude to me? The implications were frightening.

And there was a separate, but potentially embarrassing issue in the background. Ramadan Guney, the Turkish Cypriot businessman who had stood bail for Asil Nadir, had claimed that he did not have to forfeit his surety because the bail order had not been properly dealt with at the time Asil Nadir's case had tranferred to the Crown Court. This was a highly technical issue involving court procedures, but Guney's case against forfeiture was upheld by the Court of Appeal, and the SFO then took it to the House of Lords. I wondered who in the end would be held responsible if there had been such an extraordinary oversight. As my trial started I discovered that the Law Lords had already made their final judgement, but that it would not be made public until my case was over. I wondered why.

At the end of June I went down to Bristol for the first of my pre-trial hearings, sessions held before the main trial to argue any points of law, such as what evidence will be admissible. As soon as I got to court, Peter Krivinskas greeted me with the news that a huge, 300-page file of 'evidence' had been delivered by the prosecution the day before. This was the third time this had happened. Moreover it appeared that the SFO were still interviewing and reinterviewing witnesses eight months after they had charged me. They had just spoken to my former secretary for the third time, who ironically, was now taking a law degree at Bristol University. I was upset that five years after they had lost their jobs in the most unpleasant circum-stances, the old SAM staff were still being pestered by the SFO.

When we all finally got into court, Geoffrey Robertson told everyone in no uncertain terms that for Mrs Forsyth to be found guilty of any handling charge Mr Nadir would first have to be proved guilty of stealing the £400,000 in question. And that since this money was not apparently linked to any of the offences with which Asil Nadir had been charged, he felt the SFO might find it hard to substantiate their case. I was delighted to see that the SFO contingent looked utterly miserable. They had been told that they faced the Nadir trial by proxy, and my defence threatened to air, very publicly once again, their handling of Mr Nadir's case. Judge Tucker announced that trial would take place in mid-January 1996, which would, he agreed, give the defence time to study the half-a-million documents accumulated in Mr Nadir's case.

Meanwhile there was another pre-trial hearing set for November. Over the summer Peter Krivinskas and I were hard at work trying to identify the crucial documents that would reveal the reasons for the raid on SAM that had precipitated the collapse of PPI. We were entitled to documents under the disclosure rules, provided it could be shown they were relevant to my defence. Since I had been chairman of SAM, I felt that I was entitled to know the background to the raid. No one had even seen the warrant for the raid on SAM.

We were particularly interested in the meeting called by the SFO for 23 August 1990, which we knew about because the Inland Revenue had shown Peter Knight the note of the confidential telephone conversation between the then SFO deputy director Michael Chance and a senior Inland Revenue official. According to the note, Chance had phoned and invited the Inland Revenue to attend and indeed chair the meeting. We could only assume that the meeting, which involved the Department of Trade and the police, had taken place despite the refusal of the Inland Revenue. So we asked the SFO for the minutes of the meeting, which appeared to us to be a crucial one.

They wrote back to Peter Krivinskas saying that there were no minutes of the meeting, but there was a document, which they refused to give us, contending that it was not relevant to my defence. They indicated that, in any event, they might seek a Public Interest Immunity Certificate. I was furious. I had by now read quite a lot about the use and abuse of PIICs to prevent the disclosure of evidence, although few people had ever heard of them before the dramatic collapse of the Matrix Churchill case, when it emerged that Government Ministers had signed PIICs that enabled the prosecution to withhold from the defence vital evidence that showed that the defendants' activities had been known to and approved by the authorities. The justification for their use was the protection of national security or the workings of government. I could not believe that the document I was asking for fell into either of those categories. Mr Nadir, of course, was always convinced that there were political machinations behind the attack on him and his company, and he saw this as proof of it. I was convinced that the document had more likely originated from the London Stock Exchange.

We knew that the Exchange had passed its report on the abortive bid of August 1990 to the SFO. It had said so publicly. Two successive Attorney-Generals had also told Michael Mates that the PPI investigation had started as a result of a referral by the Stock Exchange. I was convinced by now that the Stock Exchange had, in turn, obtained information from the Inland Revenue. I was sure this document would also demonstrate that the SFO had relied on the tax investigation as 'evidence' linking Mr Nadir to the Rhone Finance companies whose dealings in PPI shares seemed to have been the starting-point for the SFO investigation. Once I had it, I could show that the assumptions were wrong.

My lawyers planned to ask for this document at the November pre-trial hearing, where, once again, I found myself sitting in a magnificently wood-panelled courtroom – the Central Criminal Court is a truly lovely building. But by then I felt I had made some progress. The day before the hearing the SFO had finally sent Peter Krivinskas the warrant and supporting affidavit for the raid on SAM. They had been forced to do so. Geoffrey Robertson had suggested that the raid might have been unlawful, and that therefore any evidence found there would be inadmissible in my trial. This had prompted the sending of the elusive warrant.

It told me much of what I wanted to know: that the raid had indeed been mounted on the erroneous assumption that SAM was a conduit for dealings in PPI shares by the Rhone Finance companies. Safiye Nadir's two trust companies, Tristan and Forum, were wrongly alleged to have been administered by Rhone Finance and it was clear that Jason Davies's share purchases for both groups of companies had been assumed to reflect common ownership.

At the pre-trial hearing it was agreed that the contentious document for which we had asked would be disclosed on a 'counsel to counsel' basis. Only the defence and prosecution QCs would look at it, and a decision would be taken about whether or not to ask for disclosure. It was not the only document that the SFO had failed to deliver to us, however. They claimed that three other documents we had asked for were missing – simply not in the files.

I was even more furious when David Calvert-Smith said that my trial could not start in the middle of January because he would be involved in another case until then. The last thing I wanted was a delay, and Judge Tucker was none too pleased either as we had all agreed to the January date the previous summer. The Judge had already stated that he had read the SFO's witness statements and could not quite understand the relevance of many of them. Extra-ordinarily, the bulk of them had been taken in relation to Mr Nadir's prosecution, which had not involved the money I was now accused of handling. And many of them seemed to focus on transactions in PPI shares. I was rather in agreement with Judge Tucker in failing to see their relevance to the precise charges against me. The SFO wanted to infer that the money allegedly stolen from PPI had been used for some kind of share-support operation by Mr Nadir. This was what my trial was really going to be about.

Meanwhile a new trial date had to be set, and Judge Tucker was very amusing when he actually asked if there was anyone who could replace David Calvert-Smith for the prosecution. He peered at the QC over his glasses like an owl sizing up a mouse and wondered aloud whether Mr Owen QC might be available. That caused a few giggles. Robert Owen had been the lead prosecutor against Mr Nadir. It was he who had originally brought up the bribery allegation involving Judge Tucker in court. And he had told the Judge that he might be interviewed in the course of the police investigations. In the event it had been the hapless David Calvert-Smith who had been required to apologise to Judge Tucker over the groundless allegations that had so dramatically disrupted his courtroom. I couldn't help feeling that the Judge would have relished an opportunity to have Robert Owen QC appear before him in my case. Alas, it was not to be. The trial date was moved to the middle of February instead, when Mr Calvert-Smith was sure he would be available.

I was in constant touch with Asil Nadir, who had had his own battles to fight. Just before Christmas 1994, the TRNC Government had seized his hotels in order to try and force the tax payments. The administrators had been trying to do a deal with the TRNC – or that part of it that opposed Mr Nadir over the assets. Then there had been a last-minute truce with him. I could never fathom Cypriot politics even when I lived there, but 2000 miles away it was quite impossible to know what was really going on. It seemed, however, that he was losing ground, particularly when it was announced that the administrators had managed to sell the Jasmine Court and Palm Beach hotels, plus the packaging company, to some local businessman.

By Easter 1995 it was clear that Mr Nadir himself was actually behind the company that had bought the assets. The clue was in the name of the company, Learned, which is the meaning of his sister Bilge's name in Turkish. He had bought the assets, unknown to the administrators, with the financial backing of a Turkish business woman friend. Well, he had always said he would get them back – and he did.

Even more extraordinary was the letter he received from the Coopers' administrator, Christopher Barlow, a few months later, requesting a meeting with him. The administrators had accused him of taking money from the company, and Touche Ross had tried to sue him and his family and freeze their assets. It was clear that the administrators thought Asil Nadir was behind the attacks on their personnel in Istanbul. Now they were writing to him asking for his cooperation. An extract follows:

Dear Mr Nadir

It has been some time since the Administrators of PPI were in direct contact with you. As you will be aware, I have taken over from Michael Jordan and Richard Stone the day to day running of the administration. It seems to me that it would be helpful for us to meet shortly, so as to enable me to improve my understanding of what it is you wish to achieve in relation to the remaining parts of the Polly Peck group.

It was an admission of failure. The administrators wanted to wind up the PPI affair, which had caused them such frustration, not to mention indictments in a Turkish court against three of the UK's best-known accountants. Mr Nadir had bought back his Cypriot assets. Now the remaining Turkish companies were being offered to him.

It was a relief when the big day dawned, and my trial finally started at Chichester Rents, where the Maxwell brothers had stood in the dock only a few weeks before. The Serious Fraud Office was alleging that in October 1989 Asil Nadir had needed a large sum of money to pay off personal debts, that he had stolen the cash from PPI and that I had laundered the money for him. The SFO had to prove two things. First, that the money – £400,000 – had been stolen. Second, that I knew it was stolen at the time I dealt with it. Clearly it was enough for me to show that I could not possibly have known the money was stolen back in the autumn of 1989. But I wanted to demonstrate that the £400,000 was not stolen at all – to get right to the heart of the matter.

I did not intend to base my defence on the fact that I was obeying orders. I felt that if I could show, through my trial, that this £400,000 was not misappropriated, but had been paid into Unipac by the Nadirs before it was paid out of Polly Peck, then it would help demonstrate that the transactions that had been the basis of Asil Nadir's charges had been entirely proper. The key to this lay in Northern Cyprus, where the SFO had refused to go and look at evidence. As my QC, Geoffrey Robertson, told the court, the SFO had not been concerned to find the truth about this transaction.

When I was arrested and questioned by the SFO on my arrival back in the UK in September 1994 I had practically forgotten the

197

circumstances surrounding the £400,000. I had been in Switzerland on business at the time. Jason Davies, who by then was resident in Geneva looking after Nadir Investments, had an urgent payment to make to the stockbrokers A. J. Bekhor. There was £400,000 coming to the Restro account at the Zurich branch of Warburg Soditic. Restro held the Nadir family shareholding, and I assumed the payment was interest on the loan account. Jason Davies needed the money in a hurry. I must have assumed this was some kind of a foreign-exchange deal, and that it had been arranged to divert the money.

Jason Davies asked me to go to Warburg in Geneva, collect the money and arrange for £310,000 of it to be paid to A. J. Bekhor in London. I had deposited the £310,000 at the Geneva branch of my own bank, the Midland, since I thought this was the quickest way to transfer it to London. I took the remaining cash – £88,000 – back to the UK, arranging for it to be collected at the airport and credited to the Baggrave farm account. No attempt had been made to conceal the money or the route of it. And I was prepared for it to go through my own bank, for heaven's sake. As Geoffrey Robertson told the court: 'If she's a launderess, she's not much of a washerwoman, because she leaves her name all over the shirts.'

One of my problems was that I could not remember exactly why I had gone to Geneva on 15 October 1989, which was a Sunday. The prosecution claimed that I had gone there specially to 'launder' the £400,000. All I recalled was that Mr Nadir had phoned me from the USA that weekend and told me to go to Switzerland. He feared there was going to be some kind of international financial crisis, and I should be on hand for the bankers who had extended large margin loans to the Nadir family against the security of their PPI shares.

I soon discovered that the financial markets had indeed wobbled rather alarmingly that weekend. There had been a sharp fall in share prices on Wall Street on the Friday, and the markets were nervous about what would happen on the Monday. Funnily enough there was an identical stock-market crisis one weekend during my trial.

Quite why anyone should think Asil Nadir needed £400,000 so desperately in October 1989 was hard to fathom. He was on the crest of a wave after the successful purchase of Del Monte – PPI had just become a FTSE-100 company, by now valued at over £1 billion. And he and his family owned a quarter of the shares, making him one of the richest tycoons in the UK. There was no reason for him to steal £400,000 – nor did the prosecution ever offer any evidence why he should do so. It was ridiculous.

I knew only that Jason Davies needed £310,000 to pay A. J. Bekhor, but I probably assumed it was to finance some of the PPI shares bought for Safiye Nadir's trust. I had no idea that it was to be used, presumably with Mr Nadir's approval, for one of Jason's other clients, Gateway, one of the Rhone Finance companies that had featured so prominently in the warrant for the raid on South Audley Management.

I can only guess that Jason Davies knew some Nadir family money was due from London and had arranged to divert it for his other clients. It was just this sort of contra deal that had brought SAM to the attention of the Inland Revenue in the first place – and that had led the Stock Exchange and the SFO to believe that Asil Nadir was behind the Rhone Finance companies. In autumn 1989 I knew nothing about Gateway. But clearly the SFO was now going to try and justify that wretched warrant by linking me to the Rhone Finance companies at my own trial.

As the trial started, it was obvious that the prosecution was relying heavily on the assumption that there was something inherently dubious about the way PPI was run. They were trying, by inference, to suggest that Asil Nadir had stolen money, even though they couldn't prove it. Asil Nadir could transfer PPI money on the basis of his signature alone. The prosecution alleged that he resisted attempts to introduce a dual-signature system. Seven former PPI directors were called as prosecution witnesses. They revealed that all the main board directors could transfer money with just a single signature, and the change to dual signature had indeed been discussed at board meetings but had not been implemented until well into 1990. I didn't know much about this issue, but it emerged that Asil Nadir had not been particularly opposed to the introduction of the dual-signature system.

I had little idea what attitude these former directors now had to Azil Nadir – the events of 1990 when PPI collapsed had been traumatic for them. I nearly burst into tears when the first witness, Norbert Wirsching, who had run PPI's Capetronics subsidiary, praised Asil Nadir for his hard work and dedication to the company. 'Sometimes we directors felt embarrassed,' he told the court, 'that we as a board should get credit, whereas he did not.' He declared that Asil Nadir had not resisted the idea of changing the single-signature system.

David Fawcus, the last and most senior of the former PPI directors to be called, told the court how Asil Nadir worked seven days a week, even Christmas Day. He pointed out that there was a very good reason why Mr Nadir retained the single signature. PPI was a truly international company, and money often needed to be moved around outside normal UK banking hours.

All the directors knew that they had worked with a remarkable person – and they said so. I was really delighted. If the prosecution had thought that they would manage further to smear Asil Nadir's reputation through my trial, they were sorely disappointed. What emerged was the portrait of a very dedicated businessman, with immense charm, who made decisions quickly, but, as one director said, took every step to make sure his directors had access to information.

More to the point the directors explained the currency and foreign-exchange problems confronted by PPI and, in particular, the problems with the Turkish lire. As a banker I knew that the Turkish lire was simply not dealt in easily like dollars or sterling, and that foreign-exchange transactions through the local banks were slow and expensive as a result. I now knew to what extent Unipac, the Cypriot company, had developed a key banking and foreign-exchange role within the company and had acquired the Turkish lire it needed locally directly from individuals, including the Nadir family, who received the equivalent in sterling. Unipac in Cyprus was a major PPI profit-earner, but the finance came from London. The company needed the local currency to pay its growers and employees – PPI had set up the Niksar bottling plant in Turkey to generate local currency. The secondary banking operation in Unipac fufilled a real corporate need, and as I understood it the company benefited financially.

The charges against Asil Nadir as well as me had been based on the third-party transactions. In 1990 the SFO investigators had seen money paid out from PPI in London but had not visited Cyprus to see what had happened at the other end. Funds had been paid into Unipac, its subsidiary, and it was there they would have found the matching payments. The point was made loudly and clearly by David

Fawcus, PPI's former Finance Director, when David Calvert-Smith asked him about the depositing of third-party funds with Unipac.

Q 'Where were these notifications kept at Polly Peck?'

A 'Which notifications?'

Q 'The notifications that money had been paid in Cyprus.'

A 'They would be in Cyprus.'

Q 'Did Polly Peck have any record whatever?'

A 'No, it wouldn't do.'

From the testimony of the directors it was clear that the PPI auditors, Stoy Hayward, had known about Unipac's third-party banking business since September 1989, when they had been asked about it by the Inland Revenue. Stoy had not then raised the issue with any of the PPI directors, nor did they until September 1990 when the audit partner made it clear to David Fawcus that the third-party payments were unusual but broke no laws, either here in the UK or over in Northern Cyprus.

David Fawcus also confirmed that Mr Nadir kept a PPI account for his personal use, which Fawcus himself used to check to ensure was always in credit. He also said that he understood that Asil Nadir had a similar current account in Unipac in Cyprus, which had a credit balance of between £6 million and £9 million over the years 1988, 1989 and 1990. I was fascinated by this. What on earth was I doing sitting in the dock, accused of handling money stolen from PPI, when Mr Nadir had reserved that much cash on deposit with the company? The prosecution trundled on with its case. Many of the witnesses were the same as those lined up for Asil Nadir's trial. Now we were having his trial by proxy.

One of the saddest things for me was to see people I had known, and with whom I had dealt, sitting in the witness-box. Two of SAM's former tax advisers from Rawlinson & Hunter, Phillip Prettejohn and Simon Jennings, now appeared as prosecution witnesses. They were top flight accountants and had been retained by me to advise us on setting up the right tax structure for the Nadir family interests.

Phillip Prettejohn spent all day in the witness-box as Geoffrey Robertson treated us all to a comprehensive seminar on the subject of tax and the extraordinary structures devised quite legally to protect the capital of wealthy, non-domiciled individuals such as Asil

Nadir from the UK taxman. It was important for the jury to understand that the structure of which SAM was a part had been perfectly above board and developed on the best advice. The prosecution was making out that because money went a rather circuitous route, there had to be something wrong about it. In fact it was all to do with tax regulations and devising legal ways of keeping money out of the UK. To hear him you would think my QC was a leading member of the tax bar – the way in which he got Phillip Prettejohn to explain the finer points of international tax was quite brilliant.

The prosecution then called a number of stockbrokers who had worked at A. J. Bekhor. They wanted to demonstrate that I was somehow responsible for Gateway and, by implication, the other Rhone Finance companies – we were back to the reason for the raid on SAM all those years ago. The raid that collapsed PPI had been ordered on the basis of wrong information, and now we would see the proof of that.

Dennis Wilson was the broker who actually carried out all Jason Davies' stock-market transactions through the firm. He was effectively Jason's partner, and we had met only twice – once when he was waiting at SAM for Jason Davies to join him for a lunch appointment and on another occasion when he came along to one of our Christmas parties. My QC cross-examined the former Bekhor stockbrokers very closely. We knew that one witness had claimed in a statement that I phoned Jonathan Bekhor from Switzerland three or four times a week to buy shares, and that Asil Nadir had visited Bekhor's offices.

The allegations had been so alarming that I had travelled to New York to see Bekhor himself. A few weeks before my trial the Serious Fraud Office had also gone out to interview Bekhor, and he had rubbished both the allegations made by this witness. As five former Bekhor stockbrokers filed in and out of the witness-box, it was clear that none of them had ever seen or heard of Asil Nadir's visits to Jonathan Bekhor. As my QC pointed out, it would have been something of an event at the time, because Mr Nadir had been at the height of his fame then.

Some ex-Bekhor employees had seen me when I had gone round to Bekhor's once for lunch. One even recalled talking to me once on the phone about settlement. That wasn't surprising. A substantial number of PPI shares had been purchased for Safiye Nadir's trust companies, Tristan and Forum, through A. J. Bekhor, and I was ultimately responsible for ensuring that these transactions were settled.

There remained the final Bekhor witness, a woman called Marilyn Nash. She had been Jonathan Bekhor's personal assistant and had alleged, quite contrary to everything we had heard so far from the other five former Bekhor employees, that not only had Mr Nadir visited Bekhor's but that I had also telephoned frequently from Switzerland. When the SFO had interviewed Jonathan Bekhor, he had denied having ever met Mr Nadir or being phoned by me as claimed.

But the prosecution would not ask Jonathan Bekhor to testify, despite the fact that it called to the witness stand half a dozen of Bekhor's employees. Bekhor was, of course, an important prosecution witness in another case, although the SFO chose to disregard him. It was a crazy situation, where some Crown prosecutors considered Bekhor a good witness, and others – the SFO – thought him unreliable. As my trial started a number of uncomplimentary newspaper stories suddenly appeared about Jonathan Beckhor, who, it was now known, was a possible defence witness in my case.

When Marilyn Nash eventually appeared she gave evidence about my phone calls and Mr Nadir's visits up the back stairs to the Bekhor offices. She had not herself been present at these meetings. She claimed that Jonathan Bekhor had told her the Nadirs did not like to discuss business in front of women. The prosecution had gone to some pains to establish that I was Asil Nadir's 'right-hand woman'.

My QC put it to Nash that she had a grudge against Jonathan Bekhor. That she was involved in sending a wreath to his wife following one of the attacks on him in the USA. This she denied. She did, however, admit that Jonathan Bekhor owed her now estranged husband, Henry Nash, money – some £185,000.

Even so the prosecution had not succeeded in linking me to the Gateway company, its share-dealing debts or the activities of any of the other companies administered by the Geneva-based Rhone Finance that had been clients of Jason Davies. At one point the court was adjourned for four days because the prosecution was waiting for Rhone Finance's two principals, Roger Leopard and Ian McNeill, to turn up to give evidence. Leopard was going to come to London, McNeill was to be allowed by the Judge to give his evidence by video link from Switzerland because he had been ill. In the event neither of them gave evidence, not even from Switzerland. Not that I was at all worried about what they might have had to say.

In fact there was a good reason why I wanted Roger Leopard of Rhone Finance to come to court, and it had nothing to do with my charges. I wished my QC to question him about a fascinating piece of information he had revealed in a statement given to the SFO in Switzerland in October 1991. One of the policemen, Andy Barnes, who had been investigating Mr Nadir, had formally interviewed Leopard before a Swiss magistrate under oath. Leopard was answering questions about the ownership of the 'Geneva airport' companies. During this interview he told Barnes that he had taken the decision to send an agent to Northern Cyprus to try and retrieve the documentation on Riverbridge and Gateway – and the other companies being investigated – from their owners, who had been Jason Davies's Turkish Cypriot clients.

This information was not included in the evidence against me produced by the prosecution. It was contained in the 'unused' material to which I, as the defendant, had enjoyed access – the full version of the Swiss interview. Finding the name of his agent popping up in 1991 begged a series of interesting questions. Michael Francis, who had invented the allegations of a plot to bribe the Judge, had a number of aliases, which included the name of this agent.

The SFO had claimed that they had engaged in no dealings with him before late summer 1992 when he had first been arrested at Gatwick Airport. But I knew that this agent's name had been one his many aliases, and I realised that the police knew this as well. Some of the so-called 'witnesses' who had given statements to the police back in 1993, supporting Francis's allegations that Mr Nadir had a 750 million DM account in Lichtenstein even referred to Francis by the agent's name. Francis had also spent a lot of time in Switzerland. And here was the same name referred to in an SFO interview dated autumn 1991 – a year before Michael Francis was supposed, according to the SFO, to have entered the picture. Could he possibly be the same person?

We were all keen to know from Roger Leopard of Rhone Finance exactly who this person was. We had a photograph of Michael Francis all ready for him to identify. But despite Judge Tucker's demands that he should come to give evidence and the subsequent delay of my trial proceedings, Roger Leopard stayed away. It was desperately disappointing, particularly for my QC Geoffrey Robertson, who had been looking forward to this particular cross-examination and the prospect of livening things up.

If the agent were indeed Michael Francis, why had the SFO claimed that they knew nothing about him until mid-1992? The implications were, and are, devastating in the context of Asil Nadir's prosecution. I thought we might still have a chance to find out more, since policeman Andy Barnes, who had interviewed Roger Leopard in 1991, and had also interviewed Michael Francis later, was on the list as the final prosecution witness. Alas, he was suddenly withdrawn.

The prosecution now embarked on proving its second charge, concerning the £88,000 I had put into the Baggrave Farm account. It was quite distressing to see the women I had employed at SAM dragged into the witness-box. They were all nice people – we had been a happy group there at 24 Berkeley Square. I knew that over the years some of them had been interviewed as many as four times by the SFO or the police. One ex-employee, now expecting a baby, looked terrified. She even took her witness statement into the box with her.

The prosecution was claiming that the Baggrave Farm account was short of money. They had produced a bank statement showing an overdraft in mid-October 1989. But there were three different bank accounts for Baggrave Farm: one was for petty cash, the other two were major accounts. One of the major accounts was submitted as evidence by the SFO, and the other showed that a payment of £125,000 was made to it from SAM's parent company in Jersey on 20 October 1989. There had clearly been no problem with the flow of funds from the Nadir family's trust companies, and it emerged the bank was prepared to give an unsecured overdraft of up to £400,000 to the Nadir personal companies at this time.

In autumn 1989 we had just bought a herd of Charolais cows for Baggrave, and we were intending to buy two bulls to service them. The court now heard about the delicacies of pedigree-cattle rearing – some of the money had been spent on semen for Asil Nadir's bulls. Part of the £88,000 cash had gone in a £68,000 cheque to Jack Young at United Auctions, who advised us on stocking the farm. The prosecution claimed that he had been pressing for payment. In fact, as Jack Young himself declared when he got into the witness-box, he was not pushing us for his money at all. United Auctions, as he explained proudly, was the Sotheby's of the cattle market, and Baggrave had been an excellent customer.

The last week in October 1989, when I returned from Geneva, I went up to Perth livestock show to meet Jack Young, who was auctioning there, and I took the cheque with me. It was at that show that we purchased Crackerjack, which became the prizewinning bull that adorned the front cover of the brochure we produced for Baggrave. Crackerjack duly became a jury exhibit – and, it turned out, a great help in my defence.

When he cross-examined me, Mr Calvert-Smith asked, 'Mrs Forsyth, did you enjoy being seen at the Perth show buying the best bull?' The implication was that I would have been prepared to launder money because Baggrave and its pedigree herd had been so close to my heart. I pointed out that Crackerjack had not been a prizewinner before he came to Baggrave. I had decided not to splash out on one of the top bulls – I had gone round at six o'clock on a freezing morning in Perth to seek out unknown, cheaper bulls with potential.

Less colourful, but much more important, was the accounting evidence concerning the £400,000 transaction. One of the Peat Marwick accountants who had been investigating for the SFO, with the consent of the company at the PPI offices in October 1990, now gave evidence. Seeing him was a shock. He looked so young. I saw from his witness statement that he had been qualified as a chartered accountant for less than two years when he had been drafted into the PPI inquiry as a 'forensic specialist'. He produced the documents showing the £400,000 transfer to S. G. Warburg on behalf of Unipac. He admitted that there had been no attempt to conceal the payment in the PPI intercompany accounts, but that he had found no matching payment coming back from Unipac in the books of Polly Peck. The point was, of course, that the match for an intercompany transaction like this would not be apparent in the PPI books – nor would it be expected to be seen there.

Under cross-examination the accountant conceded grudgingly that the payment match might indeed be more likely to be found in the books of the subsidiary, Unipac. 'You wouldn't expect to find a match in the books of Polly Peck. What happens in the subsidiary's account – and what they do with the money and whether it is matched – is essentially their business,' he told the court.

So there we had it. Asil Nadir and I had been charged because money had left PPI. But the SFO had never inspected the books of Unipac to see the payments coming into its subsidiary. As David Fawcus had said, the records would be in Cyprus, not in London

We had already retained a forensic accountant, Chris Hines of Baker Tilley, as an expert witness to trace this £400,000 payment. He had satisfied himself that the payment had indeed been properly registered in Unipac's books and associated accounting documents, as would have been normal practice. It had been entered as an equivalent payment by Asil Nadir to Unipac in Cyprus in Turkish lire on 14 October 1989 – just a few days before the money had left PPI in London. But we had to demonstrate conclusively, once and for all, that these third-party transactions that had been the basis of the charges against Asil Nadir and I were genuine.

While the trial was taking place we organised a forensic expert to go to Northern Cyprus to check the documents for this £400,000 transaction. Leslie Dick had been there once before, in 1991, to check the documents seen by Binder Hamlyn when they had investigated the transactions that had been the basis of the first charges against Mr Nadir. Now he went again – with vastly more sophisticated forensic equipment occupying the seat on the aircraft next to him. That very weekend there was an international drama when a flight from Northern Cyprus was hijacked – just my luck, I thought. I heaved a sigh of relief when I realised that it was not his plane that had been seized. But little did I realise that the real ambush would take place in court a few days later when the SFO argued that neither Mr Dick's evidence, nor indeed any accounting evidence from Cyprus, should be placed before the jury.

I was stunned. I just could not believe that this was possible. Sitting in court without the jury, listening to Calvert-Smith as he argued against the vital evidence being admitted in court, I just broke down in tears. I couldn't help myself. I so desperately wanted to show that this money had not been stolen – that the SFO had only 'half the picture' when they charged Asil Nadir.

The prosecution was alleging that I should have known the money was stolen because of its 'circuitous route' around countries and bank accounts. But I hadn't directed that money. Those who had, PPI accountant Ersin Tatar in London and Jason Davies in Switzerland, could not be called as defence witnesses because their names had been listed as wanted by the UK police. This was never made clear to the jury, who only knew that the prosecution had not applied for their extradition. My best defence, and indeed my only defence apart from my own testimony, was to show that the money was not stolen. That it had been a payment from PPI on behalf of Unipac, which had received the money in Turkish lire several days before it was paid out at PPI. I had a sleepless night while Judge Tucker pondered the SFO's submission and was overjoyed when he refused it.

Leslie Dick put his forensic evidence before the jury. He had checked the £400,000 in Unipac's books and bank documents, where it was shown paid in Turkish lire on 14 October 1989 – three days before I had collected it in Switzerland. He had examined a number of documents looking for signs of forgery or fabrication, including the Unipac 1989 cash ledger, a bound volume recording all the transactions for that year. As he pointed out, pages could conceivably be manufactured for loose-leaf ledgers, but it was hard to see how a bound volume could be successfully tampered with. The ledger bore all the hallmarks of a book that had been well used on a continual basis. It would, he said, be virtually impossible to fabricate a record such as this – it was simply not feasible.

Mr Calvert-Smith invited us all to ponder what he called his 'total fabrication theory' – that everything could have been forged over a period of years. I don't know what the jury made of this, but the idea was incredible, as Leslie Dick told the court:

> The scale of the operation. The fact that different people, in different organisations, would have had to have been involved. I mean, people in the bank, people at Unipac and, indeed, for some of the documentation people, in banks in Jersey and people in banks here in the UK.

Dick believed that a fabrication on this scale was impossible. I was overjoyed. The search for the 'stolen' £400,000 I had handled had finally stripped the SFO's prosecution of Asil Nadir and me of my credibility. I now felt I had achieved what I had set out to do in September 1994 when I had returned to the UK on the fourth anniversary of the raid on SAM.

The SFO had destroyed Polly Peck when they raided my company. They had produced charges against Asil Nadir that could only be sustained by refusing to go to Northern Cyprus to see the evidence – evidence that had now been brought into court, despite their objections.

The SFO had allowed Asil Nadir's trial to be derailed by false allegations that he was planning to bribe his trial judge. Asil Nadir had been vilified by the media before he had received the opportunity to present his defence. All this had happened because the blunderings of the authorities had destroyed Polly Peck, and no one wanted to admit they had made a colossal mistake when they caused the biggest corporate collapse the UK has ever seen. The whole affair had been to justify the fact that the SFO destroyed PPI when they raided SAM. I had seen with my own eyes the way they had fought to keep this evidence out of court.

Over the next few days there would be the summing-up of my trial and the jury's verdict. For me it was over. I already felt that I had won a moral victory. I stepped out into the cold March wind of Chancery Lane that evening, happier than I had felt for years.

My joy was short-lived, however. The prosecution had produced the bizarre possibility that the Turkish lire had been paid in the form of 50 lire notes and that payment of this sum would have involved some 29 million pieces of paper. This amused Judge Tucker, who enquired if this would require a lorry. The cash receipt showed the number 50, but this meant 50,000 Turkish lire – the number of notes required could be fitted into a briefcase not much larger than the one I had used to carry the £400,000 in Switzerland. There was in fact no 50 Turkish lire note in circulation in 1989 – this was a complete fiction.

But in his summing-up Judge Tucker went back to the 50 lire note and the 29 million pieces of paper required. He told the jury that it was difficult to envisage what would be needed to transport all those notes, leaving them with the overwhelming idea that the cash might not have been paid in and that 'the total fabrication theory' was a possibility. It was extraordinary. And it is dreadful to be found guilty when you know that you are innocent. But I still believe in British justice, for both me and Asil Nadir.

Index